EVANGELICALS AND CATHOLICS TOGETHER

# Evangelicals and Catholics Together

## Toward a Common Mission

Charles Colson

Richard John Neuhaus

Editors

WORD PUBLISHING

DALLAS LONDON VANCOUVER MELBOURNE

PUBLISHED BY WORD PUBLISHING,
DALLAS, TEXAS

Scripture references are from the following sources:

*The New International Version* of the Bible (NIV),
copyright © 1983 by the International Bible Society. Used by permission
of Zondervan Bible Publishers.

*The Revised Standard Version* of the Bible (RSV),
copyright © 1989 by the Division of Christian Education of the National Council
of the Churches of Christ USA. Used by permission.

*Project Editor: Terri Gibbs*

*Book design by Mark McGarry*
*Set in Monotype Dante*

LIBRARY OF CONGRESS CATALOGING-IN-PUBLICATION DATA

Evangelicals and Catholics together: toward a common mission/
Charles Colson, Richard John Neuhaus, editors.
p. cm. Includes bibliographical references and index.
ISBN 0-8499-3860-0 (alk. paper)
1. Evangelicals and Catholics together. 2. Catholic Church —
Relations — Evangelicalism. 3. Evangelicalism — Relations — Catholic Church.
4. Evangelicalism — United States. 5. Catholic Church — United States.
6. Mission of the church. 7. United States — Civilization — 20th
century. 8. United States — Church history — 20th
century. I. Colson, Charles W. II. Neuhaus, Richard John.
BR1641.C37E94 1995 280'.042 — dc20 95-24750 CIP

567899 RRD 654321

PRINTED IN THE UNITED STATES OF AMERICA

*Where Christ is, there also is the Church.*

# Contents

# Introduction

IT WAS OUR PRAYER that "Evangelicals and Catholics Together: The Christian Mission in the Third Millennium" would generate serious discussion. As we all discover from time to time, people should be careful what they pray for. We were not prepared for the intensity of the discussion—and the controversy—that greeted the declaration when it was issued at the end of March, 1994. Looking back on it now, it seems obvious that we should not have been surprised. After all, ECT is an invitation to reexamine stereotypes, prejudices, and conventional ideas that have been entrenched, in some cases, for almost five hundred years.

We are regularly asked whether we are pleased with the response to ECT. Pleased is not the word for it. We are immeasurably grateful to God for what he has done and continues to do through this initiative. We cannot know what will be the final significance of ECT for relations between evangelical Protestants and Roman Catholics, and for the Christian mission in the third millennium. We do know that a conversation has been started, and that conversation bears the promise of multiplying the power of gospel proclamation to a world increasingly threatened by a culture of decadence and death.

ECT is a beginning. We cannot emphasize that too much. The

declaration and the essays in this book lift up what has been accomplished, but their greater importance is to point us toward what we must do together, by the grace of God, in the years ahead. If this is the work of God—and with many thousands of others we believe it is—we cannot grow weary in advancing the pattern of convergence and cooperation affirmed by ECT. The cause by which we are claimed is not our cause, nor does it belong to our several traditions or denominations. It is the cause of God in Christ "reconciling the world to himself, not counting their trespasses against them, and entrusting to us the message of reconciliation" (2 Cor. 5:19 RSV). We are at most, if we are found faithful, his ambassadors, and the final test of ECT will be whether it strengthens the church's witness to that gospel of reconciliation.

ECT is a beginning, and perhaps it is appropriate at the beginning of this book on ECT to say something about how this beginning began. While we knew one another's work, the two of us became acquainted personally in 1985. The year before, Neuhaus had published his book, *The Naked Public Square: Religion and Democracy in America.* Colson invited Neuhaus, together with our mutual friend Carl Henry, to address a distinguished gathering of Christian leaders at the DeMoss House of the Prison Fellowship in Virginia. That memorable evening brought together members from the House and Senate and Cabinet, plus distinguished preachers, writers, and activists to reflect and pray together about what we believed to be a historic moment of responsibility for Christians in America. As was to happen on subsequent occasions, we sensed the Holy Spirit moving us to do more, although we knew not quite what.

In 1987, Colson published *Kingdoms in Conflict,* a well-received book that aimed to build upon and advance the argument of *The Naked Public Square.* Obviously, the two of us—sometimes in conversation, sometimes not knowing what the other was up to—were being led in similar directions. Our concern for Christian witness in "the public square" was growing, but the problems were formidable. For one thing, the Christian political activism that had emerged in the late 1970s had fallen on difficult days, with the national media orchestrating an orgy of contempt for a "religious right" that had become embroiled in one personal scandal after another. It became evident that Christian engagement in the great cultural, social, and political tasks of our time would be largely futile, even counter-productive, unless that engagement was grounded in shared spiritual commitment and gospel truth.

At the same time, both of us were frequently approached by evangelicals and Catholics who had been finding one another as Christian brothers and sisters in various activities, notably in the pro-life movement and the charismatic renewal. For Colson, the encounter between evangelicals and Catholics was most dramatically evident on the front lines of evangelism in prisons around the world. "God is doing something new," these people were telling us. "Isn't it time for evangelicals and Catholics to get together to explore what God might have in mind for us?" We discussed all this from time to time, but we did not know what to do, nor was it evident to us that we were the ones to take the initiative. We waited, and we prayed. Then, in 1992, Colson published *The Body: Being Light in Darkness.* That reflection on biblical themes of the Church and unity in Christ captured the evangelical imagination, strengthening our intuition that the time had come to take the initiative that would eventually produce ECT.

There was another factor. Along with many other evangelicals and Catholics, we were anguished by the growing conflicts between our communities in various parts of the world, especially in Latin America. That was the original focus of the meeting that we convened in New York City in September, 1992. Our concern was (and is) that animosities between evangelicals and Catholics threatened to mar the image of Christ by turning Latin America into a Belfast of religious warfare. Three noted sociologists of religion were part of that first meeting— Peter L. Berger of Boston University, and two British scholars, David Martin, author of *Tongues of Fire: The Explosion of Protestantism in Latin America,* and his wife, Bernice Martin.

In addition, the core working group that would in time produce ECT was composed of seven Roman Catholics and eight evangelicals (listed as participants following the ECT text reproduced in this volume). We invited these participants for their leadership positions in our several communities and for their eminent qualifications as theologians, evangelists, missiologists, and directors of Christian ministries. These people brought very different perspectives to the table. Throughout the ECT process, there has been a shared determination to respect differences. That is true also of the chapters in this book. The authors speak for themselves, but each speaks in a respectful awareness of the convictions of others.

At the September, 1992, meeting, the discussions about evangelical-Catholic relations in Latin America were marvelously productive, yet it soon became evident that we had to address a prior question. How could we speak a useful word to our brothers and sisters elsewhere if we had not in a more careful and comprehensive way addressed our relationship with one another here in North America? Perhaps, it was suggested, the most important gift that we could offer others would be the example of our common commitment to Christian faith, life, and mission. In the course of our conversation, it dawned upon a number of participants, almost simultaneously, as though by the prompting of the Holy Spirit: "Here is the Church. Here around this table. Christ is here, his gospel is being spoken, and therefore his Church is here. How do we make that simple but wondrous truth clear to our fellow believers? What does that truth mean for us and our ministries?"

We then turned to the task of addressing those questions. At the end of two days of intensive discussion, debate, and prayer, we had a general sense of the direction in which we were being led, and of the specific issues that must be included in whatever we might publicly say together. We can report that those days were not easy. We were determined to take on the hard questions in our disagreements and divisions as evangelicals and Catholics. The arguments were frequently sharp and sometimes painful. We knew that any statement that might come out of this would have to stand up to the most severe critical examination. All of the participants evidenced a robust skepticism about "ecumenical" statements that hedge on important differences. Again and again it was said that the only unity we could seek, the only unity that is pleasing to God, is unity in the truth.

Tired but gratified, the participants knew what they wanted to say and appointed a drafting committee to say it as precisely and effectively as possible. That committee included: Kent Hill, President of Eastern Nazarene College in Massachusetts, an accomplished evangelical theologian, educator, and authority on religion in Russia and Central Europe; George Weigel, a lay Catholic theologian, President of the Ethics and Public Policy Canter in Washington, D.C., and expert on religion-and-society questions in the U.S. and abroad; and the two of us. A first draft was circulated and thoroughly criticized by participants in the fall of 1992. The work was delayed when Neuhaus, who served as secretary to the committee, underwent emergency cancer surgery in

January, 1993. (Now, thank God, he appears to be completely recovered.) By spring of 1993, the enterprise was back in full swing, and over the course of the next year seven drafts were circulated, criticized, and revised in accord with suggestions received. After a final meeting of the drafting committee at DeMoss House and a final approval by all participants, ECT was released in New York on Tuesday, March 29, 1994.

Colson wants to acknowledge the inestimable help of Dr. Daryl Charles throughout this process. Charles, who received his Ph.D. from Westminster Seminary, provided a scholarly expertise on Reformation theology that was invaluable. Similarly, Neuhaus notes that Father Avery Dulles, probably the most respected Catholic theologian in America, was for all practical purposes a member of the drafting committee and was unstinting in his help at every step of the way. It should be noted that drafts of ECT were also circulated among evangelical and Catholic leaders and theologians beyond the circle of original participants. It has not escaped our attention that some who were sent drafts of the declaration in advance and offered no criticism at the time have since become vocal critics of ECT.

Our work is far from done. As we said, ECT is only a beginning. We do believe this effort has been blessed by God, and we are gratified beyond measure by the reception it has received from innumerable evangelical and Catholic Christians. It is our prayer that this book will further advance a God-pleasing unity in the proclamation of the saving gospel of Jesus Christ, and greater cooperation among his disciples in the moral and spiritual renewal of our culture. In prison ministries and elsewhere, there are wonderful signs of a new openness and cooperation in winning people to Christ.

There is still much to discuss about differences and commonalties in what evangelicals and Catholics believe, teach, and confess. We have learned from the many responses, both positive and negative, to ECT. Certainly it did not deal with all the questions that need to be addressed, and no doubt we might have avoided some misunderstandings by being more explicit at various points. As proposed by ECT, plans are underway for continuing theological conversations. These conversations will be independent of the official conversations between the Roman Catholic Church and various evangelical Protestant bodies. It is our hope, however, that the ECT conversations will usefully complement the more official activities. We are greatly encouraged in that hope by officials in both communities who have expressed their gratitude for ECT in advancing the encounter between evangelicals and Catholics.

A beginning has been made. This book builds on that beginning. The authors offer it to you, the reader, in the spirit of ECT's concluding affirmation that "this is a time of opportunity—and, if of opportunity, then of responsibility—for evangelicals and Catholics to be Christians together in a way that helps prepare the world for the coming of him to whom belongs the kingdom, the power, and the glory forever. Amen."

CHARLES COLSON
RICHARD JOHN NEUHAUS
MAY, 1995

# ECT Statement:

## "Evangelicals and Catholics Together: The Christian Mission in the Third Millennium"

WE ARE EVANGELICAL PROTESTANTS and Roman Catholics who have been led through prayer, study, and discussion to common convictions about Christian faith and mission. This statement cannot speak officially for our communities. It does intend to speak responsibly from our communities and to our communities. In this statement we address what we have discovered both about our unity and about our differences. We are aware that our experience reflects the distinctive circumstances and opportunities of Evangelicals and Catholics living together in North America. At the same time, we believe that what we have discovered and resolved is pertinent to the relationship between Evangelicals and Catholics in other parts of the world. We therefore commend this statement to their prayerful consideration.

As the Second Millennium draws to a close, the Christian mission in world history faces a moment of daunting opportunity and responsibility. If in the merciful and mysterious ways of God the Second Coming is delayed, we enter upon a Third Millennium that could be, in the words of John Paul II, "a springtime of world missions" (*Redemptoris Missio*).

As Christ is one, so the Christian mission is one. That one mission can be and should be advanced in diverse ways. Legitimate diversity, however, should not be confused with existing divisions between Christians that obscure the one Christ and hinder the one mission. There is a necessary connection between the visible unity of Christians and the mission of the one Christ. We together pray for the fulfillment of the prayer of Our Lord: "May they all be one; as you, Father, are in me, and I in you, so also may they be in us, that the world may believe that you sent me" (John 17). We together, Evangelicals and Catholics, confess our sins against the unity that Christ intends for all his disciples.

The one Christ and one mission includes many other Christians, notably the Eastern Orthodox and those Protestants not commonly identified as Evangelical. All Christians are encompassed in the prayer, "May they all be one." Our present statement attends to the specific problems and opportunities in the relationship between Roman Catholics and Evangelical Protestants.

As we near the Third Millennium, there are approximately 1.7 billion Christians in the world. About a billion of these are Catholics and more than 300 million are Evangelical Protestants. The century now drawing to a close has been the greatest century of missionary expansion in Christian history. We pray and we believe that this expansion has prepared the way for yet greater missionary endeavor in the first century of the Third Millennium.

The two communities in world Christianity that are most evangelistically assertive and most rapidly growing are Evangelicals and Catholics. In many parts of the world, the relationship between these communities is marked more by conflict than cooperation, more by animosity than by love, more by suspicion than by trust, more by propaganda and ignorance than by respect for the truth. This is alarmingly the case in Latin America, increasingly the case in Eastern Europe, and too often the case in our own country.

Without ignoring conflicts between and within other Christian communities, we address ourselves to the relationship between Evangelicals and Catholics, who constitute the growing edge of missionary expansion at present and, most likely, in the century ahead. In doing so, we hope that what we have discovered and resolved may be of help in other situations of conflict, such as that among Orthodox, Evangelicals, and Catholics in Eastern Europe. While we are gratefully aware of ongoing efforts to address tensions among these communities, the shameful reality is that, in many places around the world, the scandal of conflict between Christians obscures the scandal of the cross, thus crippling the one mission of the one Christ.

As in times past, so also today and in the future, the Christian mission, which is directed to the entire human community, must be advanced against formidable opposition. In some cultures, that mission encounters resurgent spiritualities and religions that are explicitly hostile to the claims of the Christ. Islam, which in many instances denies the freedom to witness to the Gospel, must be of increasing concern to those who care about religious freedom and the Christian mission. Mutually respectful conversation between Muslims and Christians should be encouraged in the hope that more of the world will, in the oft-repeated words of John Paul II, "open the door to Christ." At the same time, in our so-called developed societies, a widespread secularization increasingly descends into a moral, intellectual, and spiritual nihilism that denies not only the One who is the Truth but the very idea of truth itself.

We enter the twenty-first century without illusions. With Paul and the Christians of the first century, we know that "we are not contending against flesh and blood, but against the principalities, against the powers, against the world rulers of this present darkness, against the spiritual hosts of wickedness in the heavenly places" (Ephesians 6). As Evangelicals and Catholics, we dare not by needless and loveless conflict between ourselves give aid and comfort to the enemies of the cause of Christ.

The love of Christ compels us, and we are therefore resolved to avoid such conflict between our communities and, where such conflict exists, to do what we can to reduce and eliminate it. Beyond that, we are called and we are therefore resolved to explore patterns of working and witnessing together in order to advance the one mission of Christ. Our common resolve is not based merely on a desire for harmony. We reject any appearance of harmony that is purchased at the price of truth. Our common resolve is made imperative by obedience to the truth of God revealed in the Word of God, the Holy Scriptures, and by trust in the promise of the Holy Spirit's guidance until Our Lord returns in glory to judge the living and the dead.

The mission that we embrace together is the necessary consequence of the faith that we affirm together.

## We Affirm Together

Jesus Christ is Lord. That is the first and final affirmation that Christians make about all of reality. He is the One sent by God to be Lord and Savior of all: "And there is salvation in no one else, for there is no other name under heaven given among men by which we must be saved" (Acts 4). Christians are people ahead of time, those who proclaim now what will one day be acknowledged by all, that Jesus Christ is Lord (Philippians 2).

We affirm together that we are justified by grace through faith because of Christ. Living faith is active in love that is nothing less than the love of Christ, for we together say with Paul: "I have been crucified with Christ; it is no longer I who live, but Christ who lives in me; and the life I now live in the flesh I live by faith in the Son of God, who loved me and gave himself for me" (Galatians 2).

All who accept Christ as Lord and Savior are brothers and sisters in Christ. Evangelicals and Catholics are brothers and sisters in Christ. We have not chosen one another, just as we have not chosen Christ. He has chosen us, and he has chosen us to be his together (John 15). However imperfect our communion with one another, however deep our disagreements with one another, we recognize that there is but one church of Christ. There is one church because there is one Christ and the church is his body. However difficult the way, we recognize that we are called by God to a fuller realization of our unity in the body of Christ. The only unity to which we would give expression is unity in the truth, and the truth is this: "There is one body and one Spirit, just as you were called to the one hope that belongs to your call, one Lord, one faith, one baptism, one God and Father of us all, who is above all and through all and in all" (Ephesians 4).

We affirm together that Christians are to teach and live in obedience to the divinely inspired Scriptures, which are the infallible Word of God. We further affirm together that Christ has promised to his church the gift of the Holy Spirit who will lead us into all truth in discerning and declaring the teaching of Scripture (John 16). We recognize together that the Holy Spirit has so guided his church in the past. In, for instance, the formation of the canon of the Scriptures, and in the orthodox response to the great Christological and Trinitarian controversies of the early centuries, we confidently acknowledge the guidance of the Holy Spirit. In faithful response to the Spirit's leading, the church formulated the Apostles' Creed, which we can and hereby do affirm together as an accurate statement of scriptural truth:

> I believe in God, the Father almighty, creator of heaven and earth.

> I believe in Jesus Christ, his only Son, our Lord. He was conceived by the power of the Holy Spirit and born of the virgin Mary. He suffered under Pontius Pilate, was crucified, died, and was buried. He descended into hell. On the third day he rose again. He ascended into heaven, and is seated at the right hand of the Father. He will come again to judge the living and the dead.

> I believe in the Holy Spirit, the holy catholic Church, the communion of saints, the forgiveness of sins, the resurrection of the body, and the life everlasting. Amen.

## We Hope Together

We hope together that all people will come to faith in Jesus Christ as Lord and Savior. This hope makes necessary the church's missionary zeal. "But how are they to call upon him in whom they have not believed? And how are they to believe in him of whom they have never heard? And how are they to hear without a preacher? And how can men preach unless they are sent?" (Romans 10). The church is by nature, in all places and at all times, in mission. Our missionary hope is inspired by the revealed desire of God that "all should be saved and come to a knowledge of the truth" (1 Timothy 2).

The church lives by and for the Great Commission: "Go therefore and make disciples of all nations, baptizing them in the name of the Father and of the Son and of the Holy Spirit, teaching them to observe all that I have commanded you; and lo, I am with you always, to the close of the age" (Matthew 28).

Unity and love among Christians is an integral part of our missionary witness to the Lord whom we serve. "A new commandment I give to you, that you love one another; even as I have loved you, that you also love one another. By this all men will know that you are my disciples, if you have love for one another" (John 13). If we do not love one another, we disobey his command and contradict the Gospel we declare.

As Evangelicals and Catholics, we pray that our unity in the love of Christ will become ever more evident as a sign to the world of God's reconciling power. Our communal and ecclesial separations are deep and long standing. We acknowledge that we do not know the schedule nor do we know the way to the greater visible unity for which we hope. We do know that existing patterns of distrustful polemic and conflict are not the way. We do know that God who has brought us into communion with himself through Christ intends that we also be in communion with one another. We do know that Christ is the way, the truth, and the life (John 14) and as we are drawn closer to him—walking in that way, obeying that truth, living that life—we are drawn closer to one another.

Whatever may be the future form of the relationship between our communities, we can, we must, and we will begin now the work required to remedy what we know to be wrong in that relationship. Such work requires trust and understanding, and trust and understanding require an assiduous attention to truth. We do not deny but clearly assert that there are disagreements between us. Misunderstandings, misrepresentations, and caricatures of one another, however, are not disagreements. These distortions must be cleared away if we are to search through our honest differences in a manner consistent with what we affirm and hope together on the basis of God's Word.

## We Search Together

Together we search for a fuller and clearer understanding of God's revelation in Christ and his will for his disciples. Because of the limitations of human reason and language, which limitations are compounded by sin, we cannot understand completely the transcendent reality of God and his ways. Only in the End Time will we see face to face and know as we are known (1 Corinthians 13). We now search together in confident reliance upon God's self-revelation in Jesus Christ, the sure testimony of Holy Scripture, and the promise of the Spirit to his church. In this search to understand the truth more fully and clearly, we need one another. We are both informed and limited by the histories of our communities and by our own experiences. Across the divides of communities and experiences, we need to challenge one another, always speaking the truth in love, building up the Body (Ephesians 4).

We do not presume to suggest that we can resolve the deep and long-standing differences between Evangelicals and Catholics. Indeed these differences may never be resolved short of the Kingdom Come. Nonetheless, we are not permitted simply to resign ourselves to differences that divide us from one another. Not all differences are authentic disagreements, nor need all disagreements divide. Differences and disagreements must be tested in disciplined and sustained conversation. In this connection we warmly commend and encourage the formal theological dialogues of recent years between Roman Catholics and Evangelicals.

We note some of the differences and disagreements that must be addressed more fully and candidly in order to strengthen between us a relationship of trust in obedience to truth. Among points of difference in doctrine, worship, practice, and piety that are frequently thought to divide us are these:

· The church as an integral part of the Gospel or the church as a communal consequence of the Gospel.

· The church as visible communion or invisible fellowship of true believers.

· The sole authority of Scripture (*sola scriptura*) or Scripture as authoritatively interpreted in the church.

· The "soul freedom" of the individual Christian or the magisterium (teaching authority) of the community.

· The church as local congregation or universal communion.

· Ministry ordered in apostolic succession or the priesthood of all believers.

· Sacraments and ordinances as symbols of grace or means of grace.

· The Lord's Supper as eucharist sacrifice or memorial meal.

· Remembrance of Mary and the saints or devotion to Mary and the saints.

· Baptism as sacrament of regeneration or testimony to regeneration.

This account of differences is by no means complete. Nor is the disparity between position always so sharp as to warrant the "or" in the above formulations. Moreover, among those recognized as Evangelical Protestants there are significant differences between, for example, Baptists, Pentecostals, and Calvinists on these questions. But the differences mentioned above reflect disputes that are deep and long standing. In at least some instances, they reflect authentic disagreements that have been in the past and are at present barriers to full communion between Christians.

On these questions, and other questions implied by them, Evangelicals hold that the Catholic Church has gone beyond Scripture, adding teachings and practices that detract from or compromise the Gospel of God's saving grace in Christ. Catholics, in turn, hold that such teachings and practices are grounded in Scripture and belong to the fullness of God's revelation. Their rejection, Catholics say, results in a truncated and reduced understanding of the Christian reality.

Again, we cannot resolve these disputes here. We can and do affirm together that the entirety of Christian faith, life, and mission finds its source, center, and end in the crucified and risen Lord. We can and do pledge that we will continue to search together—through study, discussion, and prayer—for a better understanding of one another's convictions and a more adequate comprehension of the truth of God in Christ. We can testify now that in our searching together we have discovered what we can affirm together and what we can hope together and, therefore, how we can contend together.

## We Contend Together

As we are bound together by Christ and his cause, so we are bound together in contending against all that opposes Christ and his cause. We are emboldened not by illusions of easy triumph but by faith in his certain triumph. Our Lord wept over Jerusalem, and he now weeps over a world that does not know the time of its visitation. The raging of the principalities and powers may increase as the End Time nears, but the outcome of the contest is assured.

The cause of Christ is the cause and mission of the church, which is, first of all, to proclaim the Good News that "God was in Christ reconciling the world to himself, not counting their trespasses against them, and entrusting to us the message of reconciliation" (2 Corinthians 5). To proclaim this Gospel and to sustain the community of faith, worship, and discipleship that is gathered by this Gospel is the first and chief responsibility of the church. All other tasks and responsibilities of the church are derived from and directed toward the mission of the Gospel.

Christians individually and the church corporately also have a responsibility for the right ordering of civil society. We embrace this task soberly; knowing the consequences of human sinfulness, we resist the utopian conceit that it is within our powers to build the Kingdom of God on earth. We embrace this task hopefully; knowing that God has called us to love our neighbor, we seek to secure for all a greater measure of civil righteousness and justice, confident that he will crown our efforts when he rightly orders all things in the coming of his Kingdom.

In the exercise of these public responsibilities there has been in recent years a growing convergence and cooperation between Evangelicals and Catholics. We thank God for the discovery of one another in contending for a common cause. Much more important, we thank God for the discovery of one another as brothers and sisters in Christ. Our cooperation as citizens is animated by our convergence as Christians. We promise one another that we will work to deepen, build upon, and expand this pattern of convergence and cooperation.

Together we contend for the truth that politics, law, and culture must be secured by moral truth. With the Founders of the American experiment, we declare, "We hold these truths." With them, we hold that this constitutional order is composed not just of rules and procedures but is most essentially a moral experiment. With them, we hold that only a virtuous people can be free and just, and that virtue is secured by religion. To propose that securing civil virtue is the purpose of religion is blasphemous. To deny that securing civil virtue is a benefit of religion is blindness.

Americans are drifting away from, are often explicitly defying, the constituting truths of this experiment in ordered liberty. Influential sectors of the culture are laid waste by relativism, anti-intellectualism, and nihilism that deny the very idea of truth. Against such influences in both the elite and popular culture, we appeal to reason and religion in contending for the foundational truths of our constitutional order.

More specifically, we contend together for religious freedom. We do so for the sake of religion, but also because religious freedom is the first freedom, the source and shield of all human freedoms. In their relationship to God, persons have a dignity and responsibility that transcends, and thereby limits, the authority of the state and of every other merely human institution.

Religious freedom is itself grounded in and is a product of religious faith, as is evident in the history of Baptists and others in this country. Today we rejoice together that the Roman Catholic Church—as affirmed by the Second Vatican Council and boldly exemplified in the ministry of John Paul II—is strongly committed to religious freedom and, consequently, to the defense of all human rights. Where Evangelicals and Catholics are in severe and sometimes violent conflict, such as parts of Latin America, we urge Christians to embrace and act upon the imperative of religious freedom. Religious freedom will not be respected by the state if it is not respected by Christians or, even worse, if Christians attempt to recruit the state in repressing religious freedom.

In this country, too, freedom of religion cannot be taken for granted but requires constant attention. We strongly affirm the separation of church and state, and just as strongly protest the distortion of the principle to mean the separation of religion from public life. We are deeply concerned by the courts' narrowing of the protections provided by the "free exercise" provision of the First Amendment and by an obsession with "no establishment" that stifles the necessary role of religion in American life. As a consequence of such distortions, it is increasingly the case that wherever government goes religion must retreat, and government increasingly goes almost everywhere. Religion, which was privileged and foundational in our legal order, has in recent years been penalized and made marginal. We contend together for a renewal of the constituting vision of the place of religion in the American experiment.

Religion and religiously grounded moral conviction is not an alien or threatening force in our public life. For the great majority of Americans, morality is derived, however variously and confusedly, from religion. The argument, increasingly voiced in sectors of our political culture, that religion should be excluded from the public square must be recognized as an assault upon the most elementary principles of democratic governance. That argument needs to be exposed and countered by leaders, religious and other, who care about the integrity of our constitutional order.

The pattern of convergence and cooperation between Evangelicals and Catholics is, in large part, a result of common effort to protect human life, especially the lives of the most vulnerable among us. With the

Founders, we hold that all human beings are endowed by their Creator with the right to life, liberty, and the pursuit of happiness. The statement that the unborn child is a human life that—barring natural misfortune or lethal intervention—will become what everyone recognizes as a human baby is not a religious assertion. It is a statement of simple biological fact. That the unborn child has a right to protection, including the protection of law, is a moral statement supported by moral reason and biblical truth.

We, therefore, will persist in contending—we will not be discouraged but will multiply every effort—in order to secure the legal protection of the unborn. Our goals are: to secure due process of law for the unborn, to enact the most protective laws and public policies that are politically possible, and to reduce dramatically the incidence of abortion. We warmly commend those who have established thousands of crisis pregnancy and postnatal care centers across the country, and urge that such efforts be multiplied. As the unborn must be protected, so also must women be protected from their current rampant exploitation by the abortion industry and by fathers who refuse to accept responsibility for mothers and children. Abortion on demand, which is the current rule in America, must be recognized as a massive attack on the dignity, rights, and needs of women.

Abortion is the leading edge of an encroaching culture of death. The helpless old, the radically handicapped, and others who cannot effectively assert their rights are increasingly treated as though they have no rights. These are the powerless who are exposed to the will and whim of those who have power over them. We will do all in our power to resist proposals for euthanasia, eugenics, and population control that exploit the vulnerable, corrupt the integrity of medicine, deprave our culture, and betray the moral truths of our constitutional order.

In public education, we contend together for schools that transmit to coming generations our cultural heritage, which is inseparable from the formative influence of religion, especially Judaism and Christianity. Education for responsible citizenship and social behavior is inescapably moral education. Every effort must be made to cultivate the morality of honesty, law observance, work, caring, chastity, mutual respect between the sexes, and readiness for marriage, parenthood, and family. We reject the claim that, in any or all of these areas, "tolerance" requires the promotion of moral equivalence between the normative and the deviant. In a democratic society that recognizes that parents have the primary responsibility for the formation of their children, schools are to assist and support, not oppose and undermine, parents in the exercise of their responsibility.

We contend together for a comprehensive policy of parental choice in education. This is a moral question of simple justice. Parents are the primary educators of their children; the state and other institutions should be supportive of their exercise of that responsibility. We affirm policies that enable parents to effectively exercise their right and responsibility to choose the schooling that they consider best for their children.

We contend together against the widespread pornography in our society, along with the celebration of violence, sexual depravity, and antireligious bigotry in the entertainment media. In resisting such cultural and moral debasement, we recognize the legitimacy of boycotts and other consumer actions, and urge the enforcement of existing laws against obscenity. We reject the self-serving claim of the peddlers of depravity that this constitutes illegitimate censorship. We reject the assertion of the unimaginative that artistic creativity is to be measured by the capacity to shock or outrage. A people incapable of defending decency invites the rule of viciousness, both public and personal.

We contend for a renewed spirit of acceptance, understanding, and cooperation across lines of religion, race, ethnicity, sex, and class. We are all created in the image of God and are accountable to him. That truth is the basis of individual responsibility and equality before the law. The abandonment of that truth has resulted in a society at war with itself, pitting citizens against one another in bitter conflicts of group grievances and claims to entitlement. Justice and social amity require a redirection of public attitudes and policies so that rights are joined to duties and people are rewarded according to their character and competence.

We contend for a free society, including a vibrant market economy. A free society requires a careful balancing between economics, politics, and culture. Christianity is not an ideology and therefore does not prescribe precisely how that balance is to be achieved in every circumstance. We affirm the importance of a free economy not only because it is more efficient but because it accords with a Christian understanding of human freedom. Economic freedom, while subject to grave abuse, makes possible the patterns of creativity, cooperation, and accountability that contribute to the common good.

We contend together for a renewed appreciation of Western culture. In its history and missionary reach, Christianity engages all cultures while being captive to none. We are keenly aware of, and grateful for, the role of Christianity in shaping and sustaining the Western culture of which we are part. As with all of history, that culture is marred by human sinfulness. Alone among world cultures, however, the West has cultivated an attitude of self-criticism and of eagerness to learn from other cultures. What is called multiculturalism can mean respectful attention to human differences. More commonly today, however, multiculturalism means affirming all cultures but our own. Welcoming the contributions of other cultures and being ever alert to the limitations of our own, we receive Western culture as our legacy and embrace it as our task in order to transmit it as a gift to future generations.

We contend for public policies that demonstrate renewed respect for the irreplaceable role of mediating structures in society—notably the family, churches, and myriad voluntary associations. The state is not the society, and many of the most important functions of society are best addressed in independence from the state. The role of churches in responding to a wide variety of human needs, especially among the poor and marginal, needs to be protected and strengthened. Moreover, society is not the aggregate of isolated individuals bearing rights but is composed of communities that inculcate responsibility, sustain shared memory, provide mutual aid, and nurture the habits that contribute to both personal well-being and the common good. Most basic among such communities is the community of the family. Laws and social policies should be designed with particular care for the stability and flourishing of families. While the crisis of the family in America is by no means limited to the poor or to the underclass, heightened attention must be paid those who have become, as a result of well-intended but misguided statist policies, virtual wards of the government.

Finally, we contend for a realistic and responsible understanding of America's part in world affairs. Realism and responsibility require that we avoid both the illusions of unlimited power and righteousness, on the one hand, and the timidity and selfishness of isolationism, on the other. U.S. foreign policy should reflect a concern for the defense of democracy and, wherever prudent and possible, the protection and advancement of human rights, including religious freedom.

The above is a partial list of public responsibilities on which we believe there is a pattern of convergence and cooperation between Evangelicals and Catholics. We reject the notion that this constitutes a partisan "religious agenda" in American politics. Rather, this is a set of directions oriented to the common good and discussable on the basis of public reason. While our sense of civic responsibility is informed and motivated by Christian faith, our intention is to elevate the level of political and moral discourse in a manner that excludes no one and invites the participation of all people of good will. To that end, Evangelicals and Catholics have made an inestimable contribution in the past and, it is our hope, will contribute even more effectively in the future.

We are profoundly aware that the American experiment has been, all in all, a blessing to the world and a blessing to us as Evangelical and Catholic Christians. We are determined to assume our full share of responsibility for this "one nation under God," believing it to be a nation under the judgment, mercy, and providential care of the Lord of the nations to whom alone we render unqualified allegiance.

## We Witness Together

The question of Christian witness unavoidably returns us to points of serious tension between Evangelicals and Catholics. Bearing witness to the saving power of Jesus Christ and his will for our lives is an integral part of Christian discipleship. The achievement of good will and cooperation between Evangelicals and Catholics must not be at the price of the urgency and clarity of Christian witness to the Gospel. At the same time, and as noted earlier, Our Lord has made clear that the evidence of love among his disciples is an integral part of that Christian witness.

Today, in this country and elsewhere, Evangelicals and Catholics attempt to win "converts" from one another's folds. In some ways, this is perfectly understandable and perhaps inevitable. In many instances, however, such efforts at recruitment undermine the Christian mission by which we are bound by God's Word and to which we have recommitted ourselves in this statement. It should be clearly understood between Catholics and Evangelicals that Christian witness is of necessity aimed at conversion. Authentic conversion is—in its beginning, in its end, and all along the way—conversion to God in Christ by the power of the Spirit.

In this connection, we embrace as our own the explanation of the Baptist-Roman Catholic International Conversation (1988):

> Conversion is turning away from all that is opposed to God, contrary to Christ's teaching, and turning to God, to Christ the Son through the work of the Holy Spirit. It entails a turning from the self-centeredness of sin to faith in Christ as Lord and Savior. Conversion is a passing from one way of life to another new one, marked with the newness of Christ. It is a continuing process so that the whole life of a Christian should be a passage from death to life, from error to truth, from sin to grace. Our life in Christ demands continual growth in God's grace. Conversion is personal but not private. Individuals respond in faith to God's call but faith comes from hearing the proclamation of the word of God and is to be expressed in the life together in Christ that is the Church.

By preaching, teaching, and life example, Christians witness to Christians and non-Christians alike. We seek and pray for the conversion of others, even as we recognize our own continuing need to be fully converted. As we strive to make Christian faith and life—our own and that of others—ever more intentional rather than nominal, ever more committed rather than apathetic, we also recognize the different forms that authentic discipleship can take. As is evident in the two-thousand-year history of the Church, and in our contemporary experience, there are different ways of being Christian, and some of these ways are distinctively marked by communal patterns of worship, piety, and catechesis. That we are all to be one does not mean that we are all to be identical in our way of following the one Christ. Such distinctive patterns of discipleship, it should be noted, are amply evident within the communion of the Catholic Church as well as within the many worlds of Evangelical Protestantism.

It is understandable that Christians who bear witness to the Gospel try to persuade others that their communities and traditions are more fully in accord with the Gospel. There is a necessary distinction between evangelizing and what is today commonly called proselytizing or "sheep stealing." We condemn the practice of recruiting people from another community for purposes of denominational or institutional aggrandizement. At the same time, our commitment to full religious freedom compels us to defend the legal freedom to proselytize even as we call upon Christians to refrain from such activity.

Three observations are in order in connection with proselytizing. First, as much as we might believe one community is more fully in accord with the Gospel than another, we as Evangelicals and Catholics affirm that opportunity and means for growth in Christian discipleship are available in our several communities. Second, the decision of the committed Christian with respect to his communal allegiance and participation must be assiduously respected. Third, in view of the large number of non-Christians in the world and the enormous challenge of our common evangelistic task, it is neither theologically legitimate nor a prudent use of resources for one Christian community to proselytize among active adherents of another Christian community.

Christian witness must always be made in a spirit of love and humility. It must not deny but must readily accord to everyone the full freedom to discern and decide what is God's will for his life. Witness that is in service to the truth is in service to such freedom. Any form of coercion—physical, psychological, legal, economic—corrupts Christian witness and is to be unqualifiedly rejected. Similarly, bearing false witness against other persons and communities, or casting unjust and uncharitable suspicions upon them, is incompatible with the Gospel. Also to be rejected is the practice of comparing the strengths and ideals of one community with the weaknesses and failures of another. In describing the teaching and practices of other Christians, we must strive to do so in a way that they would recognize as fair and accurate.

In considering the many corruptions of Christian witness, we, Evangelicals and Catholics, confess that we have sinned against one another and against God. We most earnestly ask the forgiveness of God and one another, and pray for the grace to amend our own lives and that of our communities.

Repentance and amendment of life do not dissolve remaining differences between us. In the context of evangelization and "reevangelization," we encounter a major difference in our understanding of the relationship between baptism and the new birth in Christ. For Catholics, all who are validly baptized are born again and are truly, however imperfectly, in communion with Christ. That baptismal grace is to be continuingly reawakened and revivified through conversion. For most Evangelicals, but not all, the experience of conversion is to be followed by baptism as a sign of new birth. For Catholics, all the baptized are already members of the church, however dormant their faith and life; for many Evangelicals, the new birth requires baptismal initiation into the community of the born again. These differing beliefs about the relationship between baptism, new birth, and membership in the church should be honestly presented to the Christian who has undergone conversion. But again, his decision regarding communal allegiance and participation must be assiduously respected.

There are, then, differences between us that cannot be resolved here. But on this we are resolved: All authentic witness must be aimed at conversion to God in Christ by the power of the Spirit. Those converted—whether understood as having received the new birth for the first time or as having experienced the reawakening of the new birth originally bestowed in the sacrament of baptism—must be given full freedom and respect as they discern and decide the community in which they will live their new life in Christ. In such discernment and decision, they are ultimately responsible to God, and we dare not interfere with the exercise of that responsibility. Also in our differences and disagreements, we Evangelicals and Catholics commend one another to God "who by the power at work within us is able to do far more abundantly than all that we ask or think" (Ephesians 3).

In this discussion of witnessing together we have touched on difficult and long-standing problems. The difficulties must not be permitted to overshadow the truths on which we are, by the grace of God, in firm agreement. As we grow in mutual understanding and trust, it is our hope that our efforts to evangelize will not jeopardize but will reinforce our devotion to the common tasks to which we have pledged ourselves in this statement.

## Conclusion

Nearly two thousand years after it began, and nearly five hundred years after the divisions of the Reformation era, the Christian mission to the world is vibrantly alive and assertive. We do not know, we cannot know, what the Lord of history has in store for the Third Millennium. It may be the springtime of world missions and great Christian expansion. It may be the way of the cross marked by persecution and apparent marginalization. In different places and times, it will likely be both. Or it may be that Our Lord will return tomorrow.

We do know that his promise is sure, that we are enlisted for the duration, and that we are in this together. We do know that we must affirm and hope and search and contend and witness together, for we belong not to ourselves but to him who has purchased us by the blood of the cross. We do know that this is a time of opportunity—and, if of opportunity, then of responsibility—for Evangelicals and Catholics to be Christians together in a way that helps prepare the world for the coming of him to whom belongs the kingdom, the power, and the glory forever. Amen

PARTICIPANTS: **Mr. Charles Colson,** Prison Fellowship; **Fr. Juan Diaz-Vilar, S.J.,** Catholic Hispanic Ministries; **Fr. Avery Dulles, S.J.,** Fordham University; **Bishop Francis George, OMI,** Diocese of Yakima (Washington); **Dr. Kent Hill,** Eastern Nazarene College; **Dr. Richard Land,** Christian Life Commission of the Southern Baptist Convention; **Dr. Larry Lewis,** Home Mission Board of the Southern Baptist Convention; **Dr. Jesse Miranda,** Assemblies of God; **Msgr. William Murphy,** Chancellor of the Archdiocese of Boston; **Fr. Richard John Neuhaus,** Institute on Religion and Public Life; **Mr. Brian O'Connell,** World Evangelical Fellowship; **Mr. Herbert Schlossberg; Archbishop Francis Stafford,** Archdiocese of Denver; **Mr. George Weigel,** Ethics and Public Policy Center; **Dr. John White,** Geneva College and the National Association of Evangelicals.

*Concern over the public impression that the Southern Baptist Convention had officially endorsed ECT led Richard Land and Larry Lewis to withdraw their signatures in April, 1995, while, at the same time, making clear that they maintain their strong personal endorsement of the declaration.

ENDORSED BY: **Dr. William Abraham,** Perkins School of Theology; **Dr. Elizabeth Achtemeier,** Union Theological Seminary (Virginia); **Mr. William Bentley Ball,** Harrisburg, Pennsylvania; **Dr. Bill Bright,** Campus Crusade for Christ; **Professor Robert Destro,** Catholic University of America; **Fr. Augustine DiNoia, O.P.,** Dominican House of Studies; **Fr. Joseph P. Fitzpatrick, S.J.,** Fordham University; **Mr. Keith Fournier,** American Center for Law and Justice; **Bishop William Frey,** Trinity Episcopal School for Ministry; **Professor Mary Ann Glendon,** Harvard Law School; **Dr. Os Guinness,** Trinity Forum; **Dr. Nathan Hatch,** University of Notre Dame; **Dr. James Hitchcock,** St. Louis University; **Professor**

Peter Kreeft, Boston College; Fr. Matthew Lamb, Boston College; Mr. Ralph Martin, Renewal Ministries; Dr. Richard Mouw, Fuller Theological Seminary; Dr. Mark Noll, Wheaton College; Mr. Michael Novak, American Enterprise Institute; John Cardinal O'Connor, Archdiocese of New York; Dr. Thomas Oden, Drew University; Dr. J. I. Packer, Regent College (British Columbia); Rev. Pat Robertson, Regent University; Dr. John Rodgers, Trinity Episcopal School for Ministry; Bishop Carlos A. Sevilla, S.J., Archdiocese of San Francisco.

**Numerous other evangelical and Catholic leaders have asked to be listed as endorsers of ECT, but in order to prevent the above list from becoming unwieldy, it is limited to those who endorsed the declaration prior to its release on March 29, 1994.

# Contributors

CHARLES COLSON, founder and chairman of Prison Fellowship Ministries. Recipient of the Templeton Prize for Progress in Religion in 1993.

AVERY DULLES, S.J., Laurence J. McGinley Professor of Religion and Society, Fordham University, and Professor Emeritus, The Catholic University of America, is an internationally known theologian and lecturer, and the author of seventeen books and over six hundred articles on theological topics.

RICHARD JOHN NEUHAUS, president of The Institute on Religion and Public Life. Editor-in-chief of *First Things: A Monthly Journal of Religion and Public Life.*

MARK NOLL, McManis Professor of Christian Thought at Wheaton College, is the author of *A History of Christianity in the United States and Canada* (Eerdmans, 1992) and the editor of *Confessions and Catechisms of the Reformation* (Baker, 1991).

J. I. PACKER, Sangwoo Youtong Chee Professor of Theology, Regent College, Vancouver.

GEORGE WEIGEL, president of the Ethics and Public Policy Center, Washington D.C. Author or editor of fourteen books on religion and public life.

# The Common Cultural Task:
# The Culture War from a Protestant Perspective

### Charles W. Colson

> Truth demands confrontation;
> loving confrontation, but
> confrontation nevertheless.
>
> *Francis Schaeffer*

IN 1987 A GROUP of men, each chained and blindfolded, huddled together in a small, dreary room in a crowded neighborhood of battle-scarred Beirut. As hostages held by Shiite Muslim terrorists, the little group must have experienced the very depths of despair. They didn't know where they were, but they knew that they had little hope of being rescued and that their captors were armed fanatics. Hours dragged into days, all in darkness.

But one of the captives, Father Lawrence Jenko, saved bits of bread and water from his meager ration. When the guards left the men alone for a few minutes, Jenko blessed the bread and water and offered communion to his fellow captives, one of whom was a Presbyterian minister, Benjamin Weir. Of course Jenko and Weir held vastly differing understandings of what was happening—whether those elements were the real body and blood of Christ or symbolic—but at that moment, such a theological distinction was not their concern. They took the elements and experienced what they later described as one of their most profound moments of intimacy with Jesus Christ their risen Savior. And this intimacy enabled them to endure horrifying months of captivity and eventually to emerge with their faith deepened and strengthened.

It was a dramatic example of what Baptist theologian Timothy George describes as "an ecumenism of the trenches." And believers of all traditions are discovering what that means as our culture grows increasingly hostile to Christianity.

In front of abortion clinics, Catholics join hands with Baptists, Methodists, and Episcopalians to pray and sing hymns. Side by side they pass out pamphlets and urge incoming women to spare their babies. Occasionally, like Jenko and Weir, they even share prison cells.

Both evangelicals and Catholics are offended by the blasphemy, violence, and sexual promiscuity endorsed by both the artistic elite and the popular culture in America today. On university campuses, evangelical students whose Christian faith comes under frequent assault often find Catholic professors to be their only allies. Evangelicals cheer as a Catholic nun, having devoted her life to serving the poor in the name of Christ, boldly confronts the president of the United States over his pro-abortion policies. Thousands of Catholic young people join the True Love Waits movement, in which teenagers pledge to save sex for marriage—a program that originated with Baptists.

This new ecumenism bears no relationship to liberal ecumenism, which seeks unity by disregarding doctrinal differences. Conservative evangelicals and Catholics understand and maintain the distinctives of their respective traditions. All the same, they take united stand on the common ground of Scripture and the ancient confessions—what C. S. Lewis called "mere Christianity."

Some dismiss this new ecumenism as a mere political alliance, part of the agenda of the much-maligned Religious Right. This is nonsense. Believers on the abortion picket lines are not risking arrest for the sake of their political views: They are willing to face such a risk for the sake of their deepest Christian conviction that all human life is precious and created in the image of a holy God. Believers who resist the onslaught of pornography and the radical homosexual agenda are not politically motivated; they are committed to the moral order of the universe as God has established it.

This is a theologically rooted alliance—not one hammered out in the ivory towers of academia or the well-lit conference rooms of church bureaucracies, but one lived out on the battlefield. This is the origin of and justification for "Evangelicals and Catholics Together."

Increasing numbers of evangelicals and Catholics are discovering that today's much-discussed "culture war" is more than a series of battles over issues. Instead, it is a clash of worldviews that involves fundamental differences about truth and ultimate reality, the nature of God, the created order, the moral law, and the human condition. And in this clash, these two communions stand shoulder to shoulder.

As we enter the new millennium, believing evangelicals and believing Catholics—together—must rediscover, defend, and live out the biblical worldview that they rightfully share. This is not merely a political necessity, as though evangelicals and Catholics should form a coalition (perhaps with the aid of Mormons and Muslims) to elect better candidates and enact better laws. Our culture's sickness is far too deep for mere political remedies. Our contemporary culture needs to be reevangelized. The Christian worldview must be brought to bear in new form and forcefulness on the intellectual and moral framework of contemporary life. This is a task for all true Christians, whether evangelicals, Catholics, or members of other traditions.

The task is urgent. Make no mistake: The culture war is real, and we who believe in the Bible are losing it—largely, I believe, because of our failure to understand the true nature of the forces arrayed against us. For the real assault is coming at the deepest and most dangerous level.

## The Cultural Crisis: The Assault on Truth

The social issues that have galvanized Christians over the last two decades—legalized abortion, violence and sexual permissiveness in entertainment, dissolution of the family, euthanasia, and the other battles of the culture war—are symptoms of a profound transformation at the deepest philosophical and religious levels from which our culture springs. Our society is experiencing the throes of this cultural shift. Assumptions about right and wrong, the human condition, and reality itself are undergoing a profound change. Our culture is drifting away from its Judeo-Christian foundations and adopting an entirely different set of presuppositions.

It seems odd that believing in the value of human life, in chastity, in the sanctity of the family, and in the reality of the moral law should be controversial today. Only a few decades ago almost no one would have disputed such basic principles of our civilization. Christians of different traditions—Catholics and Protestants, Calvinists and Arminians—could argue theology, but they could take for granted their common worldview. Even those who rejected Christianity tacitly agreed with the philosophical assumptions of the Judeo-Christian tradition. But today the Christian consensus about the nature of existence and the moral structure of human life is no longer culturally dominant. While the influence of Christianity—Catholic, Protestant, and Orthodox—has been profound throughout Western and some Eastern societies, today the Christian influence in many areas is being silenced, even rooted out, with devastating consequences.

We Christians in America now live in a society that has rejected not just Christian truth but any conception of truth. Those in academic positions and in the media and entertainment businesses who insist that there are no intellectual or moral absolutes are undermining the very possibility of civil society in their exaltation of the concept of the autonomous individual given to incessant pleasures. The whole of Western civilization is therefore facing a cultural crisis of historic magnitude. The collapse of truth and the loss of moral criteria threaten to unravel the moral consensus that has enabled us, in spite of all our differences, to live together in freedom. As Michael Novak tersely put it in his Templeton address: "Truth matters."

*Roots of the Crisis*

Christianity's exile from the dominant culture began with the Enlightenment of the late 1700s. At that time the intellectual founders of the modern era argued—successfully—that human reason autonomous from religious revelation should be the basis of social and political order and of the very meaning of life for individuals. By material "progress," these Enlightenment thinkers insisted, through scientific technologies and social programs, every human problem would be solved. Christianity, in its insistence on human fallenness and the universal need for supernatural grace, was denounced as an impediment to the self-assertiveness and self-fulfillment of natural human impulses. In his new

*An Intellectual History of Liberalism*, the French scholar Pierre Manet actually locates the origins of modernism generally, and liberalism specifically, in Enlightenment thinkers' determination to "divorce everyday life from the pervasive influence of the Catholic Church." They thus created the ideology of liberalism to separate politics "from all notions of cosmological order." What followed, Manet suggests, "was the evolving concept of an individual with no goals outside the confines of the self and a state with no purpose but to prevent individuals from dominating one another."[1]

A similar analysis has been provided by Owen Chadwick in his *The Secularization of the European Mind in the Nineteenth Century*. Chadwick also finds in "the declining hold of the church and its doctrines on European society" the origin of "a major shift in Western life and thought." That shift played itself out in horrific wars and the rise of totalitarianism in Europe—and it is that same shift that accounts for the peaceful but no less momentous confrontation between secularism and Christian faith in America today.[2]

Yet while advocating the abandonment of Christian faith for two hundred years, the proponents of modernism still believed in a single, universal truth about human nature and the meaning of life that would unite all peoples in a common vision of reality. They even held to a concept of universal morality, though they based its hold on the concepts of natural rights instead of natural law, and on the social contract instead of a common good.

In short, modernists believed in truth, and they believed truth could be discovered and defined by human reason without the guidance of biblical revelation or church doctrine. They were wrong. The first modernists—the French Revolutionaries—enthroned the goddess of reason in Notre Dame Cathedral, but their "reforms" quickly turned into a reign of terror. In the wake of the French Revolution's failures, Karl Marx offered a purportedly scientific analysis of culture grounded in dialectical materialism and the moral principles of social justice, but Marxist socialism led inexorably to police states and murder on a scale never previously known in all of history.

Today it is widely acknowledged that the tenets of modernism have not only failed but have been proved false. Reason has not solved all human problems. Science and technology have not ushered in utopia. Marxist socialism has failed in Europe and the therapeutic welfare state has failed in America. Technology continues to accelerate social change, but faith in the ability of the political ideologies and social programs grounded in modernism has all but disappeared. But instead of reconsidering the Christian tradition, which in appropriating classical philosophy gave birth to Western civilization in the first place, intellectual elites in abandoning modernism have effected a merely lateral movement: This transitional period, marked by a decay of cultural modernism, has been variously described as postmodernity or postmodernism.

At the intellectual heart of postmodernity are poststructuralists who reject the traditional logocentric view of language, radical multiculturalists and new historicists who engage in a sort of psychotherapeutic historiography, critics of science who call for new "paradigms," neo-Marxists who share an equal or greater disdain for free-market capitalism than their predecessors, deep ecologists who view nature rather than human beings as sacred, and radical feminists who equate "hateful" thoughts and speech with hateful deeds.

Postmodernity rejects the modernist ideals of coherency, uniformity, rationality, progress, and conventional morality, while exhibiting an unflinching commitment to radical egalitarianism, subjectivity, and disorder. Also characteristic of postmodern culture, as Frederick Turner has well noted, is its implicit but conspicuous distrust of the democratic process.[3]

For Gertrude Himmelfarb, who has examined the effects of the postmodern spirit on culture and society in her book *On Looking Into the Abyss,* the great transgression of postmodernity is that it actively proselytizes on behalf of the Nietzchean abyss (hence, the title of her book).[4] The abyss, Himmelfarb observes with utmost sobriety, has grown deeper and more terrifying. The beasts of modernity have mutated into beasts of postmodernity—relativism into nihilism, amorality into immorality, irrationality into insanity, sexual deviancy into polymorphous perversity.

Gene Edward Veith, Jr., has admirably explored the meaning and implications of postmodern thought in his excellent *Postmodern Times: A Christian Guide to Contemporary Thought and Culture.* "The modern worldview constructs rationally designed systems in which human beings find it impossible to live," Veith writes. "The new secular solution [of postmodern thinkers], however, is not only to blow modernism to smithereens but to explode all stable forms, including Christianity."[5] As Veith later points out, "According to the postmodernists, the problem with the Enlightenment is not its uncritical dependence upon human reason alone, but its assumption that there is such a thing as objective truth. . . . When postmodernists say, 'There are no absolutes,' this is no frivolous claim. The course of modern secular thought has led them to this conclusion."[6]

The consequences of this intellectual and moral predicament are all around us, affecting our every personal and public pursuit, our every social, political, and educational institution, and they have become the motive force of our very economy, in which entertainment is the principal industry and in which self-help therapies are prominent in every profession.

But if the consequences of the postmodern condition are all-encompassing, they also are incurable—except by a culturewide rediscovery of the foundations of our civilization in the Judeo-Christian tradition. Even a cursory examination of the intellectual cul-de-sac in which postmodernism has captured our cultural elite demonstrates the validity of this assertion. For the first consequence of postmodernism is the loss of belief in the existence of truth itself. And without a belief in truth, any culture inevitably descends into decay and disorder.

## The Consequences of Postmodernism

### The Worship of Power

In America, one of the most prominent scholar-evangelists for postmodernism is Stanley Fish, a professor of English at Duke University who also teaches law. In his book *There's No Such Thing as Free Speech, and It's a Good Thing, Too,* Fish argues that, since there are no objective, universal standards for truth, all "truth claims" are merely manipulations of language to achieve social or political power. All so-called principles are, according to Fish, merely personal preferences, so debates over *truth* are really power games. "Someone is always going to be restricted next," Fish writes, "and it is your job to make sure that the someone is not you."

Fish goes so far as to declare he does not believe in free speech—one of our most cherished constitutional rights. He bases his conviction on the postmodern thesis that, since there is no truth, there is no rational force to argument. All that is involved in public discourse is the quest for power—so restricting free speech or free maneuverings for "power"—is "a good thing."

## The Loss of Cultural Identity and Integrity

The loss of truth leads naturally to the second consequence of postmodernism: the loss of cultural integrity and the destruction of our own heritage.

Western civilization flourished on the foundations of truth about human nature and destiny under God. Confidence about first principles of existence enabled Western societies to experience a flowering of culture, resulting in magnificent expressions of social order, political organization, and the fine arts. Because the truth exists, and could be known, the truth also could be expressed in language and established in social custom, law, and political economy. The modern era has in one sense lived off the capital of this cultural inheritance. But today that cultural inheritance has been exhausted, and in the exhaustion we have lost confidence in the integrity of our own way of life. In this vacuum postmodern infatuation with ideological *multiculturalism* is flourishing.

The postmodern devotion to radical multiculturalism is perfectly understandable, given the loss of truth. For if there is no truth, language, too, is, as Stanley Fish remarks, only a construct of power. Traditional proclamations of truth and traditional cultural artifacts are only masks for oppressive power. In fact, postmodernist scholars maintain that because truth is only a construct by classes of people who want power over other classes of people, the language of Western moral discourse is only a reflection of the biases of a Western quest for power. We are, to cite a postmodernist slogan, in "a prison house of language." As a result, every aspect of Western tradition and teaching has to be deconstructed. And one way to deconstruct the West is to denigrate the traditions and institutions that have been the West's greatest contribution to civilized moral life.

This hostility to the Western tradition and its manifestation in multiculturalism reaches far beyond the ivory towers of academe. Indeed, they are affecting discourse at every level of American life—including the teaching of our children, as I learned to my horror with my eleven-year-old granddaughter.

I happened to be visiting our son and daughter-in-law the day school began last year. My granddaughter came home, proudly displaying a beautifully illustrated history book. The cover featured an attractive Norman Rockwell painting.

"Who wrote the Bill of Rights?" she asked. "We were studying about that in class." Having pursued doctoral studies in constitutional law, I gave her a detailed answer. Then I suggested we turn to the section on the Bill of Rights and see what the book said. There under a picture of the document was the following caption: "The Bill of Rights provided protection for most Americans but not native Americans, black Americans, and women." My granddaughter was horrified. "That's unfair to exclude blacks and native Americans and women," she said indignantly.

I told her it would be unfair, but it was also untrue. The Bill of Rights excluded no one. "Oh yes it does," she replied. "It says so right here." Then I remembered my own youth—what the teacher or textbook said had to be true.

I proceeded to find the actual text in the book, put my granddaughter beside me, and read each one of the first ten amendments to the Constitution of the United States. At the end of each one I would ask, "Now does that exclude women, native Americans, or blacks?" Each time she shook her head: no.

At the end of the tenth amendment, with no reference made to any exclusions, my granddaughter looked at me in amazement and said, "The book is wrong." It was a moment of real awakening for her.

I then explained that when viewed by today's standards, we could find many shortcomings in our system in its earliest days—the lack of universal franchise for example—but ours was the greatest experiment in human freedom ever undertaken for all time. It is unfair, as these authors attempted to do, to judge what was done two hundred years ago by today's revised standards.

Many Americans are unaware that the skepticism of multiculturalism now extends to the textbooks used in many of our schools. Eventually, unless the loss of cultural integrity that this skepticism fosters is countered, and the moral integrity of our culture reaffirmed, our children and grandchildren will not inherit the wisdom of their own rightful heritage.

Civilizations are destroyed when they become separated from their own heritage and lose an understanding of their shared values, accumulated wisdom of tradition, and debts to the past—to what G. K. Chesterton called "the democracy of the dead." Normally cultures are cut off from their own heritage principally through military defeat or political revolution. We are in peril of being the first people consciously to do this to ourselves—to sever ourselves from our own heritage in quest of absolute autonomy. That is a potential consequence of postmodernism that we must do everything to prevent.

### The Loss of Moral Order and Political Consensus

Just as the loss of truth leads to the loss of cultural integrity, so the loss of cultural integrity results in the disintegration of common moral order and its expression in political consensus. These joint losses—of moral order and political consensus—constitute the third consequence of postmodernism.

The postmodernist rejection of truth naturally has profound consequences for moral conduct. Moral principles are no longer based in transcendent and universal truths but are deemed to be arbitrary constructs of a now-vanquished cultural tradition. The personal lifestyle as a matter of choice supplants the adoption of a common universal code of moral conduct. And this is perfectly logical. For if there is no God, and no truth, all moral codes must be man-made. If you make up your rules, I can make up my own.

The shallowness and the increasing violence of the abortion debate is but one of the serious manifestations of this loss of common moral order. Not unexpectedly, proponents of abortion on demand have attempted to confine debate to the postmodern concept of *choice* in behalf of autonomous individuals who are responsible to no one, not to God, not to their fellow human beings, not even to the child whose life they end. If one woman *chooses* to bear a child, another woman can just as rightly *choose* to have an abortion. The intention of a woman's decision on the issue is irrelevant; the only possible validation of either decision is said to be *choice*. Some advocates for abortion rights go so far as to oppose debate even about purely scientific matters, such as fetal development or ultrasound images of a fetus that reveal it to be a living human person. They do so on the ground that facts might interfere with the exercise of choice.

This utter separation of moral conduct from convictions grounded not in personal preference but in transcendent truth has now become the very law of the land in America. In *Casey v. Planned Parenthood*, the

Supreme Court in 1992 declared, "At the heart of liberty is the right to define one's own concept of existence, of meaning, of the universe, of the mystery of life." As Justice Antonio Scalia warned in his dissent to the Court's majority opinion, the Court's ruling eventually could be expanded to declare a universal right to "homosexual sodomy, polygamy, adult incest, and suicide." In other words, the very moral order of American society could be threatened by the judicial adoption of the intellectual and moral relativism of postmodern thought.

Freedom depends on individuals governing themselves by internalizing commonly accepted moral principles. But if there is no truth, if culture is only a construct of the class in power, there are no common moral principles, and the individual man or woman is left to conclude that self-government is slavery, self-expression the very essence of freedom, even the highest good of life. This is why postmodern ideologies not only give little support for political order but encourage a kind of individualism that is a formula for anarchy and, inevitably, totalitarianism.

Historically, the concern of the American legal system and its courts has not been private metaphysical or religious beliefs that are protected by the First Amendment, but public justice. People of different beliefs —from Christians to atheists to devotees of New Age systems—are free to disagree over the meaning of life. Yet all are able to agree on standards of public order and justice, just as all can agree to stop when a traffic signal is red. In other words, we may subscribe to a common public moral order for reasons based on vastly different religious or philosophical convictions, but we all stop. But even a common practice or policy as simple as stopping when a traffic light is red depends in the final analysis on a widely shared conviction that there is an objective truth that all people may know and to which all people owe allegiance.

After all, if truth does not exist, if no cultural norms are grounded in truth, and if there is no moral law, freedom, too, is an illusion, and, ipso facto, there can be no basis for limiting the power of the state. If cultural values are only a mask for arbitrary power, how are individuals to be restrained from seeking absolute power for themselves, at the expense of political order for all?

Already we are witnessing this dark side of the purportedly "tolerant" propaganda of postmodernism. Traditional views about human sexuality, for example, are routinely ridiculed by cultural elites in our universities and the media and even by high officials of the federal government. Politically correct notions of what may and may not be discussed influence teaching in our schools and have been incorporated into law and the employment policies of many major corporations. As exit polling after the November 1994 elections demonstrated, millions of Americans now deem their own federal government, through its policies and agencies, to be an enemy of traditional cultural values—and traditional American liberties. What these polls reflect is a correct—albeit instinctive—fear that as the traditional moral consensus crumbles, the state becomes arrogant and overreaching, and they show that millions of people attribute the cause of cultural permissiveness and decay to liberal politicians.

## The Loss of Liberty

It would be tragic as well as ironic if the postmodern stress on utter individual freedom apart from all traditional concepts of truth and moral conduct were to end in the loss of freedom through totalitarianism. I am no alarmist, but it stands to reason—albeit a reason whose appeal is rejected by postmodern thinkers—that the state will rush in to impose its absolute power and to quench freedom completely when enough individuals have lost the very ability to lead moral, disciplined lives.

We already see signs of this. Since the 1960s, which marked the ascendancy of postmodernist thought in American life, the rate of violent crime has risen 560 percent. When I got out of prison twenty years ago, there were 230,000 men and women behind bars in America; now there are over 1 million. Moral relativism has had both a quantitative and qualitative effect on the frequency of criminal conduct. To a large extent, criminal behavior in the past was motivated by some recognizable human emotion, such as envy, greed, or hatred. But today, youths commit murder without apparent motive—and without remorse. In the hard lines of their faces, we see among criminals of all ages today the evidence of a new, terrifying threat to society: crime without conscience. Over the next decade, a dramatic rise in the number of youths in crime-prone age groups could result in a crime wave that would dwarf the already-explosive rise in crimes committed by youthful offenders.

Because of my visits to hundreds of prisons in this country and around the world, I am convinced that the exploding rates of violent crime will never be lowered simply by enacting more stringent penalties, employing more police, or building more prisons. The only real solution to the increase in senseless violent crime is a recultivation of conscience. And throughout the history of our own society, the cultivation of conscience, both among individuals and within social and political institutions, has been provided in large measure by men and women of Christian faith.

This is why the disappearance of a national consensus on the very existence and nature of truth and the erosion of our former moral and political consensus have ominous implications for our political order. Millions of Americans have become so fearful of violent crime that they are beginning to clamor for public safety at all costs—even at the expense of fundamental rights and responsibilities. For example, a poll of the residents of Miami showed that 71 percent would favor random search-and-seizure by police if suspension of Fourth Amendment protections would result in lower crime rates.[7] The implication is obvious: When people are forced to choose between liberty and security, many will choose security—at the expense of liberty. In other words, when moral chaos sets in, many people will gladly surrender their liberties to secure a sense of peace.

Postmodernists may shun appeals to reason or revelation, but the lessons of history are inescapable. One of the principle lessons of history is that when truth retreats tyranny advances. Postmodernist ideologies give little theoretical support for political freedom. The fourth consequence of postmodernism may very well then prove to be the loss of liberty.

The purpose of civil authority, according to Romans 13, is to restrain evildoers, lest original sin sweep away the social order. The postmodernist state—including our own American government at present—falls short of this purpose when it fails to restrain either evildoers or its own appetites. As a result, policies proposed to control everything from violent crime to the abortion debate, and even the very concept of religious freedom itself, as proven by the tragic conflagration of the Branch Davidians' sect in Waco, Texas, wrench back and forth between license and tyranny.

Christians have always insisted that truth and morality cannot be maintained apart from God. The history of the modern era and now of the nascent postmodern era bears witness to the immutability of this conviction. The original consequences of the Fall of our race as they are described in Genesis are repeated time and again in history whenever the human intellect and human will attempt to act autonomously from the laws of God established in our very nature and declared in the revelation of his Word. Yet these restraints, grounded in the eternal truths of God's will for humankind, have once again been cast off. This is the crisis of postmodern society. And in it, in our own society today, nothing less is at stake than the very possibility of a civilized social order and the political freedoms that it alone allows.

## Beyond the Culture War

By definition, those who belong to a particular culture share certain assumptions—a vision of the world. Because of this consensus, the people who comprise a culture can agree on how to live together, how to communicate with each other, and how to govern themselves. Today, however, the West is experimenting with a new kind of individual autonomy that threatens to render culture impossible.

In his book *Culture Wars*, sociologist James Davison Hunter argues that the current controversies over abortion, sexual morality, and school textbooks finally manifest the profound split in American culture made inevitable by the Enlightenment and long since apparent in once-Christian Europe.[8] No longer can Americans agree on foundational moral and intellectual assumptions or even on a common methodology or a common language for discussing these issues. On one side of these and other significant issues are those who appeal to objective criteria, such as biblical teaching, principles of natural law, or traditional custom. On the other side are those who, having rejected every appeal beyond mere self-interest, rely solely on subjective criteria: *How do you feel about it?* or *Everybody has to have a choice.*

In his more recent book, *Before the Shooting Begins,* Hunter points out that culture wars often end in shooting wars. He asks correctly whether American democracy can long survive if Americans no longer share a moral consensus.[9]

At root, every issue that divides the American people is religious in essence. In one respect of course, religion transcends culture. Christianity, for example, is a catholic or universal faith that manifests itself in every culture in the world. In another respect, though, religion is the very basis for culture and is both the origin and sustaining authority of a culture's moral principles, social customs, and political institutions. As historian Christopher Dawson often pointed out, religious *cult* is the very origin of social and political culture.[10]

It is a historic fact that Western civilization is a consequence of Christian culture. Christian teaching has given rise to the West's traditional insistence on the eternal moral worth of the individual and also to the West's confidence in the rational order of creation. Just so, the United States, though not wholly in fact a Christian nation, owes its very existence to the Christian principles that emerged in Europe through nearly two millennia of Christian influence.

But Christianity is no longer the cultural force either in Europe or in America that it once was. Indeed, as I have attempted to demonstrate, entire schools of secular thought are laboring to eradicate the last remaining vestiges of Christian influence from contemporary life.

In this much-discussed "culture-war," Christians are losing. With the forces arrayed against us—a contemptuous media, unrestrained consumerism, sexual libertinism, a hostile academia, and an omnipresent hedonistic entertainment industry—Christians are both surrounded and outnumbered. As James Hunter indicates in the very title of his recent book, *Before the Shooting Begins*, the phrase "culture war" is a metaphor that signifies a struggle that eventually could descend into a violent civilizational confrontation.[11] Already, for example, some pro-life advocates have resorted to assassinating abortionists, apparently in the dreadfully misguided belief that avenues to peaceful political change have been foreclosed. But violence is forbidden to Christians for many reasons—not the least because violent means could never address the origins of our moral and political crises. These origins are to be found in spiritual rebellion.

## The Church and Culture

Where does this leave evangelicals, Catholics, and other Christians who believe in objective truth and a transcendent morality? What can the church do to renew American culture?

Ironically the Church must first remember that its principal obligation is *not* to renew the culture. The task of the Church is to be the Church, to proclaim the gospel of Jesus Christ, and to make disciples.

The Church is called to be faithful to God, to live out his Word, to proclaim his truth, and to assist men and women in growing spiritually as part of a holy, righteous community. Whenever the Church has made culture its first priority, its message has become politicized and the Church has been swallowed up by the surrounding culture. Whenever the Church has focused on being faithful to Christ, it has been used powerfully to influence the culture.

This is a question of maintaining priorities. Our first obligation is to be the people of God, but that does not mean we are to ignore politics. To the contrary. As citizens we are to take a keen interest in the political process: As Augustine argued, Christians ought to be the best of citizens because we act in the love of God, whereas others act because they are forced to do so. So both as citizens and as Christians, acting as salt and light, we are to be fully involved in the political process. But unlike our secular friends, we recognize that the problems in our culture cannot be solved by political power alone.

And we must always guard the independence of the gospel from secular ideologies. A politicized gospel, whether in the form of liberation theology on the left or nationalism on the right, is not biblical. When the Church is acting as the Church, it will avoid partisan alignment. Otherwise, politicians of both the right and the left would exploit the Church for their own ends. (I know. When I was in politics, I used to do it.)

Christians must also have a realistic view of the limits of politics. Governmental solutions at their best can never address problems that are essentially spiritual. In 1980 most Christians were euphoric over the election of a conservative president in Ronald Reagan. But families continued to fall apart, the abortion rate soared, sexual promiscuity blossomed into the AIDS epidemic, and postmodernist philosophies took over the universities. Some of the key Supreme Court votes in decisions such as *Casey v. Planned Parenthood* that have affirmed the right to an abortion and enshrined other postmodernist principles, were cast by justices appointed by conservative presidents. Our cultural problems are not so much political as, in order, spiritual, intellectual, and moral in origin.

Christians need to contribute to the public debates; they need to be zealous in protecting religious freedom and other human rights and to promote the rule of law. But their faith must always be centered in Christ, never in political power, much less in politicians.

For many reasons, Christians can expect to be increasingly unwelcome in postmodern cultures. Some politicians and many in the media in America, for example, are stirring up fear of the so-called Religious Right. Catholics and evangelical Protestants are experiencing together the bitter sting of cultural ostracism.

Beyond ostracism, committed evangelicals and Catholics may expect to experience downright hostility as American culture enters more deeply into a postmodern frame of reference. For example, George Gallup found in a 1992 poll that 50 percent of the American people fear fundamentalist Christians. Nearly 30 percent would not want a fundamentalist—that is, a conservative Christian—as a neighbor.

No doubt evangelicals and Catholics could improve their image by being more Christlike. But I think the hostility is more substantially grounded. (Christ was not very popular either.) The message of the Church is that there is truth, whether people like it or not—intellectual, moral, and spiritual truth. The Church is proclaiming Christ, "the way, *the truth,* and the life" (John 14:6). This message cannot fail to be offensive to those who reject the very concept of truth. The more the Church proclaims that message, the more it is challenging the postmodern desire for autonomy and pleasure, for the right to choose one's own reality.

But we can also expect to break through the defenses of some of our antagonists, forcing them to confront their own condition and to be convicted of their sin so that they can know, first, the reality of God, and, second, the love of God through our Lord Jesus Christ. Despite the cultural animosity Christians face, the Church must still do the work of evangelism. God has promised that his Holy Spirit will always bring people to faith.

The apostle Paul proclaimed the gospel to an alien and antagonistic culture that had no background in the Scriptures and in which abortion, infanticide, violence, and homosexuality were rampant. The Romans went so far as to erect one more obstacle to evangelism: Potential converts knew that if they embraced the Christian faith they would face death. Yet the gospel spread like wildfire.

That age of martyrdom long ago was in many respects the golden age of the Church. The early Church had its share of mistakes and divisions, yet it demonstrated a purity of faith, love, and devotion that our critics find it hard to fault. Unworthy actions of the Church have come most often when Christianity has become culturally acceptable. Perhaps we may hope that the postmodern age will herald a return to the virtues and vitality of the early Church.

## Challenges of the Faithful Church

### Disciple Members

The Church faces a series of daunting challenges.

First, it must disciple its own members. A 1994 poll by George Barna found that 72 percent of Americans do not believe there exists an absolute truth about God, the origin and nature of the human race, or standards of moral conduct.[12] An even more frightening statistic is that 62 percent of Americans who identify themselves as evangelical Christians do not believe in absolute truth. In other words, postmodern intellectual skepticism has infiltrated the Church. Other polls find that only 37 percent of Christians know what the word *gospel* means; only 40 percent know that Jesus gave the Sermon on the Mount; only 9 percent can identify the Great Commission.

Moral relativism also has infected the Church. A poll by Father Andrew Greeley found that 56 percent of single fundamentalists engage in sex outside of marriage—about the same rate as for liberals (57 percent), while 66 percent of single Catholics are sexually active.[13] Remarkably, Father Greeley found that American Catholics may be more permissive than secular Americans: whereas 67 percent of all those he polled said they believe that premarital sex is morally permissible, an astonishing 83 percent of Catholics do so—in direct defiance of their church's teaching. This is scandalous—a reflection on how many are simply nominal in their faith.

These polls show that both believing evangelicals and believing Catholics must place a higher priority on Christian education and spiritual formation. Christians must be taught what being a Christian means. Christians must also be trained to *think* biblically, so they understand their faith and can defend it against doubt, drift, and actual attack. They need to be taught to understand their times, to recognize that they are living in a hostile moral environment, and to develop spiritual discernment to sort out the true from the false and the good from the evil.

The Church in the postmodern age cannot afford the luxury of anti-intellectualism and sentimentality, of downplaying doctrine and relaxing the rigor of God's moral demands. Standing up for the truth of God's Word, as did Athanasius against heterodox dissenters in the early Church, may be costly. Churches that make demands on their members may well shrink in membership (though it is also possible that people are yearning for a definite spiritual structure that can give order to their lives). The Church *must* put its own house in order. Otherwise, it will have nothing to offer postmodern culture.

## Defend the Truth

Second, the Church must make a powerful apologetic in defense of truth. We have to demonstrate that there is *a* truth before we can pronounce *the* Truth. Recently on an airplane I sat across the aisle from a young woman. She had attended a fundamentalist college and recognized me from having read my book *Born Again*. She had turned away from the faith. She said, "I don't believe that I can say *this is true*. How do I know? I don't believe anything is true. How do I know anything is true?" We talked about the whole concept of truth—if there is truth, and, if so, how it must affect our lives. Only then was she ready to listen to me talk about God.

During the modern era, discussions with non-Christians usually hinged on questions of truth: Is there a God? Is the Bible reliable? Is Jesus who he said he is? Today non-Christians do not object to Christianity because they doubt its claims are true; they object to Christianity because it claims to be true. "Christianity may be true for you," they will say, "but it isn't true for me." "Jesus works for some people, but other religions work just as well for others." Or the ultimate postmodernist put-down, "You Christians think you have the only truth."

Though proponents of postmodernism realize that they have no conceptual basis for truth, Christians do have a foundation for truth on which they can build, as for centuries they have been building. Once again, however, the Church needs scholars who can recover and revitalize the rich intellectual tradition that is such a precious but now neglected part of our culture's heritage. But it is the task of every Christian, not just scholars and clergy, to cultivate a biblically informed mind and to be prepared to defend what we believe. All Christians need to cultivate a comprehensive biblical worldview—a view of all of life informed by Scripture.

## Make a Cultural Apologetic

Third, Christians need to make a powerful *cultural* apologetic. Believing evangelicals and believing Catholics need to unmask the inadequacies of contemporary culture and show that Christianity offers a compelling alternative.

The polls, for what they are worth, keep telling us bad news, but they are also starting to reflect rays of hope. A recent opinion poll by Richard Wirthlin found that 62 percent of Americans believe this country is on the wrong track.[14] A *Times Mirror* survey found that 71 percent are dissatisfied with the way things are going in America.[15] Their complaint is no longer with the economy. They are worried about crime, about the breakdown in society, about the loss of moral values. *Newsweek* found that 76 percent of Americans believe we are in a spiritual and moral decline.[16] Something is crying out from the soul of America; people are sensing that postmodernism is a formula for personal, social, and moral ruin.

This dissatisfaction, this disillusionment with relativism, provides an important opening for the Church. In every human heart there is something—the image of God—that cries out for truth, even when the surrounding culture says there is no truth. There is a craving for human dignity, even when the culture says individual identity is an illusion. There is a struggle with guilt and meaning, even when the culture says guilt is a Christian contrivance to deny people the pleasures of a good time.

When President Clinton appeared on MTV before a group of teens, the big news was the question about whether he wore boxers or briefs. That the president of the United States was asked such a question—and, even more, that he answered it—shows how the very notion of public authority has been trivialized. But the most significant moment of the evening came when a seventeen-year-old said, "Mr. President, it seems to me that singer Kurt Cobain's recent suicide exemplified the emptiness that many in our generation feel. How do you propose to teach our youth how important life is?"

Her question was profound, but neither the President nor the press understood it. The *New York Times* reported that "Mr. Clinton did not seem to have an immediate legislative solution at hand." (We can be thankful at least for that—one can imagine a "Meaning of Life" bill being sent to Congress from the White House.) Apparently taken aback,

Clinton gave a therapeutic answer about the need to feel good about yourself. But that did not answer the question. Kurt Cobain took pills and drugs to make him feel good. The young woman was asking whether life has any objective meaning: Is there truth?

And of course she was asking the wrong person. That kind of question can be answered only by the Church.

The fact is, postmodernism is refuting itself. Its intellectual relativism has shut down learning in many of our schools, turning education into a mockery and giving us a generation of functionally illiterate channel-surfers. Its concomitant moral relativism has soured personal relationships and broken families apart. Its rhetoric of permissiveness has born bitter fruit in pervasive despair, violence, and crime. These and other failures of our culture represent irrefutable evidence that contemporary alternatives to traditional religious faith—to the Christian principles from which our culture sprang—are not only inadequate but destructive. Human beings do indeed require for civilized living a higher conceptual framework than is being provided by ideologies of the modern era.

Christianity addresses these and all other legitimate concerns of modern thought, and especially of postmodern thought, without falling prey to their respective dangers. For example, yes, reason alone is limited, but objective truth still exists. Yes, humanism is a mirage, but human beings still have worth and dignity. Yes, human beings exist in great cultural diversity, but they all share a common nature and a common spiritual need. It has been observed that there is, in fact, only one truly multicultural institution: the Church. On every continent, in nearly every tribe and language, in every race and ethnic group on the face of the earth, Christians are worshiping the same God and sharing the same faith in Jesus Christ.

## Demonstrate Christian Living

Demonstrated Christian living is critical to our witness to the truth and to our cultural apologetic. Postmodernists tend to be oblivious to abstract arguments, but they can see and be moved by Christian *life*. Christians, in their concern for human life and compassion for the suffering, brought hospitals to America. Christians, committed to truth, opened the first schools and universities. Christians, aware of a moral law that transcends the culture, were instigators of social reform.

About the only moral value postmodernists seem to be able to advance is total, undiscriminating tolerance, but being able to tolerate anything is a formula for accepting the status quo. Those who accept people as they are have no interest in helping them change, even when their condition and behavior is ruining their lives. Those who think one culture as good as another have no motivation to work to improve society. Mere tolerance is a weak and passive virtue compared to the active energy of Christian love. It is hard to see how postmodernism could ever inspire people to embrace the virtues of compassion, self-sacrifice, and service to others. It takes Christianity to marshal the spirit we see in our prison ministry that motivates volunteers to go into prisons, to work patiently with killers and child molesters, to care for those who are dying of AIDS, or to work among the poor and suffering in the inner cities.

The pro-life message is not taken very seriously by the media and the cultural establishment. But when Mother Teresa at the National Prayer Breakfast stood and confronted the nation's power elite over the injustice of abortion, people paid attention. The image of this frail nun, barely able to peep over the podium, gently but boldly chastising the president of the United States, the most powerful man in the world, captures well the position of the Church in the postmodern age—powerless, marginalized, weak by the world's standards, yet in possession of a truth that can bring powers and principalities to their knees.

After Mother Teresa's speech, it was President Clinton's turn to address the assembly. What could this pro-choice president say in response to Mother Teresa? In the tense atmosphere, President Clinton said something extraordinarily significant. He paid homage to the example of her life. In light of Mother Teresa's *life*, her work among the poor and the dying, he was defenseless against her pro-life message. Mother Teresa's example gives her a moral authority that goes beyond eloquence and argument. Her fiery love for the dying beggars in Calcutta, the way she and her followers wash the sores of the suffering, and the Christlike spirit she radiates through all of her words and actions lend her a singular credibility.

We in Prison Fellowship experience this same attentiveness when we demonstrate our faith in simple acts of Christian love and when the power of Jesus Christ transforms the lives of hardened criminals in ways that astonish psychiatrists and social workers. It is also the power of Jesus

Christ that sends our army of volunteers into prisons, bringing the love of Christ to the most repugnant of sinners.

Christians are also working with pregnant women to give them an alternative to abortion: paying their medical bills, taking them into their homes, and helping care for the children they bear. Christian ministries are giving genuine help to the poor—not just by giving them handouts as the government does, but by helping them personally to escape the lifestyle of poverty. Christians are on the front line whenever there is a disaster or a famine across the world.

The Church must intensify its efforts to demonstrate the beneficial consequences of the Christian faith, not only in institutional ways, but also in the way ordinary Christians relate to their families, friends, and co-workers. The Church must equip its members for works of service, sending them out into the mainstream of life, carrying with them the truth of God's Word. If we can show that our faith makes a difference in our lives and in the way we treat others, we can make our faith credible, even in the postmodern age.

To urge the Church to respond to our contemporary culture by discipling its members, cultivating truth, engaging the culture, and demonstrating our faith in action—this is to propose nothing new. This is what the Church at its best has always done. From a Protestant perspective, this is the proudest heritage of the Reformation and our evangelical tradition.

## The Evangelical Heritage

The term *evangelical* embraces a wide range of diverse theologies. For example, Calvinists, who do not believe that the human will has any role in salvation, consider themselves to be evangelical, as do Arminians, who believe that salvation and obedience derive from a free decision. Some evangelicals are charismatic or Pentecostal, believing that the Holy Spirit communicates directly to individuals and empowers Christians with miraculous gifts. Other evangelicals believe the charismatic movement to be perilously subjective. Some evangelicals come from the holiness tradition, with its strict taboos on worldly behavior; others emphasize the freedom of Christians from legalistic rules of conduct. Politically, some evangelicals are conservative; others are liberal; still others, drawing from the pacifism and separatism of the Anabaptist tradition, could be described actually as radical. Indeed, it is significant that 30 percent of those who describe themselves as evangelical are Roman Catholic.

While evangelicals of different traditions seriously defend and debate their respective theological systems, they enjoy a remarkable degree of peace with one another. Their similarities and common purposes—as well as the rise of parachurch ministries that mobilize Christians outside of denominational structures—have enabled evangelicals to present something of a common front.

This is possible because evangelicals share a commitment to the *evangelium* or "good news" that Jesus Christ died for our sins and offers salvation to all who put their faith in him. As a result, evangelicals are dedicated to *evangelism,* that is, the proclamation of the gospel to non-Christians, to those who do not know Jesus Christ and so are lost in their sins. Because of this emphasis on conversion, many members of evangelical churches, myself among them, have been converted to the Christian faith as adults. This fact may explain the zeal and intensity of our convictions. After all, converts—those who have embraced the faith in a conscious and informed manner—tend to be critical of the sinful lifestyles or shallow religiosity they practiced before their conversion, and they also tend to be committed, rather than nominal, Christians.

All evangelicals also have a high regard for the Bible, the infallible Word of God, which tells us of Christ and of God's will for our lives. Though evangelicals may disagree about how parts of the Scriptures should be interpreted, all agree that we have a final and complete authority—God's self-revelation in human language.

## An "Evangelical Catholic"

While some would derive the common use of the term *evangelical* initially from the sixteenth century, evangelical belief is rooted in the creeds and convictions of the first centuries, in which the subapostolic Church sought to affirm and reaffirm the essence of the *evangelion*. In his reaffirmation of the gospel of grace, however, contrary to the common misconception, Luther did not intend actually to start a new church. Rather, his was a call to *restore* the purity of the apostolic Church. Luther's protest was simultaneously an exhortation to *return* to historic Christian orthodoxy.

To employ the term used by many Lutherans today, Luther was, in fact, an "evangelical Catholic." For example, he held a high view of the sacraments and insisted on the baptismal regeneration of infants and the Presence of Christ in the Eucharist. But Luther also believed that the gospel—the good news of salvation by grace through faith alone made possible by Christ's death and resurrection—had become obscured in the medieval and late-medieval Church (specifically: (1) apostolization of extra-biblical traditions, (2) divinization of papacy, and (3) obscuring of the doctrine of justification). He believed that Christians should have a personal faith, a genuine relationship with Jesus Christ. He also believed that the Bible should be available not only to clergy but to everyone—not so that everyone could devise private theologies, but so that each Christian could encounter, in an intimate way, God's law and gospel. In short, Luther opposed only what he deemed to be corruptions within the medieval Catholic Church, and, for his pains, he and those who agreed with him were excommunicated.

As a result, the unity of Western Christendom was broken. Protestantism and Catholicism went their separate ways, falling into antagonism and war. Protestantism, too, fragmented into denominations holding to widely diverse theologies, as Luther's evangelicals were challenged by the reformed Calvinist theologians, as well as by the protocharismatic enthusiasts and the socially radical Anabaptists. Nevertheless, the Reformation churches, for all their theological diversity, had an impact on every aspect of European culture.

For example, the Reformation doctrine of vocation helped break down the barriers between the sacred and the secular, bringing all of life under the lordship of Christ. Just as they stressed the role of every Christian—not just the clergy—as part of Christ's Church, the Reformers saw all vocations—sacred and secular, intellectual and manual—as ways of serving God. The works of monks and priests, wrote Luther, "in God's sight are in no way whatever superior to the works of a farmer laboring in the field, or of a woman looking after her home." What mattered was that each individual should understand his or her calling, and in so doing collaborate with God in the grand design of the universe, working for God's glory, the common good, and his or her own fulfillment.

This theological insight bore fruit in social, political, and economic change. The view that scrubbing floors possessed a sacred dignity democratized the work ethic. The conviction that individuals should follow their own God-given talents instead of conforming to an inherited trade helped to shatter rigid social castes. Until the Reformation, most forms of trade carried on for profit were seen as inherently immoral, but the insistence that all work, including that of tradesmen and businessmen, could be pleasing to God liberated business. Profit was no longer viewed simply as a means of accumulating wealth, but as a way to help others. Calvin encouraged workers to produce more than they needed so they could give the surpluses to those in need. In this way the Reformation paved the way for democratic capitalism.

The Reformation's emphasis on a personal relationship with Christ also meant that every person should be able to read God's Word. The poor as well as the rich, women as well as men, servant girls and plowboys, all began to be taught how to read the Bible. Reformed or Protestant churches began schools that were open to all. Once peasants learned how to read the Bible, they could read everything else. This access to knowledge meant that people could improve their lives. Education led to social mobility. As the invention of the printing press made Bibles—and then every other kind of book—available to everyone, Western culture was on its way to achieving a general literacy that provided incalculable personal and social benefits.

Individuals who knew their own worth and had access to knowledge soon demanded the right to govern themselves. Their Bibles taught them that there is a moral law that transcends the state, that kings themselves could be judged according to an objective law. The Scottish Presbyterian Samuel Rutherford explored this notion in his classic treatise *Lex Rex: or The Law and the Prince* (1644). *Lex Rex* means literally that law is king. Rutherford argued that no one is above the law—that even kings and other rulers, while agents of God, are under the higher authority of God's law. Though this belief was implicit in Catholicism, Rutherford was the first to employ it to condemn the concept of the divine right of kings. For example, Rutherford argued that a ruler who violates the moral law is no longer God's agent but a tyrant. Therefore, though Christians are obliged to obey their legitimate rulers, they may challenge and if need be even disobey and rebel against tyrannical state power.

Rutherford's political theory, augmented by the Reformed churches' developing practice of the congregational form of governance, paved the way for the Puritan revolution in England, which resulted in the execution of Charles I and the establishment of the first modern parliamentary republic. Eventually, Rutherford's ideas were expanded by John Locke into a powerful argument for self-government that was profoundly influential among Americans of the eighteenth century, especially among leaders of the American Revolution and drafters of the United States Constitution. Thus did the Reformation provide the original conceptual basis for political freedom and democratic government.

Theories of human perfectibility and social and political organization that were promulgated by Enlightenment thinkers gradually supplanted this Reformation tradition, so that wholly secular notions about human existence came first to challenge, and eventually to displace, the religious influence of heirs of the Reformation. However, at the same time, the Wesleyan revivals in England and the Great Awakening in America effected a resurgence of evangelical belief and practice. Christians who remained committed to the Scriptures and to the gospel returned to the forefront of social and political reform in both Europe and the United States.

To me, an especially inspiring example of this evangelical heritage within the modern era is William Wilberforce. A member of the British House of Commons, Wilberforce converted to evangelical Christianity in 1784. He then founded an organization called the Proclamation Society for the "reformation of manners," that is, for the moral reawakening of society. His major objective was the abolition of slavery in the British dominions. Motivated by his evangelical faith, Wilberforce worked night and day, speaking to groups large and small, to educate citizens of the evils of slavery while endeavoring as a legislator to change the law. Finally, in 1807, his bill to abolish the slave trade was passed. Thereafter, and for the remainder of his life, he devoted his energies to abolishing the very existence of slavery in English law. In 1833, only days after the second reading in Parliament of the bill to achieve that noble end, Wilberforce died. Slavery in British dominions effectively died with him.

Wilberforce exemplifies the way in which an individual Christian, through living the love of Christ, can have influence—can even change—the whole of a culture. Other evangelicals throughout the nineteenth century, especially in America, were in the forefront of efforts to help the poor, to improve the lot of women and children, to fight the drunkenness and sexual immorality that were devastating families, and to challenge society to abide by its highest ideals.

Of course the record of evangelicals is not perfect. The gospel sometimes was taken hostage by political ideology—in the United States, for example, Northern evangelicals denounced slavery in the South, while Southern evangelicals defended the institution. Both based their claims on the Bible. For other Christians of the nineteenth century, social activism eventually overshadowed their original commitment to the gospel, and their focus shifted away from spiritual salvation to the so-called social gospel. This transformation gave rise to a liberal or modernist Protestantism that eventually eclipsed the influence of the evangelical tradition, which by the twentieth century was beginning to be defined as "fundamentalism."

By the advent of the twentieth century, the hegemony of higher critical assumptions about Scripture and related attacks against the authority of Christian revelation had compelled conservative Christians to rally in behalf of what they called "the fundamentals" of Christian faith and to defend them with sophisticated scholarship. Nearly every Protestant denomination in America was racked by this controversy between modernists and fundamentalists. In the end, modernists prevailed, assuming control of most mainline denominations and seminaries. The fundamentalists, unfairly ridiculed as both anti-intellectual and out of touch with the times, were forced to form a kind of subculture. They established independent congregations and denominations and, for a while, retreated from full engagement with American culture.

This retreat had many ramifications. For example, in shifting their attention from the classical Christian and Reformation emphasis on virtue, which looks outward upon the world, many fundamentalist Christians concerned themselves primarily with personal piety, which of course looks inward upon the self. This turn to a narrow, private pietism meant that many conservative Protestants, concerned only with doctrinal purity, failed to participate in the great intellectual and cultural debates of the early twentieth century. Though the first defense of fundamentalism had been provided by the learned faculty of Princeton University, adherents of fundamental beliefs came increasingly to hold anti-intellectual views of Christian faith and practice. In this way, ironically, fundamentalists unwittingly abetted the outright secularists who were striving to make orthodox Christianity of marginal importance in American life.

In recent decades, however, this has changed. In 1947, for example, one of the towering figures of our era, theologian Carl F. H. Henry, wrote *The Uneasy Conscience of Modern Fundamentalism,* which challenged the internal weaknesses of fundamentalism. Henry was joined by a new generation of conservative Protestant theologians who articulated a renewed, more sophisticated defense of orthodoxy. Henry also founded *Christianity Today,* which helped popularize the new movement. Eventually, these able scholars achieved intellectual respectability for their defense of the faith, and in doing so reappropriated the designation of *evangelical,* for the very term *fundamentalist* had become burdened with problematic connotations.

Another important figure in this transition from separatist fundamentalism to culturally engaged evangelicalism was the late Francis Schaeffer, who in my judgment was one of the great prophets of the twentieth century. Schaeffer looked like anything but a typical preacher. Indeed, with his goatee and knickers he looked more like an eccentric from the mountains, which in fact he was, for his ministry was centered not in the Bible Belt of America but on a mountainside in Switzerland. Yet, perhaps more than anyone else, Schaeffer jolted conservative American Protestants out of their parochialism and complacency and showed them how to challenge the surrounding culture with the truth of God's Word.

Schaeffer accomplished this through L'Abri, a center he established in the Alps where people studied the Bible in depth and explored the consequences of the biblical worldview. L'Abri became a major center of Christian thought, evangelism, and discipleship. Schaeffer developed a powerful critique of the ways in which Western culture had fallen away from the biblical worldview. He encouraged Christians to use their minds, to study secular thinkers, and to analyze works of art. Schaeffer also urged Christians to create art of their own, and to think and to act Christianly in every dimension of life.

During the intellectual confusions and social upheavals of the 1960s and 1970s, young people throughout Europe and the United States flocked to L'Abri, where they were introduced to a vigorous Christianity and challenged to bring their faith to bear upon culture. Schaeffer's books became popular on many college campuses and were best-sellers in Christian bookstores. His film series *How Shall We Then Live?* extended Schaeffer's cultural critique to local churches. His condemnation of abortion, conveyed in another film series, *Whatever Happened to the*

*Human Race?* helped to mobilize evangelicals for the pro-life movement.

In this way Schaeffer's ministry at L'Abri influenced a generation of evangelical scholars, leaders, and activists. Christian students, having spent a summer at L'Abri, returned to college and evangelized their friends. Campus ministries such as InterVarsity Christian Fellowship, Navigators, and Campus Crusade for Christ were enabled to lead an evangelical renewal in the very citadels of secularism.

For one brief moment in time, then, evangelicals achieved attention and respectability. For example, *Newsweek* proclaimed 1976 the "Year of the Evangelical." In February of that year, my book *Born Again* was published. But I knew almost nothing about the evangelical world when Barbara Walters interviewed me on the *Today Show*. She wanted to talk about Watergate; I wanted to talk about Jesus. We compromised and agreed to spend seven minutes on Watergate and seven minutes on how Jesus had changed my life. At the end of the interview, she held up a copy of *Born Again* and told viewers, "This is a great book. Go out and read it." By that night almost all of the book stores in America had sold out of my book. Three days later someone asked Jimmy Carter, then a relatively obscure candidate for president campaigning in New Hampshire, if he was born again. He said he was. Within months, rock musicians, movie stars, and football teams were claiming the term *born again.*

For reasons previously explained, evangelicals since the mid-1970s have lost much of their influence in intellectual and cultural debate. However, by acquiring a renewed understanding of the role of the Church in society, that influence can be recovered—indeed, it must be recovered.

## The Evangelical Challenge—Ecumenism of the Trenches

Unfortunately, evangelicals are divided about how best to respond to contemporary culture. Some say we should tailor our message to appeal to the contemporary mind—playing down doctrine and the message of repentance, throwing out the trappings of the old-time religion in favor of pop music, entertaining worship services, and a feel-good message that caters to the consumerist impulse fostered by the American economy. Others, including myself, argue that we cannot evangelize the culture by conforming to it, and that, if we were to abandon our evangelical distinctiveness, the culture would evangelize *us* and the biblical worldview would cease even to exist in large, popular megachurches.

In my judgment, therefore, evangelicals must neither withdraw from the culture nor surrender to it. Rather, they must engage the culture with the truth of God's Word and the power of the gospel.

To do so, we must recenter ourselves on the key doctrines of historical Christianity. This means reappropriating our heritage in the Reformation as well as our heritage as Christians, which goes back even earlier, through the early Church to the time of the apostles. As we become aware of the great gulf opening up between those who believe in orthodox Christianity and those who do not, between the Church, with its supernatural foundation, and the culture, which is trying to do without any foundation at all, we suddenly discover new friends who are with us on the same side of the chasm. It is the "ecumenism of the trenches" to which I previously alluded and which "Evangelicals and Catholics Together" is intended to cement and encourage.

This is the chasm—the culture war—in the face of which evangelicals and Catholics find themselves to be allies. This is the context in which we can learn a great deal about and from each other. And we can learn from our differences as well as from our similarities.

For example, on the critical issue of truth, evangelicals tend to rely on the Reformation principle of *sola scriptura*. Our authority in matters of truth is Scripture alone. Though Protestant theologians occasionally invoke the natural law—God's will as expressed in his creation, imprinted on the conscience, and accessible through reason—for the most part evangelicals look to the Bible for all we need to know about God and his will for our lives.

This reliance on Scripture alone means that evangelicals will not have in their ranks the metaphysicians and the profound moral philosophers produced by the Catholic tradition. The reason is that our best theologians tend not to be systematic philosophers but Bible expositors. This fact accounts for the misconception common among Catholics that evangelicals read the Bible to devise their own private doctrines, thereby negating the function of the Church. However, evangelicals do not read the Bible primarily to construct private theologies but to encounter God. Consequently, while evangelicals can learn from Catholic theologians how to think deeply about spiritual truths and moral philosophy,

Catholics can learn from evangelicals about the value of close, intense Bible study.

Another significant difference is that evangelicals stress a personal faith, while Catholics, generally speaking, stress a corporate faith. Evangelicals stress the salvation of the individual, who is brought into, as we say, "a personal relationship with Jesus Christ." Catholics, by comparison, stress the salvation of the *community* of believers, with individuals coming to Christ as they take part in the corporate life of the Church.

It is true that some evangelicals develop what I have called a Jesus-and-me attitude. The temptation is to reduce Christianity to a private transaction between the individual and God, with no need for other people, for an institutional church, or for social responsibility. In fact, the democratic ethos of America leads many people to have this view of religion—from those who "feel close to God" on a golf course to politicians who say they will not let their "personal religious views" influence their policies as public officials. But the Bible makes clear the crucial importance of the Church, of individual believers joining together into a community that is no less than the body of Christ. In my book *The Body*, I explore what this means for all Christians. So, evangelicals can learn from Catholics a high view of the Church.

At the same time, since the very concept of individual identity is under such attack today, the evangelical emphasis on an individual's unique, internalized relationship with God acquires a new importance. So, Catholics can learn from evangelicals the importance of a personal faith.

There is, to be sure, a great deal of the personal piety emphasized by evangelicals among Catholics as well. This is true even though the Catholic Church in America seems to many observers to be characterized by a merely nominal faith, with members mechanically going through the motions, attending mass and receiving the sacraments without accepting or obeying the actual teachings of their Church. (I am thinking, for example, of the politicians who flaunt their Catholicism but insist that their religion will not affect their pro-choice stance on abortion. Or of the large number of American Catholics who defy their church's teaching on sexual morality.) Certainly there also are nominal Christians in evangelical churches; but, because evangelicals stress a conscious belief and commitment, undoubtedly the number of nominal believers is much lower. It is not always clear if this shared problem calls for evangelism—for actually converting people in the pew from nonbelief to a living faith—or for what evangelicals call "discipleship" and Catholics mean by "spiritual formation." Regardless, Catholics have much to learn from evangelicals about evangelism, personal commitment, and the power of the Holy Spirit to change people's lives.

Both evangelicals and Catholics also can learn together from the Reformation principle of vocation. Though heirs of the Reformation, many contemporary evangelicals have forgotten some of its lessons. These evangelicals mistakenly believe we can serve God only in church work, so they withdraw into private piety. The results include false barriers between the sacred and the secular, self-contained institutions, small-minded legalisms, and attempts to manipulate God for our own self-fulfillment—faults that resemble the medieval Catholicism that Luther condemned!

The Reformers emphasized the lordship of Christ in all of creation, including all human endeavor. This means that, while our efforts are as nothing before the sovereign, holy God, nevertheless he calls us to serve him not only in what we are but through what we do. God's plan for us in this regard is sometimes bigger than we realize. Too often we fail to recognize the part the whole of our lives can play in God's merciful designs. This reminder of the great truth that the ordinary occupations of all Christian men and women are callings from God, who has given a due share of talents to all of his children so that they can do his will in the world, has revolutionary implications for the renewal of American culture.

For example, it means that Christians must serve God not only in church but in their families, as husbands, wives, and parents; in their jobs, as factory workers or business executives, teachers or bureaucrats; as citizens, through voting and voluntary associations, righting wrongs and influencing public policy. *All* Christians, not just pastors and priests, have a ministry—to be found wherever they find themselves, which is exactly where God has placed them to contend for his lordship in everyday circumstances and relationships.

The church is the place where believers gather together, not primarily to influence the culture, but to grow in Jesus Christ. As a result of this spiritual growth, however, Christians must go out into the world to confront, convert, and renew the larger culture, taking God's truth into every highway and byway of common life.

## Reaching across the Boundaries

The ecumenical movement among liberal Protestants sought to unite various denominations by eliminating doctrinal distinctions. For those who no longer believe in the Bible or any kind of supernatural revelation, such doctrinal compromises come easily. But the deepening alliance between groups of evangelicals and Catholics that is occurring today is wholly different, because it is a cooperation among Christians who take doctrines very seriously indeed.

The new cooperation is possible because of what C. S. Lewis called "mere Christianity"—the essential elements of Christianity upheld by all theological traditions. His concise explanations of the Trinity and the Incarnation, the Fall and Redemption, the moral law and the disciplines of the Christian life enabled thousands of former skeptics to understand—and to believe—the truth of Christianity.

Lewis himself was an Anglican, but in addressing audiences consisting of unbelievers, agnostics, and actual atheists he assiduously avoided the distracting issues that divide Christendom; instead, he focused his apologetics on the truths that all Christians affirm. "Ever since I became a Christian," he explained in the preface to his *Mere Christianity,* "I have thought that the best, perhaps the only, service I could do for my unbelieving neighbors was to explain and defend the belief that has been common to nearly all Christians at all times."[17] On one level Lewis deemed himself unqualified to deal with the fine points of theology and ecclesiastical history that denominational differences often entail, preferring to leave those subjects to theologians. More importantly, he rightly understood these internal controversies to be secondary to his major purpose, which was evangelism. "I think we must admit that the discussion of these disputed points has no tendency at all to bring an outsider into the Christian fold," he wrote.

> So long as we write and talk about them we are much more likely to deter him from entering any Christian communion than to draw him into our own. Our divisions should never be discussed except in the presence of those who have already come to believe that there is one God and that Jesus Christ is His only Son.[18]

This did not mean that Lewis minimized the importance of particular theological traditions. "I hope no reader will suppose that 'mere'

Christianity is here put forward as an alternative to the creeds of the existing communions," he wrote,

> as if a man could adopt it in preference to Congregationalism or Greek Orthodoxy or anything else. It is more like a hall out of which doors open into several rooms. If I can bring anyone into that hall I shall have done what I attempted. But it is in the rooms, not in the hall, that there are fires and chairs and meals.[19]

A person who comes to believe in Jesus Christ must then join a particular church, with its distinctive doctrines and traditions.

When I first read C. S. Lewis, I knew little about evangelicalism, Catholicism, or any spiritual realities at all. Reading Lewis's marvelous books did much to confirm my own experience, that is, to demonstrate that Jesus must be the Son of God. Once I grasped this truth, other influences led me into evangelicalism. I became a convinced Baptist. But I know others who first learned about Christianity through C. S. Lewis's writings who then became Episcopalians, or Lutherans, or Catholics. This is because Lewis proclaimed the core beliefs shared by all Christians—not at all to minimize the disagreements among believers, but in the correct conviction that nonbelievers need first to hear and understand the basic elements of the Christian gospel. Today, in this same and ever more urgent task of witness and evangelism, Christians of all traditions have a unique opportunity, and in my judgment a profound obligation, to present a united front before a world captive not only to unbelief but to new forms of ancient errors ranging from the New Age to the neopagan.

One must emphasize that Lewis's "mere Christianity" was no watered-down ecumenical formula designed to promote Church unity by diminishing the importance of crucial doctrines. Indeed, though his books gained support from a broad spectrum of orthodox believers, they were harshly attacked by secularists and theological liberals alike. Even his emphasis on such "mere" Christian truths as the triune nature of God, the literal Incarnation and Resurrection of Jesus Christ, and traditional Christian ethics went squarely against the intellectual and liberal theological fashions of his time. Lewis relished the confrontation. For example, he lampooned his liberal opponents in such characters as the bishop in *The Great Divorce,* who refused to believe in a literal afterlife even when he was in hell. In turn, liberals—including leading liberals of his own Anglican tradition—vehemently attacked Lewis for his devotion to traditional doctrines of the faith.

In the preface to *Mere Christianity,* Lewis commented on his experience of being supported by conservatives from a wide range of denominations while being criticized by liberals within his own communion:

> I have met with little of the fabled *odium theologicum* from convinced members of communions different from my own. Hostility has come more from the borderline people whether within the Church of England or without it: men not exactly obedient to any communion. This I find curiously consoling. It is at her centre, where her truest children dwell, that each communion is really closest to every other in spirit, if not in doctrine. And this suggests at the centre of each there is something, or a Someone, who against all divergences of belief, all differences of temperament, all memories of mutual persecution, speaks with the same voice.[20]

Just so, the document "Evangelicals and Catholics Together" was drafted by believing Catholics and believing Protestants, people at the center of their communions, who realize that they have more in common with one another than with the borderline liberals of their own traditions.

"Evangelicals and Catholics Together" seeks to continue the legacy of C. S. Lewis by focusing on the core beliefs of all true Christians so that adherents of both major traditions can work together in the common task of evangelizing the nonbelieving world. This new cooperation requires neither evangelical nor Catholic to compromise their respective doctrinal convictions. To the contrary, we acknowledge that our differences are many and significant. We are candid about each of them, and none of those involved are willing to compromise their profession of faith.

What we emphasize is that evangelicals and Catholics affirm many of the same truths. The deity of Christ, his death on the cross for our sins, his resurrection from the dead, his Second Coming, the infallibility of Scripture—these truths, affirmed in "Evangelicals and Catholics Together," provide a solid foundation for all Christians. Those who can affirm these truths have something in common of monumental significance.

Some evangelical critics have argued that there is no need for any kind of *theological* agreement with Roman Catholics, that evangelicals can cooperate with Catholics on social and political issues, such as abortion without regard to Christian faith. Usually those who offer this view invoke John Calvin's concept of common grace, which holds that, while God grants saving grace only to true believers, he pours out his common grace to everyone: for example, that the blessings of nature, civil government, and moral order are extended to believer and nonbeliever alike, in the sense that "it rains on the just and the unjust." This is the view, widely held among evangelicals, that Christians can work with anyone—not only evangelicals and Catholics, but evangelicals and Jews, Mormons, or Muslims—in behalf of a just society and government.

In this view, evangelicals and Catholics are only cobelligerents in a common cultural war, or allies solely for tactical purposes in the face of a common challenge. This argument, I submit, undercuts the very ground on which we stand in today's cultural struggle. The doctrine of common grace is true enough, and Christians can indeed join with all other citizens solely on the basis of common citizenship in quest of a public good in our diverse society. On a similar if worldwide scale, the Vatican recently joined with Muslims to prevent a United Nations conference from promoting abortion as a means of population control. And, certainly evangelicals can join with Mormons, Jews, or Muslims in speaking against sexual immorality or political infringements of religious liberty.

But those who confess Jesus Christ as Lord, who recite the same Apostles' Creed, and who affirm the authority of Scripture, have in common something that is far more profound and durable than common grace. Political alliances based on expediency can be fleeting, as has been demonstrated by one-time allies who have abandoned the pro-life position. No, common grace does not hold soldiers fast in their trenches during battle.

Moreover, while cooperation on the basis of common grace might suffice for merely political alliances among different religious communions, it can not suffice in reestablishing Christian influence in our increasingly secular and even increasingly hostile culture. Indeed, the urgent task before all Christians today far transcends victories in political campaigns. Our task is nothing less than to articulate convincingly the biblical worldview to a culture awash in nihilism and hedonism. Neither a Baptist worldview—and I am a Southern Baptist—nor a Lutheran worldview, nor a Catholic worldview is enough to present a comprehensive, universal Christian worldview.

That theological cooperation and not merely political cooperation is crucial has already been demonstrated on the picket lines of the abortion debate. There, evangelicals and Catholics have discovered that their presence is inspired by distinctly Christian ethics that rest on a common foundation of Christian doctrine about God, human nature, the sanctity of life, and the Church's mission to the world. These pro-life champions are not only citizens who happen to oppose abortion; they are Christians—evangelicals and Catholics together—who follow Jesus Christ because they all (together) know him to be the Lord of their lives and of all life.

That there is a battle—far from won—over the very definition and protection of life itself indicates how grave the crisis within American culture has become. Christians do not have the luxury of limiting their energies to theological debate. True believers must reach across theological divides and embrace one another as brothers and sisters in Christ. Our obligation is nothing less than to join together in a defense of the truth of our shared faith. All Christians who confess that Jesus is Lord must unite for the sake of our Lord and for the sake of our culture.

In sum, those who are committed to Jesus Christ as Lord and Savior, who have experienced the transforming power of the Holy Spirit, who affirm the authority of Holy Scripture—each and all, though they understand and in worship respond to these realities differently—share more than a political or cultural agenda. They share the "one faith, one baptism, one Lord" of the Christian gospel. And they share the assumptions that proceed from faith, assumptions that form the Christian view of the world—the Christian worldview—that they must defend together.

These are the reasons for "Evangelicals and Catholics Together." Because, to bring God's truth about the public good into the public square and to resist the abortionists and mercy-killers, the relativists and the tyrants, Christians must stand together. The controversies that have divided believers for nearly five hundred years are real, to be sure, and none of them is to be minimized. However, the divisions between us are not the battle of the hour, when hosts of secularists and relativists threaten to sweep away the last trace of Christian truth, thought, and influence from our culture. Indeed, the controversies that divide us are far less significant than the common threat that confronts us.

Our call to cooperation is itself part of our heritage as evangelicals. For example, on the threshold of the twentieth century, the noted Dutch

Calvinist, Abraham Kuyper, succinctly described for European Christians the very situation all Christians now face in America:

> Now, in this conflict [against liberalism] Rome is not an antagonist, but stands on our side, inasmuch as she recognizes and maintains the Trinity, the Deity of Christ, the Cross as an atoning sacrifice, the scriptures as the Word of God, and the Ten Commandments. Therefore, let me ask if Romish theologians take up the sword to do valiant and skillful battle against the same tendency that we ourselves mean to fight to death, is it not the part of wisdom to accept the valuable help of their elucidation? [21]

Kuyper's reinvigorated Reformed theology and his development of worldview criticism proved a great influence on later evangelical thinkers, including Francis Schaeffer. In his own struggle against modernism in its manifestations at that time, Kuyper forged a coalition of fellow Calvinists and Dutch Roman Catholics led by Hermanus Schaepman. Together, they helped bring moral and social reform to the Netherlands.

A generation later, here in America, another great Reformed theologian, and a courageous defender of orthodoxy against modernists within his own Presbyterian Church and the cultural elite at large, also advocated a theological alliance with Catholics against the advancing influence of modernist doubt, skepticism, and relativism. He was J. Gresham Machen, a professor of theology at Princeton Seminary and one of the foremost champions of the Reformed tradition of his generation.

Within his own university faculty and church, Machen was banished. His modernist adversaries went so far as to expel Machen from the ministry because of his unyielding devotion to the traditional tenets of the Reformed faith. Consequently, Machen was instrumental in establishing what became the Orthodox Presbyterian Church, and he remains a major influence among evangelical churches in America. In reflecting on the threat to Christianity posed by what he alternately called modernism and liberalism, Machen wrote:

> How great is the common heritage that unites the Roman Catholic Church, with its maintenance of the authority of [S]cripture and with its acceptance of the great early creeds, to devout Protestants today! We would not indeed obscure the difference which divides us from Rome.

The gulf is indeed profound. But profound as it is, it seems almost tri-fling compared to the abyss which stands between us and many ministers of our own church.[22]

Both Kuyper and Machen believed that devout Catholics and devout Protestants have more in common with one another than with liberal theologians within their own churches or secular modernists in American culture. That such stalwart defenders of the Reformed tradition believed then, when the challenge to faith was posed by modernism, that conser-vative Protestants and Catholics must cooperate offers a profound lesson for evangelicals and Catholics today. For in this closing decade of the twen-tieth century, the challenge to Christianity is even more formidable and pervasive than the modernism encountered by Kuyper and Machen three and four generations ago. It is a challenge that issues out of postmodern assumptions about truth and ultimate reality.

## Pointing the Way

As the culture grows more and more hostile to a biblical worldview, the situation for evangelicals and conservative Catholics alike may come to parallel that of the various churches that had to live under the aggres-sively antireligious culture of communism. Admittedly, the hostility American Christians face is nothing compared to the persecutions perpetrated by communist regimes for the past seventy years. Still, the experiences of Christians who faced the atheistic materialism of Marxism-Leninism in communist Europe and Asia hold important les-sons for us all.

For example, when I was in Poland recently to start a ministry of Prison Fellowship there, my host was Father Sikorsky, the director of our ministry in Poland and chaplain-general of the Polish prison system. Since Prison Fellowship has become an international organization, with ministries in more than sixty countries, we have discovered that evangelicals and Catholics readily and amicably work together to pro-claim the life-changing gospel of Jesus Christ to sinful men and women in the prisons of the world. In fact, Roman Catholics comprise a large percentage of our volunteers abroad.

The public announcement of our new ministry in Poland was held in the church courtyard that includes the tomb of Father Jerzy Popieluszko. Father Jerzy was a young Catholic priest who in 1980 repeatedly stood on the balcony of his church to preach two messages to the one hundred thousand people who gathered each week to hear him. Because the Polish people were compelled to live under a regime based on the communist lie, Father Jerzy would proclaim, "Preach the truth. Defend the truth. Stand for the truth." His other theme was "Overcome evil with good." When martial law was declared in the winter of 1980, tanks and troops turned the entire country into one vast prison. The Poles understandably despised these troops. But Father Jerzy was determined to follow Christ's injunction to overcome evil with good, and so, on Christmas Eve, he slogged into the snow to hand out Christmas cookies to the soldiers.

In 1984 the Communists decided to silence the troublesome priest, and Father Jerzy disappeared. In churches throughout Poland, people gathered to pray for him. Steelworkers threatened to strike if he were not released. Then Father Jerzy's body was found floating in the Vistula River. His eyes had been gouged out. His fingernails had been ripped off. He had been tortured to death. The people of Poland called a national strike. The Communists sent out the tanks. The people went into the churches and started praying. They had taken Father Jerzy's preaching to heart. They marched into the streets chanting, "We forgive. We forgive."

Here was a monumental clash of worldviews—on one side the dialectical materialism, moral nihilism, and unlimited state power of communism, and, on the other, the Sermon on the Mount. Which proved stronger? The priest, faithful to what his torturers must have considered a reactionary religion and naive idealism, was martyred. But now, as always, the blood of martyrs is the seed of the Church. And so, these few years later, that one-time monolithic and monstrous communist regime has collapsed. For the truth of Christ really does overcome the lies of man; good really does, in mysterious ways, overcome evil.

Is there an evangelical who does not side with Father Jerzy? Is there an evangelical who does not think this Catholic priest was witnessing for Christ?

While Father Jerzy Popieluszko and many like him—including the man who would become Pope John Paul II—were struggling for the faith in Poland, a Reformed evangelical pastor named Laszlo Tokes was preaching the gospel in Romania. Though he was living under the regime of perhaps the most brutal of all Communist dictators, Nicolae Ceausescu, Pastor Tokes, like Father Jerzy, preached the message of truth. His church in the city of Timisoara attracted thousands of worshipers. The secret police harassed him. They broke into his church and kept records of everyone who came and went. Still the church grew.

Finally, Ceausescu decided to silence this troublesome pastor. In collaboration, the liberal church bureaucracy removed Pastor Tokes from his post. But Pastor Tokes refused to leave the ministry to which God had called him. When his ration book was taken away so that he would not be allowed to buy food, his parishioners brought food for their pastor and his family. Even when men in ski masks broke into his home and left Pastor Tokes bleeding from a knife wound in the face, he kept on preaching. Finally, an official edict was delivered, evicting the pastor from his church, and, on December 15, 1989, the secret police came to force Pastor Tokes's compliance. But they could not get to him! Surrounding the church building were thousands of his parishioners, acting as a human shield to protect their pastor. Soon more and more Romanian believers gathered around the church, among them Baptists, Adventists, Pentecostals, Orthodox, and Catholics. Pastor Tokes called out, "We are one in Christ! We speak different languages, but we have the same Bible and the same God. We are one!"

The siege lasted through the night and into the next day. The crowds grew. On December 17, the police attacked, breaking through the crowd and into the church. As Pastor Tokes took refuge near the communion table and held up a Bible, the police beat him until his face was bloody and took him and his wife out into the night. Still the crowds did not disperse. They moved into the central square. Tanks and troops filled the streets. The people shouted and sang and lit candles. Ceausescu gave orders to open fire on the protesters. Hundreds were shot. But the protest had become an uprising, and it spread throughout the country. Ordinary citizens came together in such vast numbers that the communist functionaries were overwhelmed—and Pastor Tokes and his wife were freed. Only ten days later, on Christmas Day, Ceausescu was killed. With him died the communist oppression in Romania.

An evangelical pastor and his local church stood up against the power and weaponry of a hostile culture. Once again, though at great cost, truth overcame lies and good overcame evil.

Is there a Catholic who is not on the side of Pastor Tokes? Is there a Catholic who does not think this Protestant pastor was a part of Christ's universal church? Just as surely as Pastor Tokes and Father Jerzy Popieluszko would have had vehement theological disagreements, they would have agreed about the common evil they faced in their respective societies. In sharing a common persecution, they provided a common witness.

In Romania, Catholics and Orthodox and Reformed and Baptist massed together in front of tanks to protect an evangelical pastor and his church. In America, our own confrontation with the ideologies of nihilism demand of Christians a similar unity—a similar willingness to close ranks and defend one another against a common adversary.

Francis Schaeffer foresaw the loss of our cultural foundations at the twilight of the second millennium. Until the very day he lay dying of cancer, he declared, "The great issue is truth! We have got to defend truth!" This also was the declaration of Father Jerzy Popieluszko: "Preach the truth. Defend the truth. Stand for the truth." On the threshold of the twenty-first century, this will be the task for Christians in America. It is a task for evangelicals and Catholics *together*.

## Notes

1   Pierre Manet, *An Intellectual History of Liberalism* (Princeton, N.J.: Princeton University Press, 1994), xvii, 10, 11, 82.

2   Owen Chadwick, *The Secularization of the European Mind in the Nineteenth Century* (Cambridge: Cambridge University Press, 1990), 4, 6, 26–37.

3   Frederick Turner, *Culture of Hope* (New York: Free Press, 1995), 22–23.

4   Gertrude Himmelfarb, *On Looking Into the Abyss* (New York: Alfred A. Knopf, 1994), 6.

5   Gene Edward Veith, Jr., *Postmodern Times: A Christian Guide to Contemporary Thought and Culture* (Wheaton, Ill.: Crossway, 1994), 42.

6   Ibid., 43.

7   Ana Menendez and April Witt, "Most Are Ready to Pay to Get Tough on Crime," *Miami Herald*, 15 November 1993.

8   James Davison Hunter, *Culture Wars* (New York: Basic Books, 1991), 132.

9   James Davison Hunter, *Before the Shooting Begins: Searching for Democracy in America's Culture Wars* (New York: Free Press, 1994), 4–5.

10  Russell Kirk, "Civilization without Religion," *Heritage Foundation Report,* 404 (July 1992).

11     Hunter, *Before the Shooting,* 4–5.

12     George Barna, *Virtual America* (Ventura Calif.: Regal Books, 1994), 83.

13     Andrew M. Greely, "Sex and the Single Catholic: The Decline of an Ethic," *America* (November 1991): 344.

14     Richard Wirthlin, *St. Petersburg Times,* 6 April 1994.

15     *Times Mirror, Miami Herald,* 10 April 1994.

16     Howard Fineman, "The Virtuecrats," *Newsweek,* June 1994.

17     C. S. Lewis, *Mere Christianity* (New York: Macmillan, 1958), vi.

18     Ibid., vi.

19     Ibid., xi.

20     Ibid., viii.

21     Abraham Kuyper, *Calvinism and the Future* (Princeton, N.J.: Princeton University Press, 1898), 183–184.

22     J. Gresham Machen, *Christianity and Liberalism* (New York: Macmillan, 1924), 52.

# 2

# Faith, Freedom, Responsibility:
# Evangelicals and Catholics in the Public Square

George Weigel

> If there is no transcendent truth, in
> obedience to which man achieves his
> full identity, then there is no sure
> principle for guaranteeing just
> relations between people.
>
> *Pope John Paul II*

ON SEPTEMBER 29, 1952, the National Council of Churches of Christ in the U.S.A. held a great meeting in the National Guard Armory in Washington, D.C. to inaugurate the recently completed Revised Standard Version of the Bible. The principal speaker on that occasion was neither a church official nor a prominent theologian. Rather, he was a Christian layman: the son of the late Episcopal bishop of Connecticut, to be sure, but that genealogical fact had probably eluded most of his fellow countrymen, to whom he was far better known as the secretary of state, the executor of the Marshall Plan, the negotiator of the peace treaty with Japan, and the creator of the North Atlantic Treaty Organization.

Dean Gooderham Acheson was, in the old-fashioned and honorable sense of the term, a worldly man: a man of the world. He was not given to public outpourings of piety. He had made his mark in society, not as an ecclesiastical publicist or Christian apologist, but as a highly successful lawyer and diplomat—perhaps the greatest secretary of state in the twentieth century. And yet it was not of high politics or diplomacy or law that Dean Acheson spoke on that September night. Rather, Acheson elegantly and movingly described the place of the Bible in shaping the American people and their history. To his way of thinking, Holy Scripture had played an "enormous" and "predominant" role in making the Americans who they were and in teaching Americans what they ought to be.

And what had the Americans learned from the Bible? Acheson's description is worth a longish citation:

> In the earliest days in the Northeast, the Book was All. The settlers came here to live their own reading of it. It was the spiritual guide, the moral and legal code, the political system, the sustenance of life, whether that meant endurance of hardship, the endless struggle with nature, battle with enemies, or the inevitable processes of life and death. And it meant to those who cast the mold of this country something very specific and very clear. It meant that the purpose of man's journey through this life was to learn to identify his life and effort with the purpose and the will of God. To do this he must purge his nature of its rebellious side. And this, in turn, meant that the struggle between good and evil was the raging, omnipresent battle in every life, every day.
>
> The test was not one's own will or desire, not the dictate of the government, not the opinion of the day, but the will of God as revealed by the prophets and to be found, in the last analysis, by the individual conscience—guided, instructed, chastened, but in the end, alone.
>
> Out of the travail of these lives the idea of God-fearing was given powerful content and effect. It meant a voluntary, eager, even militant submission to a moral order overriding the wills of the low and great and of the state itself. And this carried with it the notion of restraints against all, of areas blocked off into which none might enter because here the duty of the individual conscience must be performed.
>
> But this was not all. This did not exhaust the teachings of this Bible. For it taught also that the fear of God was the love of God and that the love of God was the love of man and the service of man.
>
> [For] what was written in the Book was taught also by the life of this country. Never was self-reliance so linked with mutual help as in those early days, when from birth to death neighbor turned to neighbor for help and received it in overflowing measure. No characteristic so marks

Americans to this day as this quick and helping hand, a hand offered not only to our fellow citizens but to our fellowmen.

Who are these people, the Americans? They are a people who, as we have said, hold sacred the Word of God. . . . And the source and record of the spiritual purpose of this community of men is the Holy Writ—the Book which brings us together this evening. This occasion reminds us of the tremendous vitality of these writings, which form the core, the vertebra of our society.[1]

Two generations after Dean Acheson eloquently testified to the culture-forming and community-transforming role of biblical faith in American life, it would be hard to imagine a public official making such a speech. That is not simply because statesmen of Acheson's quality are hard to come by, in this or any other era. Rather, it is because the country has changed; or, perhaps more correctly, the *interpretation* of the American experience that dominates several of the key value-transmitting centers of our society—the universities, the prestige press, the popular entertainment industry—has changed.

On all the available sociological evidence, Americans remain the most intensely religious people in the advanced industrialized world. Yet in the American elite culture's interpretation of our history and our present circumstances, that fact has come to be seen as something of a problem, an embarrassment, perhaps even a threat to the future of our liberties. Were some secretary of state to do today what Dean Acheson did in 1952, grim warnings of a terrible breach in the "wallofseparationbetweenchurchandstate"—a polysyllabic neologism in certain vocabularies—would rumble forth from the *New York Times'* editorial and op-ed pages, across the Associated Press wire, on the network news shows, and in faculty lounges from sea to shining sea. What Acheson thought was distinctive and determinative of the singular character of the American people is now regarded as problematic, at best, by many of the molders and shapers and shakers of American public opinion. The notion of Americans as a people "formed by the Book" has become, not simply controversial, but quite repellent in some quarters.

No doubt some Christians must accept a measure of blame for this. Christian churches that have accommodated the gospel to a political philosophy and program, whether of the left or of the right, have ill-served the Church and its distinctive mission by reducing Christianity to the status of being simply another "player" in the game of politics ("politics" understood in the basest terms, as the quest for power). Christians who claim divine warrant for contingent and prudential political judgments (on the merits of invading Haiti to restore the Aristide government to power; on the optimum marginal tax rate) reduce the gospel to a partisan tract. Christians who have not learned the etiquette of democratic civility, and who do not take the trouble to make their convictions known publicly in ways that can be engaged by non-Christian fellow citizens, invite the charge that their professed commitment to the achievement of a genuine pluralism is shallow and tactical. Christians who have retreated into sectarian bunkers suggest, however unwittingly, that the gospel has no public character. Christians who deny that fellow Christians are, in fact, Christians reinforce the media stereotype of Christianity as narrow, fanatical, and mean-spirited.

But to acknowledge that Christians have contributed, in their various ways, to a baleful transformation of American culture and society over the past forty years, such that a contemporary Dean Acheson who had the temerity to dedicate publicly a new version of the Bible would soon find himself beset by both lawsuits and press hostility, is not to suggest that Christians have been primarily at fault in this matter. Christians may not have responded to the secularist onslaught from the academy, the media, and the popular entertainment industry as intelligently or effectively as they might have done; but Christians did not initiate the attack, and Christians most certainly did not invent the notion that publicly vibrant and morally assertive religious faith is inimical to the American democratic experiment.[2]

## The Nature of the Crisis

Two decades into the third century of that experiment, it is no longer clear that the tricentennial anniversary of the Declaration of Independence will take place in a country living in continuity with its moral-cultural roots. Should the historic American attempt to achieve a vital democratic pluralism in which self-governance is possible (because the people have formed and sustained the moral habits—the virtues—necessary for self-governance) collapse; should the American experiment decay into a republic of established and governmentally enforced secularism; then the American experiment as understood by George Washington, James Madison, Abraham Lincoln, and Dean Acheson will have failed. The external forms of democracy—elections, legislatures, governors and presidents, courts—may remain, but they will be hollow. And their endurance over time will be dubious, at best. For the American people, required to divest themselves of their deepest convictions in order to enter public life, will no longer be able to give a persuasive public account of their commitment to democratic republicanism.

Reversing the governmentally enforced secularization of American public life, and recreating the possibility of a public square in which religiously grounded moral convictions are engaged within the bond of democratic civility, is perhaps *the* moral-cultural issue in American public life at the end of the twentieth century. And it hardly needs saying that we should not look to the forces of secularization to effect this reversal and recreation. No, this moral-cultural reformation of our republic will be the task of Christians: specifically of Roman Catholics and evangelical Protestants, the two growing ends of American Christianity on the edge of the twenty-first century.

Moreover, this is a task for *evangelicals and Catholics together*. The job is sufficiently difficult, the opposition sufficiently formidable, and the odds on success sufficiently long, that Christians of common conviction about the moral reformation of the American Republic can no longer afford to indulge their ancient biases. An ecumenism of the trenches is the order of the day in the American culture war. But there are also substantive reasons why the attempt to reclothe the "naked public square" (in Richard Neuhaus' memorable image)[3] is a joint task for evangelicals and Catholics.

Evangelicals and Catholics share a common affection for the American democratic experiment. Unlike many in the leadership of mainline / old-line Protestantism, evangelicals and Catholics do not regard America as an ill-founded republic, born in injustice and dedicated to the rape of first North America and then the world. Rather, evangelicals and Catholics tend to think, together, that America remains a providentially guided experiment in religious freedom, religious tolerance, and the possibility of constructing political community amidst luxuriant diversity. The experiment has gone awry, on more than one occasion. But that it is an honorable experiment, evangelicals and Catholics, in the main, do not doubt.

Evangelicals and Catholics (of various eschatological dispositions, to be sure) are also agreed that commitment to Christ as Lord and Savior implies—indeed, demands—commitment to the service of Christ's brothers and sisters in the world. On the other hand, evangelicals and Catholics remain resolutely (and in principle) anti-utopian. We know that the kingdom of God and its coming will be the work of God's hands, not ours; and both our communities are committed to resisting the encroachments of any political theology that empties the gospel of its specific salvific content and transforms the Church into a partisan faction.

Moreover, evangelicals and Catholics are agreed that any reclothing of the naked public square must engage the ancient moral wisdom of our elder brothers and sisters in faith, the Jewish people.

One need not have a detailed familiarity with American religious history to understand that these agreements, and the common work they have already engendered in the pro-life and profamily movements, constitute something dramatically new and different on the American scene. How evangelicals and Catholics have gotten over many of their old animosities is, however, a story for another day (and another chapter in this book). The issue here is the direction that evangelicals and Catholics together should take in reconstructing the moral foundations of American public life. Not surprisingly, the first item on that agenda is the reconstitution of genuine religious freedom in the United States.

## The Priority of Free Exercise

The principal engine motoring and legitimating the campaign to impose a governmentally enforced secularism on American public life is the Supreme Court of the United States. For almost fifty years, from *Everson v. Board of Education* (1947) through *Kiryas Joel v. Grumet* (1994), the Court has enunciated a First Amendment jurisprudence that is increasingly hostile to the free exercise of religion and that has in effect inverted the First Amendment's religion clause, such that the Court's overriding concern is "no establishment," within which religion is a life-style preference to be "accommodated."[4]

These rulings have not only made the free exercise of religious conviction, the religious education of children, and the provision of social services by religiously sponsored organizations more burdensome; they have been amplified in their public impact by the Court's substantive critique of religious conviction and practice, which has reinforced the elite-culture stereotype about the character, motivations, and behaviors of religious people. Indeed, one careful student of these matters, the Catholic legal philosopher Russell Hittinger, has argued that the Court's church-state jurisprudence has been "marked by extreme skepticism of, and often by outright hostility to, religion." Were we to imagine ourselves as anthropologists from a foreign culture, Hittinger writes, we might well conclude from "the data of the Court's holdings and dicta . . . that religion is something that belongs in the category of dangerous poisons or mental illness."[5]

That Hittinger does not exaggerate is amply demonstrated by the dicta in the Court's 1992 decision, *Lee v. Wiseman*, which struck down as unconstitutional the recitation of a nonsectarian prayer at a public middle-school graduation in Providence, Rhode Island. The Court's legal reasoning, such as it was, need not detain us here. What is of perhaps even greater interest is the Court's description of religion, which provided the substantive basis for its action in this case (and many others).

First, religion is *divisive*, or, as Justice Anthony Kennedy put it in writing the Court's decision, choosing the minister of one faith over the ministers of other faiths to deliver the graduation prayer holds "the potential for divisiveness." Nothing whatsoever in the court record indicated that this had in fact ever happened in Providence. But Justice Kennedy, believing that religious conviction, publicly manifested, was inherently "divisive," was, evidently, taking no chances. Justice Harry J. Blackmun agreed. "Religion has not lost its power to engender divisiveness," he wrote in a concurrence. Indeed, Blackmun went even farther (as was not infrequently his wont), citing an ACLU report that claimed that school prayer, along with the death penalty, "is the only issue that elicits death threats." So religion, in Mr. Justice Blackmun's view, is not only "potentially divisive," it is potentially homicidal.[6]

Second, religion is *coercive*. Prayers like those at the Providence middle-school graduation are offered before every session of Congress. So why the problem at the Providence ceremony? Because adolescents, according to Justice Kennedy, are more susceptible to "peer pressure."

Ducking the question of the congressional prayers, Kennedy wrote, "We do not address whether that choice [i.e., for public prayers at a state-sponsored event] is acceptable if the affected citizens are mature adults, but we think the State may not, consistent with the Establishment Clause, place primary and secondary school children in this position." In other words, and stripped of its legal gloss, religion is inherently dangerous for young children and, as with alcohol, tobacco, and certain salacious publications, the decision to indulge should be left to the discretion of mature adults.

Justice Souter took the issue a step farther, arguing that the congressional prayers were of no constitutional consequence because they can be "ignored." Thus Souter followed in Justice William Brennan's footsteps when the latter wrote (in the 1984 case, *Lynch v. Donnelly*) that the use of the phrase "In God We Trust" on our currency posed no constitutional problem because its "rote repetition" had emptied it of any "religious significance." Religion can be "tolerated," on this understanding, as long as its forms are emptied of significant religious content.

Third, the Court seems to think that religion is *irrational*. According to Justice Blackmun, prayer at a state-sponsored event "transforms rational debate into theological decree." (What, precisely, was being debated at the graduation in question Blackmun did not say.) Justice Kennedy, trying to orient the argument more philosophically, suggested that public prayer drains the meaning out of secular events because it suggests that "human achievements cannot be understood apart from their spiritual essence." But this, on Kennedy's view, is unjust to nonbelievers, and even to believers, for it robs the great public moments in life of their ordinary meaning and value. What the Constitution requires of us, Kennedy argued, is that we tolerate each other's religious idiosyncracies: which is to say that religion consists of so many personal quirks, like evangelical Bible software, Catholic rosaries, Jewish dietary practices, Amish horse-drawn buggies. To enter the world of religion, on this understanding, is to enter the world of irrationality.

Finally, the Court seems to think that religion is *substantively fungible*, which is to say publicly meaningless. Justice Souter thought that the rabbi's paraphrase of the Bible in his graduation prayer involved an act of discrimination against nontheistic religion, and he argued that the Constitution protected "religion in general." Thus religion, in Souter's view, can mean whatever an individual says it means. Perhaps this is

Justice Souter's private theological opinion. But it makes no constitutional sense whatsoever, for how could the state ever establish or disestablish something as nebulous as this?

Hittinger summarizes the Court's substantive view of religion in these stark terms:

> Religion is a potentially dangerous and harmful phenomenon. It is apt to engender divisiveness, even homicidal urges, in the political community. It threatens the psychological health and development of children. It tends to subvert the ordinary meanings and values of life. It is not rational, but rather subjective and idiosyncratic. It is contrary to the institutions of democracy. And whatever reality it has, it tends to elude even the most ordinary dictionary definitions.[7]

But why, then, should religion be tolerated publicly? If *that* is what religion is, why not purge the civil community of a dangerous, even noxious, activity? (As Hittinger goes on to write, "Were one to survey the Court's dicta about obscenity, he would find that obscenity is rarely described in terms as forbidding as is religion."[8]) In *Lee v. Wiseman*, then, the Court demonstrated yet again that it has no conception of religion as a public good, and indeed, the very thinnest conception of religion as a private good for individuals.

Alas, that unhappy trajectory continued in the case of *Kiryas Joel v. Grumet*, which was handed down in 1994. There, Justice John Paul Stevens claimed that the creation of a separate public school district to serve the needs of handicapped Satmar Hasidic children violated the constitutional order because it "affirmatively supports a religious sect's interest in segregating itself and preventing its children from associating with their neighbors" and "provided official support to cement the attachment of young adherents to a particular faith;" thus it "unquestionably increased the likelihood that they would remain within the fold, faithful adherents of their parents' religious faith."

As the chief legal counsel for the Satmar Hasidim, Nathan Lewin, put it in response, "I had always thought that the law that allows parents to send their children to private religious schools rather than to neighborhood public schools was designed to increase the likelihood that a family's faith would be transmitted from one generation to the next. Indeed, *Pierce v. Society of Sisters*, a 1925 Supreme Court decision, went so far as to hold that there is a constitutional *right* to cement the adherence of one's children to one's faith."[9] But that was another era, and, evidently, another America. Ours is now an America in which justices of the Supreme Court can hold it to be a social evil if children follow the religious traditions of their parents and grandparents.

On this thin and deracinated understanding, religion is not a life-shaping conviction or a lifelong commitment or condition. Rather, it is a personal life-style choice, to be taken up or laid down at whim. Justice Souter's description of the Satmar Hasidim's "religiously grounded preferences" may have made sense to him; but the phrase "religiously grounded preferences" makes no sense whatsoever to men and women of serious religious conviction, be they Satmar Hasidim, Roman Catholics, or evangelical Protestants.

## The Path Beyond the Impasse

How might evangelicals and Catholics make common cause for the restoration of a genuine religious freedom in American public life? No doubt there is important work to be done in the legal trenches, as there are local school-board arguments to be engaged and political organizing to get underway. But perhaps the most important thing that evangelicals and Catholics can offer an America being forced into the cul-de-sac of governmentally enforced public secularism is a *new understanding of the First Amendment religion clause*.

I choose the singular here deliberately. For the past fifty years the Supreme Court has insisted that there are "two religion clauses"—an "Establishment Clause" and a "Free Exercise Clause"—whose rival claims must be, somehow, balanced. But the net effect of this maneuver, as we have seen, has been to unbalance the First Amendment so that the Court's primary concern is "no establishment," in the service of which "free exercise" may be accommodated. Thus one of the most frequently used constitutional law texts, authored by Harvard professor Laurence Tribe, states that there is a "zone which the free exercise clause carves out of the establishment clause for permissible accommodation of religious interests. This carved-out area might be characterized as the *zone of permissible accommodation*."[10]

A carved-out accommodation of "religious interests": this is a reversal, indeed an inversion, of the original intention of the framers of the Constitution, and it is a "solution" that provides no solution in the context of the lived experience of the American people, yesterday, today, and, most likely, tomorrow.[11] Evangelicals and Catholics have to reverse this reversal, and the way to do that, publicly, may be to suggest a thought-experiment.

Suppose, for a moment, that the framers had added a single word to the First Amendment, such that it read "Congress shall make no law concerning an establishment of religion, or *otherwise* prohibiting the free exercise thereof"? Would that not make the situation clearer, intellectually and empirically? Why will the Americans not allow their national government to make an "establishment of religion"? Precisely in order to foster the free exercise of religion, which is both a basic human right and a building block of the civil society on which genuine democracy rests. "No establishment" in the service of "free exercise": that makes far more sense, historically and existentially, than free exercise as an "accommodation" within the overarching commitment of "no establishment," understood as state-enforced secularism in public life.[12]

The restoration of the priority of free exercise would have other salutary effects in our public life. It would clarify, for example, the meaning of that ubiquitous phrase, "the separation of church and state." America needs to be reminded that that phrase is not in the Constitution, but in fact involves an interpretation—and, arguably, a tendentious interpretation—of the Constitution. The "separation of church and state" cannot mean the separation of religion from public life, or the proscription of religiously grounded moral argument from public life, for to do so would involve a profoundly undemocratic discrimination against citizens on the basis of religious belief. The "separation of church and state" should, therefore, be understood minimally, as a description of the fact that, in the American constitutional order, the state claims no theological expertise and the Church rejects any partisan political role. Thus the state is, by definition, a limited state. And the Church, primarily for theological reasons, declines to have its truth-claims buttressed by the coercive power of the state. Attempts to read any larger meaning into "the separation of church and state," or to retroject that interpretive phrase (and a maximalist understanding of it) into the subtext of the Constitution itself, violate both history and present empirical reality.

In the course of this debate, evangelicals and Catholics should press the argument that the "separation of church and state" says something at least as important about the state and its legitimate boundaries as it does about the Church and its public role(s). That phrase and Mr. Jefferson's equally extraconstitutional "wall of separation" image have been understood in recent years as placing a limit on the Church. But "disestablishment" and "free exercise" also place crucial limits on the state. And those limits help make democracy possible.

No established Church means no sacred state. No established Church implies the *limited* or *constitutional* state. No establishment means that the state acknowledges its *incompetence* in the most important arena of life: the arena of personal conscience, in which men and women encounter God and his law. And that confession of incompetence clears the social space in which a politics of persuasion and consent can replace the politics of coercion, which is no mean accomplishment under the conditions of modernity. For the modern state—whether authoritarian, totalitarian, or democratic—is characterized by a seemingly inexorable inclination to expand the boundaries of its influence, power, and control. Thus "separation of church and state," properly understood, is an important barrier against the further encroachments of the "Nanny State."

## Toward a Genuine Pluralism

Evangelicals and Catholics committed to restoring the priority of free exercise would also help achieve that desirable end if they were to *reframe the debate over pluralism and tolerance.* As John Courtney Murray once said, pluralism, or, better, "plurality," seems written into the script of history; that the world is diverse is a basic fact about the world, this side of the kingdom. But on the Jewish and Christian understanding of these things, the script of history has a divine author. Thus it is unbecoming for Christians to chafe at the reality of plurality, diversity, difference. Rather, it is for Christians to see in the facts of plurality and difference the inexhaustibly creative love of the God who brought the world into being and sustains it by his providential care. Thus Christian attempts to create a monistic state—an antipluralist state, in which the coercive power of the state is used to enforce Christian truth-claims—are to be rejected, precisely on Christian theological grounds. For the

Church, when she is truly being the Church, acts by persuasion and witness, not by imposition through coercion.[13]

But evangelicals and Catholics must also remind America that what is often styled "pluralism" today is either massive confusion, or indifference, or state-enforced secularist uniformity in the public square. For genuine *pluralism* is not a sociological fact; genuine *pluralism* is a social and cultural accomplishment. Why? Because genuine pluralism is not the ignorance of fellow citizens shouting past each other in the darkness; nor is it indifference to our deepest religious and philosophical differences. Rather, genuine pluralism is the creation of a civil society in which men and women of conviction and decency engage each other's differences within a bond of democratic civility and tolerance. Genuine pluralism is not the avoiding of differences; genuine pluralism is the disciplined and mutually respectful conversation about those differences.

On what basis is that habit—that virtue—of tolerance formed? There are many such bases. Some of them are undoubtedly secular, even pragmatic, in nature. But evangelicals and Catholics ought to remind their fellow citizens of the fact that religious tolerance in contemporary America is often *religiously* grounded. It is not the case that Americans are religiously tolerant at the end of the twentieth century because no one denomination has a majority of citizens within its fold. No, most Americans are religiously tolerant because they believe it to be the will of God that they be religiously tolerant and democratically civil. Or, as Richard Neuhaus has so aptly put it, Americans believe that "it is the will of God that we be tolerant of those who disagree with us about the will of God."[14]

Historically, in terms of the American experience, and empirically, in terms of our present circumstances, it is simply not true that the only possible foundation for democratic tolerance and civility—the only barrier against America becoming another Bosnia or Ulster—is a benign agnosticism or benign secularism. Indeed, the opposite is more likely to be true. A religious foundation for religious toleration is a more secure foundation for toleration, because in that circumstance tolerance is perceived as a duty and obligation, rather than as a pragmatic or utilitarian accommodation to the unfortunate fact that not everybody is like "us."

Democratic deliberation in a religiously intense society is always going to be religiously informed democratic deliberation. And no doubt religiously informed public debate can be divisive. But it need not be. The alternative to the naked public square is not Ulster or Bosnia, nor is it some kind of sacred public square. Rather, the alternative is the civil public square. How might evangelicals and Catholics demonstrate to our fellow-citizens that our commitment to restoring the priority of free exercise is no threat to the rights of others? By making clear our understanding that religiously informed democratic deliberation is no danger to democracy if four conditions prevail:

1. if the political process is open to citizens of all convictions, and there are neither penalties nor rewards in terms of access to the public square based on religious conviction or the lack thereof;

2. if the Church acknowledges the limits of its competence in political and economic life and maintains a principled, firm, nonpartisan stance toward electoral politics;

3. if religious people and religious leaders, entering the public square, make genuinely public moral arguments for their views, rather than making sectarian or authoritarian claims; and

4. if a virtuous citizenry practices tolerance and works to achieve the kind of genuine pluralism described above.

## The Etiquette of Public Discourse

This third point bears development. As Lincoln's second inaugural address—perhaps the most famous political speech in American history—demonstrates, biblically derived language and biblically informed imagery can serve the ends of unity and reconciliation, even as that language and imagery calls the nation to repentance for its manifold violations of the will of God. The agitations of radical secularists notwithstanding, the enshrinement of the Second Inaugural on the wall of the Lincoln Memorial in Washington suggests that there is a permanent place in American public life for "the Book," as Dean Acheson styled it.

But our America is neither Lincoln's nor Acheson's, and in our present circumstances, the question of an *ecumenical grammar* capable of

bringing order to the public argument such that people of different theological convictions can engage each other seriously has to be pondered.
How might Christians contribute to the development of a genuine pluralism out of the plurality of vocabularies and grammars in American
public moral discourse today? How can today's cannonading between
the religious and the secularists, between Christians and Jews, between
liberal Christians and conservative Christians, and among Christians,
Jews, and Muslims be transformed into what John Courtney Murray
once called "creeds at war, intelligibly"?[15] The issue cannot be avoided,
for if we cannot talk to each other in ways that make sense to each
other—or at least enough sense to conduct the public argument that
is democracy's lifeblood—then the chances of our descending into
Hobbes' war of "all against all" are greatly magnified.

Might natural law or common grace theories of morality be helpful
here? I think so. This is not the place to survey the difference between
Roman Catholic concepts of natural law and Calvinist notions of common grace. But in both these traditions, the essential point is that, even
under the conditions of the Fall, there is a moral logic hard-wired into
the world and into us, a logic that reasonable and responsible men and
women can grasp by a disciplined reflection on the dynamics of human
action.[16] Christians of both Catholic and Protestant conviction would
agree that the grasping of that moral logic is aided immeasurably by
grace at work in human hearts; moreover, Christians on both sides of
the Reformation controversies would agree that the gospel may draw
out of the natural law certain behavioral implications that are not readily
discernible otherwise. But that such a moral logic exists, that it is accessible to all human beings through rational reflection, and that it can be
intelligibly argued in public is, I believe, a matter of moral common
sense. Could such a moral logic constitute the ecumenical grammar
necessary for public life in contemporary America?

Evangelicals and Catholics interested in pursuing that possibility
might reflect on recent history, and specifically on the debate over possible U.S. military action in the Persian Gulf and in Haiti. Across the
country, and in venues ranging from talk-radio to barber shops and taxi-
cabs, citizens of various theological dispositions argued instinctively in
the natural-law categories of the just-war tradition: Was this a just cause?
Who could properly authorize the use of force? Was there a reasonable
chance of success? Had all other nonmilitary options been tried? How

could innocent civilian lives be protected if military action were under-taken? The American people did not reach for these categories because the just-war tradition had been effectively taught in their schools. Rather, they asked those questions because they are the natural questions that any morally serious person will ask when considering the use of military force in the service of the common good. And the rather high level of the public debate on U.S. military intervention (at least in the case of the Persian Gulf War) suggests that the moral logic of the natural law has a unique capacity to bring a measure of conceptual order to a diverse so-ciety seeking to form a common moral judgment about a proposed public action.

To commend, to evangelicals and Catholics alike, the development of the skills necessary for conducting public moral argument according to the "grammar" of the natural law is not to deny explicitly Christian (or Jewish, or Muslim, or Buddhist) rhetoric a place in the public square. All Americans have the right to bring their most deeply held convictions into the debate over our common life: that is, or ought to be, the accepted understanding of the "free exercise" guarantee of the First Amendment's religion clause. But evangelicals and Catholics ought to consider whether those convictions can be most readily engaged when they are translated into an idiom that virtually all our fellow citizens can grasp. I hope to show how this can be done below, in my discussion of abortion.

## An Experiment at Risk

The naked public square is not only an offense against the religious con-victions of American citizens; it is also a danger to democracy. More is at stake here than the convenience, even the rights, of religious believers. What is at issue here is the very possibility of an experiment in self-governance in which rights are linked to responsibilities, and individual freedom to the pursuit of the common good.

If the *telos* or goal of the American experiment is the creation of the Republic of the Imperial Self, understood in radically secularist terms, then personal autonomy becomes the norm that trumps all other claims. In 1992 three justices of the Supreme Court made precisely that argument when they declared that, in America, "the heart of liberty is the right to define one's own concept of existence, of meaning, of the universe, and of the mystery of human life."[17]  One would have to go back to the *Dred Scott* decision and its assertion of a basic constitutional right to own slaves to find a federal judicial pronouncement more ominous in its implications for American democracy.

For what did Justices Kennedy, O'Connor, and Souter really say in that definition of "the heart of liberty?" They said that democracy is simply an ensemble of procedures, primarily having to do with litigation, by which we regulate the pursuit of our purely personal meanings and satisfactions. Which is to say: there is no substantive moral core to democracy. There is no community of husband and wife, understood as a solemn covenantal bond; there is only the contractual "association" of marriage, into which autonomous individuals enter in order to fulfill "personal needs." There is no civil society, no community of what Jacques Maritain called "civic friendship." There is no culture of republican virtue and no intelligible public moral conversation guiding the American experiment.

There are only The Rules of the Game.

On this understanding, we are no longer working out the public implications of what Jefferson called "self-evident truths"—which were, in fact, moral claims. Rather, the purpose of the American experiment, according to the justices, is the satisfaction of the unencumbered, autonomous, self-constituting Imperial Self: the great god I. Christians, and all men and women of elementary moral decency, will find this a chilling, indeed demeaning, construal of the human condition and possibility; it is also very bad news for democracy. Why? Because the apotheosis of "personal autonomy" carries with it—as we have already seen in the Supreme Court's substantive views on religion—the notion of the ultimate relativity (and, indeed, irrationality) of all religious and moral systems. And within that orbit of autonomy-plus-relativity, there is no satisfactory answer to the questions, Why be civil? Why be tolerant? And, finally, Why be a democrat? The naked public square in the Republic of the Imperial Autonomous Self leaves democracy naked before its enemies.

The restoration of religious freedom through the recreation of an American democracy committed to the priority of free exercise is thus not for Christians only. It is a task for all Americans who share Alexis de Tocqueville's conviction that the moral habits—the virtues—of the American people are the surest foundation of our liberties. It is a task for all Americans who understand the wisdom of Aristotle's teaching, some 2,300 years ago, that politics—the ongoing public deliberation about how we *ought* to live together—is an extension of ethics. It is a task for all Americans who have understood the culturally and politically transformative power of a biblically grounded summons to justice, as manifest in the example of Martin Luther King, Jr.

And it is a task on which evangelicals and Catholics are peculiarly well equipped to work—together.

## The Recovery of Responsibility

Throughout the United States, there is widespread agreement among people of vastly different denominations, races, and economic conditions that the country is living through a profound moral crisis. That crisis is experienced in different ways in different locales. Some communities suffer under the lethal effects of the drugs-crime-violence nexus. Still other communities are justifiably angered over tax-supported school sex-education programs that seem to regard teenage promiscuity as both normal and unavoidable; in those same communities, grave concern is expressed over a tidal wave of entertainment that celebrates sex-as-sport. Other observers of the American scene point to skyrocketing rates of illegitimacy, divorce, and sexually transmitted disease. Tax-cheating, poor job performance, and decreasing educational accomplishment are also cited, with reason, as evidence of an American moral decline. The frustration is increased by the fact, alluded to earlier, that many in the elite culture seem to think that the only moral absolute is that there are no moral absolutes. In these circumstances, Christians ask, how can we possibly have an intelligent and fruitful public discussion about what we *ought* to do as a people and a political community?

The common thread running through these multiple concerns about moral decline is the conviction that America is undergoing a *crisis of personal responsibility*. The language of "rights" is epidemic; the language of "rights and wrongs"—the language of responsibility, duty, obligation—finds it hard to get a hearing (much less a purchase on public policy).[18] One result of this celebration of personal autonomy and choice is that America has become ever more divided: between the races, between the sexes, between social classes. Two generations of emphasis on our differences, exacerbated by the notion that there is no common moral conviction to unite us (beyond the conviction of our personal autonomy!), have left many Americans wondering about the content of the *unum* in the national motto, *E pluribus unum* ("Out of many, one").

It must be emphasized that this crisis of personal responsibility is not to be found exclusively in the urban underclass (although the pathologies of the crisis are perhaps most virulently on display in those parts of our cities where the writ of the Constitution and the rule of law have, quite simply, ceased to run). Suburban shopping centers filled with teenagers for whom "mall-crawling" is their only exercise in community-building; out-of-wedlock birthrates among majority populations that have now reached the level at which, thirty years ago, social scientists began to discuss the "crisis of the black family"; college freshmen from middle America who, when asked their goal in life, respond, "I want a Lexus"; all of these phenomena are manifestations of the difficulty contemporary American culture has in forming people of character and conviction for whom the pleasuring of the Self is not the end-all and be-all of existence. How do we create (or, some would say, recreate) an America in which it is widely understood that happiness is not a function of wealth, possessions, or social status, but of faith, families, and friends? How do we come to understand, again, and as a people, that the greatest of human satisfactions are to be found in obligations fulfilled, kindnesses performed, wounds healed, insights gained?

There is no lack of diagnoses of the crisis, nor is it my intention here to adjudicate among the various competing schools of analysis in a search for The Answer to the question of America's struggle with issues of personal responsibility. Quite probably there is no one Answer. But there is one causal factor that sheds light on a lot of the rest of the crisis, and one issue that brings the crisis home inescapably: the causal factor is the sexual revolution, and the issue is abortion. How evangelicals and Catholics, together, address these matters will have much to do with our effectiveness in helping to give our country a new birth of genuine freedom.

## The "Playboy Philosophy" Disaster

Almost fifteen years ago, I interviewed a friend who was the most prominent liberal Protestant pastor in the city in which I then lived. My friend was retiring from his pulpit after many years of service, and I wanted to talk to this good man (with whom I disagreed on many, many things) about whether his mind had changed on any point of his public activism: for, during his pastorate, he had been in the forefront of the agitations for what were then called "liberalized" abortion laws, as well as for no-fault divorce, "gay rights," and so forth. So I asked my friend whether, looking back, he had had any second thoughts. He reflected for a moment and then replied that, while he couldn't bring himself to say that he'd been mistaken politically, he had concluded, as a pastor and counselor, that the sexual revolution "sure hadn't added to the sum total of human happiness."

It seemed to me a telling remark, and it helps explain why the abortion issue has been the single most fevered question in our public life for over a generation. For the abortion issue has become *the* icon of the sexual revolution, and the sexual revolution has become *the* symbol of the liberal politics in which freedom means autonomy: the right to do whatever I like, so long as no one else (or no one in whom the state declares a "compelling interest") gets hurt.

The sexual revolution—the radical challenge to the traditional sexual mores that once guided American sexual conduct—is now almost fifty years old. It has been, like most human enterprises, a complex business. Some would argue that the sexual revolution has made us more honest (meaning less hypocritical) about sex. Some would even argue that the sexual revolution has, if accidentally, helped Christians reclaim the biblical view of sexuality as a great good, a great gift of God. But whatever its modest accomplishments may have been, the sexual revolution has also had an enormous, and I would argue overwhelming, shadow side, some of whose expressions ought to be self-evidently clear by now.

The sexual revolution has, for example, been a terrific deal for predatory and irresponsible men. By promoting a contraceptive mentality that radically divides the unitive and procreative aspects of sexuality, by treating sex as a *need*, and by celebrating sex in popular culture as just another recreational activity, the sexual revolution has stacked the psychological and cultural deck in favor of men, for whom promiscuity generally has fewer and less severe biological consequences. Thus the sexual revolution has created the phenomenon of men who are perpetually adolescents in their sexuality: radically self-centered, incapable of forming and sustaining permanent commitments, "trading-in" their women for newer, sleeker models from time to time. The key to this development, legally, was *Roe v. Wade*'s legitimation of abortion-on-demand: here, at last, was unlocked for American men a permissive sexual cornucopia, for there was now a technological quick-fix for any "problems" that their predatory behavior might create. But what does it mean for a culture, and a society, when too many of its men are trapped in adolescence?

The sexual revolution (as my friend, the pastor, had discovered to his great chagrin) has also demeaned women. Rather than liberating women, a single-minded focus on sex as recreation and personal pleasure has reinforced the image of women as mere objects or instruments for the sexual gratification of men. Is the "Playmate of the Month" a liberated woman? Or is she a woman who has been reduced and debased to being nothing but an object of male sexual desire?

Moreover, by fracturing the natural linkage between sexuality and childbearing, the sexual revolution has denied and demeaned the most distinctive element of female sexuality: its natural connection to procreation. The abortion industry, a $500 million-a-year business run largely by men making considerable profits out of women's anguish, is a terrible, if appropriate, symbol of what happens when women are objectified, instrumentalized, depersonalized—and, ultimately, defeminized. What is the long-term effect on culture and society of the denial to women of a distinctive aspect of their personhood?

There is no solution to the crisis of personal responsibility in America that does not involve a frontal challenge to the sexual revolution. The sexual revolution has been bad news for women, bad news for men, and bad news for society. It has cheapened relationships. It has damaged lives. It has coarsened our public culture. And it has failed to deliver on its promise of happiness. More and more people seem to sense this; evangelicals and Catholics should help articulate this sense of discomfort, even shame, in compelling terms that reaffirm the tie between sexuality and marriage and that celebrate self-mastery and chastity inside and outside of marriage. Our national sense of moral crisis creates a moment of possibility in which some hard truths can be told, in charity, about the sexual revolution and the kind of people we ought to want to be.

Which, in turn, suggests that a reframing of the abortion debate is possible, and ought to be high on the list of works to be undertaken by evangelicals and Catholics, together.

## An Argument Reengaged

The new engagement between evangelicals and Roman Catholics in America was not the result of scholarly consultations in seminaries and graduate schools of divinity; rather, this new encounter began to be forged at the grassroots level in the 1970s, primarily in the pro-life movement. In their defense of the right to life of the unborn, and in their common commitment to service to women caught in the dilemma of crisis pregnancy, evangelicals and Catholics who had long regarded each other with suspicion (if not downright hostility) began to discover each other as allies in a common cause and partners in a common task. Out of that discovery came, over time, the even more important discovery of each other as brothers and sisters in Christ.

Viewed from one angle, the pro-life movement has been one of the great success stories of American social and political history over the past twenty-five years. Against the entrenched opposition of the media, the federal judiciary, the academy, the popular entertainment industry, the national Democratic Party, and far too many of the mainline churches, the right-to-life movement has not only survived; it has grown in numbers to the point where it now constitutes the largest movement for social reform in contemporary America. It has kept alive an issue that the nation's newspaper of record, the *New York Times*, confidently pronounced "settled" on the day after the Supreme Court handed down *Roe v. Wade* in 1973. Moreover, the movement has not been without political effect, as the defeat of the so-called Freedom of Choice Act in 1993 and the 1994 congressional elections ought to have made plain.

Viewed from within the movement, however, the pro-life cause often seems ever more fragile, even marginal. The Supreme Court, in its 1992 *Casey* decision, upheld *Roe*'s central finding of a constitutional right-to-abortion; the Clinton administration has dramatically expanded the federal government's involvement with the provision of abortion services at home, and through U.S. foreign aid programs abroad; the Surgeon-General has instructed the movement to "get over its love affair with the fetus"; the national Democratic Party remains intransigently committed to the most permissive possible pro-abortion regime; and prominent Republican leaders like Governor Pete Wilson of California, Governor Christine Todd Whitman of New Jersey, and Governor William Weld of Massachusetts have called for the national Republican Party to strip itself of its right-to-life commitment in 1996. Meanwhile, the human carnage continues, as some 1.5 million abortions are performed annually in the United States—a country that now affords less legal protection to the unborn child than it does to certain endangered species of birds in our national forests.

All of which has led to a certain exhaustion, and even a certain paranoia, in the worlds-within-worlds of the pro-life movement. Many pro-life activists, for all that they are deeply committed to a cause in which they have enlisted for the duration, seem convinced that things can only get worse. They may be right. But I don't think they are.

Careful study of the best survey research data, for example, leads to several conclusions. Even after twenty years of intense public debate, the majority of the American people do not understand that we live under the most permissive abortion regime in the democratic world; this suggests an important opportunity for education, leading to political action. Moreover, a persistent majority of Americans (on some indices, 60 percent, on others, 75 percent) reject as morally unacceptable the notion of abortion as a means of birth control; this suggests the possibility of a dramatic rollback of the abortion license, were the issue ever to be returned to the democratic deliberation of the American people. On the other hand, the research of University of Virginia sociologist James Davison Hunter indicates that the pro-life majority of Americans often feels incapable of articulating its moral views on abortion in a publicly persuasive way.[19]

This last point suggests an opportunity for evangelicals and Catholics, together, to reframe the abortion debate in terms that can engage the moral intuitions of the silent pro-life majority. Such a reframing should be done in terms of that "ecumenical grammar" of moral persuasion just discussed. In doing so, it would appeal to the moral logic of the American democratic experiment, using language and imagery more compelling than the thin language of autonomy and "choice."

Thus evangelicals and Catholics, together, should position the pro-life movement as the foremost civil rights movement of our generation and an extension of the traditional American norm of hospitality to the stranger. For the historical truth of the matter is that the abortion license violates the basic moral dynamic of American democracy. The first two hundred years of the American Republic tell an unfolding tale of aspiration, and progress, toward the ideal of liberty and justice for all. That progress was rapid in some periods, and halting in others; sometimes it suffered setbacks. But from the earliest days of the colonies down to our own times, the story of America was the story of a widening of the boundaries of the community of the commonly protected: the community of those for whom we assumed a common responsibility. The United States welcomed immigrants, freed slaves, protected workers, enfranchised women, aided the needy, provided social security for the aged, ensured the civil rights of all its citizens, and made public spaces accessible to the handicapped: all in service to its ideals of justice, in the quest for a more inclusive society.

Then came *Roe v. Wade* and its companion case, *Doe v. Bolton,* and the boundaries of the community of the commonly protected were radically constricted. Seven unelected Supreme Court justices performed the most dramatic act of exclusion in our national history: they deprived every human being, for the first nine months of his or her life, of the first of Jefferson's "inalienable" rights—the right to life. *Roe* and *Doe* were not liberalizing decisions; they were reactionary decisions. They cut against the grain of American history, and they fundamentally violated the ideals of the republic. In defending the right to life of the unborn, evangelicals and Catholics are thus working with, rather than against, the story line of the American experiment: which is to say that, on this issue, we are the party of a generous and inclusive patriotism.

In a reframed abortion debate, evangelicals and Catholics, together, should also make it clear that the abortion license has done grave damage to the moral and constitutional foundations of democracy in America. The use of privately authorized lethal violence for the ends of personal convenience or conviction is incompatible with the rule of law: indeed, it is the very antithesis of the rule of law. Just as America could not long endure half-slave and half-free, so American democracy cannot sustain itself indefinitely in circumstances in which the decision to execute innocent human beings is left to private individuals acting in private capacities but with the sanction of the state. When, in the course of the *Casey* decision, Justices Kennedy, O'Connor, and Souter instructed pro-life Americans to stop agitating the abortion issue, they took the logic of autonomy to its democratic *reductio ad absurdum*: for on this line of reasoning, citizens are forbidden, by edict of the Court, from acting democratically to compel the state to perform its most elementary function, namely, the protection of innocent human life. This is not, I dare say, what James Madison, the Father of the Constitution of 1787, had in mind.

(And we need not doubt that what is permitted at one end of the life cycle will, eventually, be permitted at the other end of physical life and perhaps at virtually every point in between. For the logic of the abortion license created by the Supreme Court leads inexorably to a constitutional right to physician-assisted suicide and indeed to the "compassionate" dispatch of all those who do not enjoy what others of us regard as a sufficient "quality of life": the severely handicapped, the comatose, the inconvenient elderly.)

To argue, then, for an America in which every unborn child is protected in law and welcomed in life is not to argue on sectarian religious grounds or in language and imagery accessible only to orthodox Christian believers. Rather, it is to argue in what once was—and what could be again—the common moral idiom of the American democratic experiment. And when these arguments are complemented by service—by making more publicly visible (and available) the care being offered to women on a daily basis by committed pro-life people running volunteer-staffed crisis pregnancy centers funded by charitable donations—then it seems to me that we have got a message that is far more powerful than the mantra of "choice."[20]

In making the case for the right to life of the unborn, then, evangelicals and Catholics, together, are making the case for a genuine freedom, nurtured within organic human communities, that is capable of reconnecting rights and responsibilities, individual freedom and the common good, and thus resisting the apotheosis of state power.[21]

## Rolling Back the Nanny State

The reconstruction of an American republic sustained by an ethic of personal responsibility will require a common evangelical and Catholic effort on a number of other social and political fronts. One such front, related to the issues underlying much of the right-to-life debate, involves the empowerment of parents to take more effective responsibility for rearing their children.

Few Americans, one suspects, are aware of Mr. Justice Stevens' queer notion that the efforts of parents to transmit their faith and their moral values to their children constitute a kind of social evil that the Supreme Court of the United States is obliged to redress. But many millions of American parents have experienced this encroachment on their natural authority directly, in the public schools, and specifically in the attempt by public-school administrators and teachers' unions to strip parents of their primary responsibilities for the moral education of the young through such curricular innovations as comprehensive sex education.[22] The rapid growth of the home-schooling movement, which now numbers hundreds of thousands of adherents, is one empirical measure of the dissatisfaction this imperialism of the educational "experts" has created. But it seems unlikely that home-schooling will become a predominant form of elementary and secondary education in the foreseeable future (for all that the computer revolution will make it ever more feasible.)

In these circumstances, an important and, I believe, morally compelling "choice" movement has emerged: the movement for full parental choice in education. That movement has been, in part, a reaction to the overweening moral arrogance of the state's educational bureaucrats and their allies in the major teachers' unions; many parents now recognize the truth of columnist George F. Will's assertion that the National Education Association is the most reactionary force in American public life today. Others have joined the movement because of their concern over declining educational performance, or their concern for the basic physical safety of their children during school hours. But the "educational choice" movement is also, and even more fundamentally, a movement to reempower parents to take responsibility for the education of their children.

That effort should commend itself to evangelicals and Catholics on grounds of principle, as well as for practical reasons. That an educated citizenry is one important aspect of the common good, no one doubts. And in the pursuit of that public good—the education of a responsible and competent citizenry—the taxing power of the state is legitimately deployed. But why should the state's authority over education extend to the delivery of educational services in what amounts to a virtual monopoly fashion? Why, in other words, should publicly collected funds be expended only in government-run schools? What norm of justice is violated if publicly collected funds are used to support other schools, sponsored by other institutions, if those schools are also contributing to the public good of educating the young? And isn't the case for such funding strengthened by the undeniable fact (at the practical level) that independent schools usually do a better educational job of educating children, especially children most at risk because of economic condition and family breakdown?

Empowering parental choice in education is thus a matter of justice, not simply a matter of convenience. The common morality has long understood that parents are the primary educators of their children—the adults primarily responsible for the development of their children's characters. For the state to use both its taxing and spending functions to arrogate to itself effective authority over elementary and secondary education violates an important norm of justice and contributes to the erosion of personal and familial responsibility in our society.

And, as we have come to see in recent years, it just doesn't work very well. The teachers' unions (which have encouraged the transformation of teaching from a vocation into a job) are, indisputably, the largest single obstacle to educational reform in America today. And to make matters worse, the politicization of the American culture war has resulted in the government school system becoming a laboratory in which all sorts of interest groups work out their agendas—many of which may be morally offensive to the parents whose children become the social lab rats. Children, not teachers and bureaucrats, should be the primary beneficiaries of the educational system; parents should take primary responsibility for determining the kind of education their children receive. That is the public moral case that needs to be argued.

What the philosophers would call the "language-game" is important here. The Catholic school in my parish, in Bethesda, Maryland, is not a *private* school. It is an *independent* school performing a *public* function for a broad cross-section of the population (in any given year, some 10 to 20 percent of the students in the school are not Catholics). St. Jane Frances de Chantal School is no less a *public* school, in the sense of *a school performing a public function*, than Bradley Hills Elementary School; the difference is that Bradley Hills is run by Montgomery County, and St. Jane's is run by my parish. Bradley Hills Elementary is thus most accurately described as a *government* school and St. Jane's as an *independent* school.

The mechanics of a comprehensive educational reform whose aims include the empowerment of parents to exercise their fundamental responsibility for the rearing of their children are the subject of legitimate debate. Some worry, and not without reason, that voucher systems (in which parents would be given, from tax-collected funds, an educational voucher to be "spent" at the school of their choice) risk embroiling independent schools with the government education bureaucracy; are vouchers-without-intrusive-government-control possible? Another proposal would permit tax credits for parents paying tuition at independent schools; but would a tuition tax credit scheme, in the lower income brackets, simply turn into another entitlement program? Still others propose to bypass the entire bureaucratic issue (and the constitutional issue created by the Supreme Court's madcap religion clause jurisprudence) by dramatically raising the federal income tax exemption for children to, say, seven thousand dollars per child (which would, adjusting for inflation, bring the exemption into line with its cash value in 1948); parents would thus have far more disposable income to be invested in independent (including religiously based) education, if they wished.

There is no one Christian answer to the mechanics of parental choice and educational reform. But there is surely a moral imperative for evangelicals and Catholics to work, together, at a radical reconstruction of American elementary and secondary education. The virtual monopoly on the public purse enjoyed by government schools must be broken. It is *prima facie* unjust. Its disempowerment of parents contributes to the breakdown of personal and familial responsibility, even as it exacerbates the problem of the Nanny State. And it has resulted in both the corruption of the teaching profession and the gross politicization of the government schools.

The recovery of responsibility and the rolling back of the encroachments of the Nanny State on the legitimate prerogatives of citizens, parents, and independent voluntary institutions will touch many other questions of public policy, including welfare reform, tort law, and the functioning of the criminal justice system. But if the family is the basic unit of society and if families stand or fall on the basis of parental responsibility, then the reempowerment of parents is a crucial part of any public reform agenda. Breaking the monopoly now enjoyed by government-sponsored education is an indispensable element of the empowerment of parents.

# The Partisanship of Truth

Some will object that this agenda for common public action by evangelicals and Catholics constitutes a partisan exercise in its own right: the mirror image of what Christian conservatives have complained about on the Christian left. And no doubt the proposals sketched here—for a restoration of religious freedom in its primary meaning of "free exercise," for a rollback of the legal endorsement of the sexual revolution, for laws protective of the unborn and supportive of the traditional family, for the empowerment of parents and the breaking of the government-school monopoly—fit more comfortably within one political party's platform than another's, at this particular juncture in American public life.

But that is an accident of history. It has to do, not with some inherent congruence between the gospel and the national Republican Party, but with the take-over of the national Democratic Party by the "McGovern Democrats" in 1972 and the subsequent transformation of that party into the party of life-style libertinism, on the one hand, and the Nanny State, on the other. Roman Catholics and Southern evangelicals were once part of the bedrock of the Democratic coalition. That that is no longer the case tells us much more about the changes in the national Democratic Party than it does about any putative changes in the moral horizons of Roman Catholicism or evangelical Protestantism.

Moreover, there is no guarantee that the Republican Party will eagerly carry the agenda for national reformation outlined above for the balance of this decade and into the twenty-first century. Indeed, were the Republican Party to abandon its pro-life commitment, I think it probable, bordering on virtually certain, that those millions of voters who were attracted to the party in the 1980s by its commitment to what came to be called "traditional family values" would head elsewhere: presumably to a new party that did not regard the social issues as untoward or embarrassing.

This reform agenda for evangelicals and Catholics working together in the public square is not partisan, save only in its partisanship on behalf of the God-given dignity of every human life from conception until natural death. Its principle reference points are biblical truth and Christian moral tradition, not electoral pragmatics—and that is precisely how it must be.

For a partisan gospel is a gospel that has been betrayed for a mess of pottage. That was true of liberation theology in its ideologically charged Marxist forms; and that is why those forms of liberation theology had to be rejected. No political ideology can ever be the bearer of the saving grace of the gospel of Jesus Christ, and no political institution can ever substitute for the Church as the privileged community called to proclaim that saving gospel to the nations. As Christians, our first allegiance is to Jesus Christ and his Church. Everything else is secondary.

But because Christian faith illuminates every aspect of life, it can brighten even the sometimes-darkened alleys of politics. Most especially, in this particular time of the testing of the American democratic experiment, Christians can remind their fellow citizens that democracy is a substantive moral experiment in a people's capacity for self-governance; democracy is not, and cannot be, simply an ensemble of institutional procedures. For the procedures of democracy will break down if they are not sustained by the kind of civil society that can only be built on the basis of shared moral convictions and commitments.

If democracy necessarily engages arguments of real moral substance, then democracy has to be tethered, ultimately, to the truth: the truth about the human person, human responsibilities, and human community. Some will ask, "Whose truth?" (Or even, in unconscious imitation of an ancient Roman procurator, "What is truth?") To which Christians must reply: The truth relevant to public life and the right ordering of our societies is the truth that is discerned through disciplined moral reflection on the human condition and on the personal and public responsibilities of human beings endowed with intelligence and free will. The cynic's question, "What is truth?" is not, as Pilate thought, the end of the conversation; it is, rather, the beginning of the necessary deliberation.

Christians believe that the truth of things is most comprehensively revealed in the gospel of Jesus Christ. But the gospel has public implications, because it addresses the totality of the human person. Not every Christian is obliged to political activism. But every Christian who engages politics ought to do so in ways that make plain that our primary concern is not to throw their rascals out in order to put our rascals in; our concern is to give democracy a new birth of genuine freedom by securing its foundations in the truth about the human person. Christian public action in service to the American republic is not, primarily, a form of domestic missionary activity. It is a form of activity that seeks to bring the moral truths of Christianity to bear on public life: not because we want to impose our values on others, but because we are convinced that the truths about goodness, justice, and virtue that we have learned through the Church can illuminate the lives of men and women of good will and moral conviction who live outside the boundaries of our religious community.

Pope John Paul II identified several of those truths in his 1993 encyclical letter on the moral life, *Veritatis Splendor* ("The Splendor of the Truth"). *Veritatis Splendor* was not a social encyclical, primarily concerned with issues of economic, political, and social life, but John Paul's discussion of the basic principles of Christian morality touched at five key points on the democratic prospect.

First, the pope provocatively argued that the most secure foundation for the bedrock democratic principle of the equality of all persons before the law is the recognition that certain acts are always morally wrong, no matter who commits them or under what circumstances they are committed. Genuine democracy can only exist, John Paul wrote, "on the basis of the equality of all its members, who possess common rights and duties. When it is a matter of the moral norms prohibiting intrinsic evil, there are no privileges or exceptions for anyone. It makes no difference whether one is the master of the world or the 'poorest of the poor' on the face of the earth. Before the demands of morality we are all absolutely equal."[23]

The principles of morality also help democracies build political community out of ethnic, racial, religious, and class diversity. The history of the post-Cold War world (indeed, the history of the world, period) has shown how difficult it can be to construct genuine pluralism out of the facts of plurality. But the task is not an impossible one, the pope writes, if "social coexistence" is based on "a morality which acknowledges certain norms as valid always and for everyone, without exception."[24] Why? Because the moral obligations of others—including racially, ethnically, and/or religiously different others—are a mirror in which I can discern my own moral obligations and thus my own humanity. That sense of common moral obligation is the basis of democratic community in a civil society: a society in which the chasms of racial, ethnic, and religious difference are bridged for purposes of achieving the common good.

Moral principles also serve democracy by creating barriers against the tyranny of the unrestrained pursuit of personal interest or pleasure, and the corrosive impacts that pursuit has on public life. Democracies, at least until very recently, have long understood that personal and commercial passions and interests have to be constrained by both law and moral-cultural habit. But what justifies legal regulation of the free market? What sustains the moral-cultural habits of self-command that can restrain personal passions? John Paul II does not believe that these justifications can be merely instrumental (that is, they are appropriate because they work). Rather, he argues, they must be grounded on certain truths about the human person that are foundational to the democratic experiment:

> If there is no transcendent truth, in obedience to which man achieves his full identity, then there is no sure principle for guaranteeing just relations between people. Their self-interest as a class, group, or nation would inevitably set them in opposition to one another. If one does not acknowledge transcendent truth, then the force of power takes over, and each person tends to make full use of the means at his disposal in order to impose his own interests or his own opinion, with no regard for the rights of others. People are then respected only to the extent that they can be exploited for selfish ends.[25]

In other words, the habits of even a virtuous citizenry are insufficient to guarantee the vitality of a civil society capable of sustaining democracy and a well-functioning market. Christians cannot be full-throttle libertarians. Legal and regulatory structures are essential for channeling the explosive energies of free people into enterprises that support genuine human flourishing and that advance the common good. But, like the moral habits of individuals, those structures will endure over time only if they are grounded, not in expedience, but in publicly acknowledged convictions about the nature and goods of human beings, as individuals and as members of the political community.

Then there is the question of ethics in government. John Paul believes, as must any American who has taken the measure of our public life over the past twenty years, that integrity in government is not simply a matter of thickening the government ethics manuals every year; for ethics is not a matter of rules and regulations alone. It has to do with convictions about who we are, and what we ought to do. As John Paul writes,

Truthfulness in the relations between those governing and those governed, openness in public administration, impartiality in the service of the body politic, respect for the rights of political adversaries, safeguarding the rights of the accused against summary trials and convictions, the just and honest use of public funds, the rejection of equivocal or illicit means in order to gain, preserve, or increase power at any cost—all these are principles which are primarily rooted in, and in fact derive their singular urgency from, the transcendent value of the person and the objective moral demands of the functioning of states.[26]

Finally, John Paul takes up the problem of decadence, which besets all advanced industrialized democracies. The individual who is shackled to his or her desires or needs is no less chained than the Christian dissidents of central and eastern Europe once were, when they went to prison or labor camp for the faith. Indeed, those Christians were more free than the American who is a captive inside the walls of his own cupidity. Christians know that in Christ our liberties have been redeemed from our desires, and that this redemption is not the denial of freedom but rather the fulfillment of freedom in goodness, in human flourishing. Christians also know about falling, and struggling, and getting up to try, with the help of grace, again. Thus John Paul reminds us of the twin imperatives of compassion and moral realism. The "clear and forceful presentation of moral truth," he writes, "can never be separated from a heartfelt respect, born of that patient and trusting love which man always needs along his moral journey, a journey frequently wearisome on account of difficulties, weakness, and painful situations."[27]

But a genuinely transforming love embraces the hard arguments, avoids moral smugness, and takes up the difficult and lengthy task of moral persuasion. It speaks truth to the power of what an earlier generation called concupiscence: to the allure of "doing it my way." Why? Because for the Christian, truth is liberating. And, as John Paul writes, an authentic liberating love of others "does not result . . . from concealing or weakening moral truth, but rather from proposing it in its most profound meaning as an outpouring of God's eternal Wisdom . . . and as a service to man, to the growth of his freedom and the attainment of his happiness."[28]

Truth serves freedom; it does not negate freedom. The founders of the American republic knew that. Too many of the inheritors of their work have forgotten it. Christians in America today are thus called to be partisans of truth. The political party or movement in which we live out that singular partisanship is an entirely secondary issue. Political parties and movements come and go. The truth remains; the truth is great; and, we believe that in Christ the truth will ultimately prevail.

Reminding America of the truths about the human person to which the founders of the republic pledged their lives, fortunes, and sacred honor, and embodying those truths in the distinctive witness we bring to public life, is the public task that history and, we must believe, Providence have set before evangelicals and Catholics together. It is a task worthy of communities gathered together by the conviction that, in knowing the truth, we shall be set truly free (John 8.32).

---

## Notes

1. Dean Acheson, "The Bible in Our National Life," in *Grapes from Thorns* (New York: Norton, 1972), 248–50, 252.

2. To be sure, some Christians have agreed with this calumny; one thinks of the Christian clergy active in the secularist lobby, People for the American Way. But these are essentially political alliances, in which secularist activism is informed not by serious theological reflection but by extreme ideological partisanship.

3. See Richard John Neuhaus, *The Naked Public Square: Religion and Democracy in America* (Grand Rapids: Eerdmans, 1984).

4. For original materials and contemporary commentary on the key cases, see Terry Eastland, ed., *Religious Liberty in the Supreme Court: The Cases That Define the Debate on Church and State* (Grand Rapids: Eerdmans, 1995).

5. Russell Hittinger,, "The Supreme Court v. Religion," *Crisis* 11, no. 5 (May 1993): 22. The balance of this section draws heavily on Professor Hittinger's research and analysis.

6. Hittinger points out the gratuity of the Court's criticism of religion as "potentially divisive": "Any number of different good and worthy human activities are potentially harmful to the civil community. Football rivalries, for example, can cause public disorder, and, in extreme cases, a breakdown of amity between different groups of citizens. Yet no one would seriously argue that football ought to be privatized merely because of its 'potential.' Rather, we tend to reserve this kind of interdiction for either inherently bad activities, or for activities which, although good and worthy, are inherently dangerous." (Ibid., 23.)

7   Ibid., 24.

8   Ibid.

9   Nathan Lewin, "The Church-State Game: A Symposium on *Kiryas Joel*," *First Things* 47 (November 1994): 39.

10  Laurence Tribe, *American Constitutional Law* (Mineola, N.Y.: The Foundation Press, 1978), 823.

11  See Mary Ann Glendon and Raul F. Yanas, "Structural Free Exercise," *Michigan Law Review* 90, no. 3 (December 1991): 477–550.

12  See Richard John Neuhaus, "Genuine Pluralism and the Pfefferian Inversion," *This World* 24 (Winter 1989): 71–86, from which this analysis is drawn.

13  Or, as Pope John Paul II put it in his encyclical letter on Christian mission, *Redemptoris Missio*, "The Church proposes; she imposes nothing" (no. 39).

14  Richard John Neuhaus, "What the Fundamentalists Want," *Commentary* 79, no.5 (May 1985): 43.

15  See John Courtney Murray, S.J., *We Hold These Truths: Catholic Reflections on the American Proposition* (New York: Sheed & Ward, 1960).

16  An ecumenically useful exploration of this claim may be found in C. S. Lewis, *The Abolition of Man* (New York: Macmillan, 1965).

17  112 S.Ct. 2791, at 2807.

18  See Mary Ann Glendon, *Rights-Talk: The Impoverishment of Political Discourse* (New York: Free Press, 1991).

19  See James Davison Hunter, *Before the Shooting Begins: Searching for Democracy in America's Culture War* (New York: Free Press, 1994), 85–121.

20  Pro-life advocacy also involves a challenge to the totalitarian temptation that lurks within the Republic of the Imperial Autonomous Self and the flight from personal responsibility. For the moral and political logic of the autonomy-based case for abortion on demand compels us to consider ourselves a nation of strangers. According to this logic, and as we have seen above, we form no communities of real consequence: whether communities of husband and wife, parents and children, mother and unborn child. We are only autonomous selves, strangers, who may even become enemies. Thus the state's primary task, in this cold universe of individual selves, is to prevent others from interfering with "my" autonomy. And so the actors in the public square are reduced to the solitary individual and the state: which is precisely the goal sought by totalitarianisms of both left and right in this century. (For a development of this argument, see "Abortion and a Nation at War," *First Things* 26 [October 1992]: 9–13.)

21  Parenthetically, a similar public case, appealing to a more powerful public idiom than that of autonomy, can be made in response to the homosexual insurgency. Orthodox Christian morality holds that homosexual acts violate the structure of the divinely created form of love by which men and women are to express their sexuality in unitive and procreative responsibility. Thus "homosexual marriage" is an oxymoron, and proposals to grant it equal

status with heterosexual marriage are an offense against biblical morality.

But how do we make that argument in public, given the confusions wrought by the sexual revolution, the plurality of moral vocabularies in America, and the disarray in the Supreme Court's "equal protection" jurisprudence? Might evangelicals and Catholics make a more powerful public policy case by arguing on natural law grounds? Thus, on this front, we might argue that it is the very nature of governments to make discriminations; that the relevant question in any contested issue is whether the discrimination proposed is invidiously unjust; and that the legal preference given to heterosexual marriage is good for society because it strengthens society's basic unit, the family, and because it is good for children. (For a development of this argument, in similar terms, see the ecumenical and inter-religious statement, "The Homosexual Movement: A Response by the Ramsey Colloquium," in *First Things* 41 [March 1994]: 15–20.)

22  On the disasters wrought by these efforts, see Barbara Defoe Whitehead, "The Failure of Sex Education," *Atlantic Monthly* 274, no. 4 (October 1994): 55–80.

23  John Paul II, *Veritatis Splendor*, 96.

24  Ibid., 97.

25  *Centesimus Annus*, 44.

26  *Veritatis Splendor*, 101.

27  Ibid., 95.

28  Ibid.

# 3

# The History of an Encounter:
# Roman Catholics and Protestant Evangelicals

Mark A. Noll

Things are not as they were!

*J. I. Packer*

I N LATE 1983 the conservative Anglican theologian J. I. Packer began a book review with a revealing bit of autobiography. Packer
had been nurtured in his faith by the robust evangelicalism of the
English Puritans; his published writings had gained him renown in Britain, Canada, and the United States as one of the most articulate modern
advocates of thoughtful, Reformed evangelicalism. Packer's remarks
about the new world heralded by the book he was reviewing, *The Born-
Again Catholic*, spoke of a momentous alteration in a long-standing
religious quarrel:

> If when I was a student you had told me that before old age struck I
> should be reviewing a popular Roman Catholic book on the new birth
> which used Campus Crusade material, carried an official *nihil obstat* and
> *imprimatur*, and was already in its fourth printing in three years, I doubt

whether I would have believed you. But that is what I am doing now. Again, if at that time you had predicted that one day an Anglican bishop would tell me how the last Roman Catholic priest to whom he talked quizzed him hard as to whether Anglicans really preached the new birth as they should, I would probably have laughed in your face. But this month it happened. Things are not as they were![1]

As true as it was in 1983 that things were not as they once had been, so a decade and more later the publication of "Evangelicals and Catholics Together: The Christian Mission in the Third Millennium" is further indication of a sea change in a once stormy relationship. A summary historical sketch, written mostly as a report on evangelical attitudes toward Roman Catholics, cannot by itself evaluate the changes played out in recent decades, but it can show the dramatic nature of what has been taking place. In particular, such a sketch is useful (1) for revealing the nature of the historic standoff between Catholics and Protestant evangelicals that existed, as if set in concrete, from the early days of the Reformation until well after the Second World War; (2) for highlighting some of the dramatic changes that have occurred in relations between Protestants and Catholics over the last three decades; (3) for showing how the Protestant perception of Catholicism's civil character—whether as threatening or supporting public moral order—has always played a large role in evangelical attitudes throughout American history; and (4) for noting some earlier anticipations of modern changes that went largely unnoticed because of the wartime footing that existed between the two camps. The story of relations between Roman Catholics and Protestant evangelicals, in short, cannot provide infallible guidance for the future, but it can provide grist for historical and theological reflection bearing on the search for Christian allies in the modern world.[2]

## Historic Standoff

Once upon a time—in fact, within the memory of many people who are still very much alive—Catholics and evangelical Protestants regarded each other with the gravest possible suspicion. That suspicion reflected a world of religious strife dramatically opposed to the situation described by J. I. Packer in 1983 or as outlined in "Evangelicals and

Catholics Together." While Roman Catholics and Protestant evangelicals are still divided by many important differences, the possibilities that now exist for communication, theological and social cooperation, and mutual encouragement are so much greater than even a generation ago as to constitute a minor revolution. To illustrate how the age of combat between Catholics and Protestants continued until the very recent past, it is necessary only to observe the general situation in the United States during the years immediately following World War II. The standoff appeared fixed, seemingly in place forever.

To be sure, by midcentury, the grosser forms of religious hostility that had prevailed widely throughout much of American history were subsiding. But the change was a matter of degree, not kind.[3] Two comments, two events, and two books suggest the extent of Protestant-Catholic disengagement in the decade and a half after World War II.

In 1945 the Presbyterian fundamentalist Carl McIntyre, who was then more centrally located on the religious spectrum than he would become, assessed the world situation in terms that some other evangelicals would have shared:

> As we enter the post-war world, without any doubt the greatest enemy of freedom and liberty that the world has to face today is the Roman Catholic system. Yes, we have Communism in Russia and all that is involved there, but if one had to choose between the two . . . one would be much better off in a communistic society than in a Roman Catholic Fascist set-up. . . . America has to face the Roman Catholic terror. The sooner the Christian people of America wake up to the danger the safer will be our land.[4]

Three years later, the Protestant church historian Wilhelm Pauck, who moved in more liberal orbits than McIntyre, took stock of the interreligious situation and concluded that "the difference between Protestantism and Roman Catholicism is so profound that it seems almost impossible to recognize them as two forms of one Christianity."[5]

These evaluations reflected a more general climate characterized by considerable mutual suspicion. In 1946 President Truman's assignment of a formal representative to the Vatican was greeted with loud protests from all along the Protestant spectrum. G. Bromley Oxnam, bishop of the Methodist Church in New York and president of the Federal Council of Churches, criticized the move as "encouraging the un-American policy of a union of church and state," which the Catholic Church pursued.[6] Nor was suspicion all on one side. When the second General Assembly of the World Council of Churches met at Evanston in 1954, Chicago's Cardinal Samuel Strich issued a pastoral letter forbidding priests to attend even as reporters and urging Catholics in general to stay far away.[7]

Even authors who attempted to write sympathetically about Catholic-Protestant differences could at best describe a cordial antagonism. When Jaroslav Pelikan, a Lutheran, published *The Riddle of Roman Catholicism* in 1959, he admitted that "the prejudices and clichés of past generations continue to dominate the image of the Roman Church current in America." His book, by contrast, was a charitable effort to dispel prejudice. Yet when Pelikan came to describe the current situation, he turned instinctively to metaphors of conflict—"unconditional surrender," "the great divide," "theological alienation." Neither did he hold out high hopes for an improvement in "what we have now . . . , on both sides, a picture of the other side that is part photograph, part old daguerreotype, and part caricature."[8] The Newman Press translated Louis Bouyer's *The Spirit and Forms of Protestantism* for American Catholic readers in 1956, the year of its original French publication. Like Pelikan, Bouyer was eager to replace prejudice with sympathy; and he was willing to concede a great deal to Protestantism. But, also like Pelikan, a point was soon reached where the language of antithesis took over, and Bouyer concluded that, while the religion of Luther, Calvin, and their theological descendants contained insights that the Catholic Church needed, it was "compromised . . . irremediably" by its fatal attachment to sixteenth-century nominalism.[9] In sum, on the very eve of Pope John XXIII's pontificate and, one might add, of the American presidential election of 1960, there seemed no particular reason to expect a quantum leap in Protestant-Catholic goodwill.

Among Protestants, differences with Roman Catholics were perceived most strongly by those who were the most evangelical. After the Second World War, evangelical publishing still maintained a steady beat of anti-Catholic polemic. New books appeared with titles like *A Priest Speaks His Mind: Why He Returned to the Protestant Faith of His Fathers* and *Catholicism Under the Searchlight of the Scriptures*. Evangelical publishers also reissued classic anti-Catholic works from the previous century including Charles Chiniquy's *Fifty Years in the Church of Rome*.[10] In 1962 the Presbyterian author Loraine Boettner published his lengthy study, *Roman Catholicism,* which came to be regarded by many evangelicals as a definitive exposition and rebuttal of the Roman Catholic faith. Boettner's conclusions summarized a very long history of evangelical complaint:

> That the Roman Church has within it much of truth is not to be denied. It teaches the inspiration of the Scriptures, the deity of Christ, the virgin birth, the miracles, the resurrection of the body, a future judgment, heaven and hell, and many other Scripture truths. In every instance, however, it nullifies these truths to a considerable extent by adding to or subtracting from what the Bible teaches. . . . The Roman Church thus has such serious inherent defects that over the broad course of history it cannot possibly emerge successful. Clearly it has lost its power to evangelize the world, and instead has become so confirmed in its present course that it cannot be reformed either from within or from without. In the main it is as antagonistic and as much an obstacle to evangelical Christianity as are the pagan religions. . . . Its interpretation of the Scriptures is so erroneous and its principles are so persistently unchristian that over the long period of time its influence for good is outweighed by its influence for evil. *It must, therefore, as a system, be judged to be a false church.*[11]

These attitudes toward Catholicism, which evangelicals maintained with something close to unanimity into the 1960s, reached back to the middle decades of the sixteenth century. A combination of attacks on church abuses and fresh articulations of biblical truths—which constituted the negative and positive poles of the Protestant Reformation—long dominated the evangelical response to Catholicism. It is possible to find slightly different points to mark the hardening of religious division—perhaps 1541 and the failure of face-to-face Protestant-Catholic negotiations at Regensburg (Ratisbon) in Germany, or, at the latest, the work of the Catholic Council of Trent (1546–63) and the full-scale responses it evoked from such Protestant luminaries as John Calvin or the Lutheran Martin Chemnitz. Exact dating, however, is immaterial, for Catholic-Protestant antagonism rapidly became a fixed planet in the Western religious sky. Already by the second half of the sixteenth century, efforts to speak sympathetically about Protestant-Catholic similarities were being met with stern opposition from both sides. Church historians of the era who tried to write with some appreciation for the opposition—like the Lutheran John Sleidan or the Huguenot Lancelot du Voisin, sieur de la Popelinière—were blasted by both Catholics and Protestants.[12]

The Protestant brief against Catholicism was expressed in a Niagara of books, pamphlets, and sermons so voluminous that no one human could possibly take the measure of it all. But the main points of that brief can be summarized quite easily. Catholics, in the Protestant view,

- taught that people earned their salvation by doing good deeds;
- prevented common people from reading the Bible and from taking their guidance for life from the Scriptures;
- manufactured extrabiblical saints, festivals, and rites that substituted human imagination for biblical patterns of worship;
- took away glory from Christ by making Mary a coauthor of salvation;
- corrupted Scripture by forcing new doctrines onto the people at the whim of popes and councils, whose supposed authority was no more than the imperialistic expression of their own selfish ambition; and
- promoted a hierarchy that stripped the faithful of their proper status as priests before God.

In their turn, Catholics gave as good as they got. Wherever Catholic communities were placed in physical or intellectual connection with Protestants, a literature sprouted that reversed the charges. Rather than rescuing Christianity from corruption, Protestantism was hastening it toward decay. In the Catholic view, Protestants

- offered a salvation by faith that denied the need for holiness before God;
- abandoned the Bible to the interpretation of every Tom, Dick, and Carrie (no matter how bizarre those interpretations might be) and thus effectively stripped it of normative, authoritative meaning;
- denied the ability of the Holy Spirit to work through ongoing

teaching officers in the Church as the Spirit had earlier worked in bringing the Church into existence;

· neglected God's gracious help provided to humanity in the person of the Blessed Virgin Mary and the exemplary saints;

· rejected the apostolic authority of bishops, councils, and popes and so abetted the rising Western tide of rationalism, secularism, and moral anarchy; and

· forsook genuine ecclesiastical leadership in favor of a political free-for-all where authority was reduced to the power of manipulation.

These polemics, which have echoed around the world since the mid-sixteenth century, arrived early in the colonies that were to become the United States. Although the number of Catholics in the thirteen colonies was small (only 25,000 by 1790), Protestant anti-Romanism was a staple of the American theological world. It was fueled especially by the background of Catholic-Protestant strife in the English Reformation. That antagonism was enshrined for English-speaking readers everywhere in the pages of John Foxe's *Book of Martyrs*, which added Catholic persecution of Protestants to the long line of sufferings endured by true servants of Christ. As merely one instance of the antagonism as it came to America, it is helpful to note the language used when the Massachusetts Judge Paul Dudley in 1750 left a legacy to Harvard College for the purpose of establishing a series of theological lectures. The third of the lectures in a rotating cycle was to be devoted to "the detecting & convicting & exposing of the Idolatry of the Romish Church, Their Tyranny, Usurpations, damnable Heresies, fatal Errors, abominable Superstitions, and other crying Wickednesses in their high Places; and Finally that the Church of Rome is that mystical Babylon, That Man of Sin, That apostate Church spoken of, in the New-Testament."[13] By the time Catholic immigration on a major scale began to the United States in the nineteenth century, anti-Catholic literature was a well-entrenched theological genre. Ray Allen Billington's study of the six antebellum decades included a bibliography of nearly forty pages devoted exclusively to anti-Catholic periodicals, books, and pamphlets.[14]

An incident from the mid-1840s illustrates how difficult it had become to maintain even the slightest respect across the Catholic-evangelical divide. With the growing numbers of Catholics in the country and the conversion of some of them to Protestantism, evangelical denominations that practiced infant baptism were faced with the question of how to regard the status of Catholic baptism. It was a poignant sign of the current state of affairs when the conservative Presbyterian theologian, Charles Hodge, brought down great wrath upon his head for defending the validity of Catholic baptism, even though that defense fully maintained Protestant arguments about the deviance of Rome. Hodge was far from being a crypto-Catholic, since throughout his long career he regularly chastised Catholicism for what he thought were its manifest theological perversions. At the same time, however, Hodge held that proper discriminations had to be made. His reasoning against the action of the Old School General Assembly in 1845, which denied the validity of Catholic baptism, is worth quoting at length, both to show the normal terms that evangelicals used in talking about Catholics and to indicate how difficult it was for even a well-respected evangelical leader to gain a hearing for even the most modest gesture of respect toward Rome:

> Baptism therefore, not being an ordinance of any particular church, but of the church catholic, and every man who professes saving truth being a member of that church, Romish baptism if administered by a man professing such truth, is Christian baptism. . . . We maintain therefore Romish baptism to be valid; that is, that it avails to make the recipient a member of the church catholic, because it is a washing with water, in the name of the Trinity, with the design to signify, seal and apply the benefits of the covenant of grace. . . . If the church of Rome is antichrist, a synagogue of Satan, how can its ordinances be Christian sacraments? This we doubt not is the difficulty which weighs most with those who reject Romish baptisms as invalid. We would ask such persons, whether they admit that a Roman Catholic can be a child of God? If he can, how can a man be a member of the synagogue of Satan and of the body of Christ at the same time? Is there no inconsistency here? If not, then there is no inconsistency in declaring that the Romish system, so far as it is distinguished from that of evangelical churches, is anti-Christian, and yet that those who are groaning under that system are in the visible church. The terms antichrist, synagogue of Satan, etc., refer not to the mass of the people, nor to the presbyters of that communion, nor the word of God, nor the saving truths which they profess, but to the Popish hierarchy and its corruptions. That hierarchy with its usurpations and errors, is the mystery of iniquity, the man of sin, which

in the church catholic, the temple of God, exalts itself above all that is called God or that is worshipped. If Roman Catholics are no part of the visible church, then the Romish hierarchy is not "the man of sin" spoken of by the apostle, for he was to rise and rule in the church. It is, therefore, one thing to denounce the Roman system, and another to say that Romanists are no part of the church catholic. And if they are in the church, their baptism being a washing with water in the name of the Trinity, is Christian baptism; just as the word of God, when read or preached by them, is still his word, and is to be received and obeyed as such.[15]

The attitudes that Hodge both reflected and combated remained particularly strong among evangelicals. Even after the momentous shifts of recent decades had begun, observers noted that conservative Protestant positions were the most resistant to change. In 1978 the ethicist James Gustafson wrote that a wide range of Protestant-Catholic dialogue was then under way in the United States, with the exception that "the most conservative Catholic and Protestant theologians do not relate to each other at all."[16] Gustafson may have been overstating things a little, but he was correct in concluding that many among the firmer sort of Protestants still retained much of their tradition's hereditary anti-Catholicism.

## Religious Standoff, Civil Mistrust

As steadily as American Protestants maintained anti-Catholicism for theological reasons, almost from the start of European settlement they were nearly as concerned about Catholicism's civil tendencies. The reputation of Catholicism as a promoter of tyranny contributed fully to the first stages of the American love affair with liberty that began in earnest with the eighteenth-century colonial wars. When warfare between France and England swept up the colonies, colonial Protestants immediately made fateful rhetorical connections and proclaimed that they were fighting for the glories of Britain against the depredations of France, the truth of Protestantism against the lies of Catholicism, and the blessings of freedom against the perils of tyranny.

Two citations, from hundreds that could be quoted, show how, even before there was a United States, American republican commitments functioned as an ally of Protestantism and an enemy of Catholicism. George Whitefield, the great evangelist, was in Philadelphia in August 1746 when news arrived that "Bonnie Prince Charles," the Jacobite (and Catholic) pretender to the British throne, had been decisively defeated at the battle of Culloden. Whitefield immediately preached a sermon to thank God for rescuing the British from the multiplied woes of a Catholic monarchy: "How soon would our pulpits every where have been filled with these old anti-Christian doctrines, free-will, meriting by works, transubstantiation, purgatory, works of supererogation, passive-obedience, non-resistance, and all the other abominations of the whore of Babylon?"[17] Ten years later, the president of Princeton College in New Jersey, Aaron Burr, Sr., rallied his evangelical audience at the start of the French and Indian Wars with a frightful vision of France's Catholic religion: "We have heard of the Policy and Perfidy of France, of her arbitrary Power, Popish tyranny and Bigotry. . . . If we view our Enemies, in a religious, as well as political Light, we shall see the Necessity of guarding against them with all possible care. Their established religion is Popery; which, beside all its other Corruptions, disposes them from Principle, to be cruel to Protestants."[18] Only two decades later, American colonists found proof positive of Britain's tyranny when they saw the British extend civil rights and historic privileges to the Catholic Church in Quebec. New England ministers saw the Act not as an overdue recognition of human rights but as an effort "to cut off all the liberties of the colonies."[19]

After the American War of Independence—and the social revolution arising from it that made liberty the center of the American ideology[20]—evangelical anti-Catholicism was given new life by the rising current of Catholic immigration into the United States. Protestant writing against Catholicism retained the historic theological animus, but it was almost always a political expression as well.

One of the main engines of the reform movements that occupied American Protestants in the period before the Civil War was anti-Catholicism, sometimes of the rabid variety. Lyman Beecher, the whirlwind Congregationalist and Presbyterian who, in a long career, spearheaded Protestant outreach in rural Connecticut, Boston, and Cincinnati, often warned Americans about the threat from the Catholic Church. Historian Sydney Ahlstrom summarized a major section of one of Beecher's most influential books, *Plea for the West* (1834), as "a 140-page tirade which depicts the pope and Europe's reactionary kings, with the Austrian emperor at their head and Catholic immigrants for agents, as engaged in an organized conspiracy to take over the Mississippi Valley."[21] When ideological controversy increased between North and South over the issue of slavery, northern Protestants knew how to put to use their long habit of linking Rome to tyranny. In the mid-1850s a broadside from the American (or Know-Nothing) Party tried to enlist anti-Catholic sentiment in the struggle against slavery: "Whereas, Roman Catholicism and slavery being alike founded and supported on the basis of ignorance and tyranny; and being, therefore, natural allies in every warfare against liberty and enlightenment; therefore, be it Resolved, That there can exist no real hostility to Roman Catholicism which does not embrace slavery, its natural co-worker in opposition to freedom and republican institutions."[22] In the two decades before the Civil War, anti-Catholicism was a staple in shaping the political actions of many Protestants in the North as well as some in the South.[23] In the postwar period of renewed Protestant enthusiasm for the future of the country, Protestants were again quick to paint Catholics as antidemocratic and antirepublican. One of the most popular works of this type, which described both the day's moral crisis as well as hope for the future, was written by a mid-Western Congregationalist, Josiah Strong. The fifth chapter of Strong's *Our Country* was entitled "Conflict of Romanism with the Fundamental Principle of our Government."[24]

A sampling of Protestant book titles can also show how central the alleged civic deficiencies of Catholicism were to evangelical polemical literature: again, from a plethora of examples, N. L. Rice, *Romanism not Christianity: a Series of Lectures in which Popery and Protestantism are Contrasted, showing the Incompatibility of the Former with Freedom and Free Institutions* (Cincinnati, 1847); Thomas Bayne, *Popery Subversive of American Institutions* (Pittsburgh, 1856); Joseph Smith Van Dyke, *Popery: The Foe of the Church and of the Republic* (Philadelphia, 1871); and Jeremiah J. Crowley, *Romanism: A Menace to the Nation; Together with my former book, The Parochial School, a Curse to the Church, a Menace to the Nation* (Wheaton, 1912), which was dedicated to "the lovers of liberty, enlightenment and progress throughout the world."

White evangelical Protestants almost universally felt that Catholics threatened the biblically based character of American civilization. Thus, the nineteenth century's active anti-Catholicism was sparked especially by the belief that the Catholic hierarchy discouraged, or even prohibited, the use of Scripture among the laity. This belief, in turn, led to the conclusion that Catholicism was inimical to the American way of life, a conclusion set out with disarming frankness by an attorney arguing in 1887 to preserve the right of a Wisconsin school board to continue daily readings from the King James Version: "The decrees of the councils, the encyclicals of the Popes, the pastoral and other letters of the Archbishops and Bishops, and the writings of learned Catholics furnish abundant evidence that the Catholic church is opposed to popular government, that it is opposed to liberty of conscience, and of worship, and that it is opposed to our public school system."[25]

It only added fuel to Protestant fires when a few well-known American Protestants actually joined the Catholic Church. Outrage at such actions was mitigated by the observation that some of the converts—like Sophia Ripley and Orestes Brownson—had already been tainted by their earlier association with the suspect Transcendentalist movement.[26]

In the twentieth century, evangelical Protestants maintained the charge that Catholicism entailed a threat to American freedoms. *The Fundamentals* of 1910–1915 included several stringent attacks on Rome, of which Bostonian J. M. Foster's was typical. His complaint was as much social and political as theological:

[The Catholic church is] the essential and deadly foe of civil and religious liberty. . . . The Roman hierarchy owns $300,000,000 in America. They have a parochial school system and clamorously demand a share in the public school fund. Their policy is the refinement of duplicity. They join the Jews, infidels and skeptics in driving the Bible from our public schools, on the ground that the State is only a secular corporation and has no right to teach morals and religion. . . . The answer which the organic people should return is: "This is a Christian State; the public school system is its agency for building up a Christian citizenship; morals and religion, so far as they are essential for discharging the functions of Christian citizenship, shall be taught in our public schools; and the school funds shall not be divided."[27]

The charge that Catholics could not be fully American because of their allegiance to the pope and their promotion of religious error played a large part in shaping Protestant voting during the presidential elections of 1928 and 1960, when Catholic candidates Al Smith and John

F. Kennedy ran for the Democrats.[28] Just after the 1960 election, Loraine Boettner's evangelical attack on Catholicism featured the charge that "Roman Catholicism [is] a poor defense against communism." Very near the conclusion of his book, Boettner repeated the stock evangelical assertion that "in general it [the Catholic Church] has sought to weaken or destroy free governments."[29]

In sum, the fixed Protestant opinion was that Catholicism was such a flawed version of Christianity as to be hardly Christian at all. In the United States, moreover, evangelical Protestants were leaders in arguing that Catholicism was not only a religious threat, but that it also subverted the free political institutions of the United States. Well after World War II, the anti-Catholic polemic went on. Into the late 1950s almost no one could have predicted that change was in the air.

## Dramatic Change

That was then. Only short decades later, the situation has become very different. Four major factors help explain why the Catholic-evangelical climate has changed and why that change has been so dramatic. First was a one-time political occurrence, second a far more important series of developments within the Catholic Church, third a political reorientation among evangelicals, and fourth a theological breakthrough. Even a sketchy account of these factors can show that, while there remains much to discuss between evangelicals and Catholics, the basis for that discussion is dramatically different than it has ever been in American history.

1.   The most visible public signal of a shift in the United States was the election of a Catholic as president in 1960. John F. Kennedy's victory was itself a milestone for overcoming Protestant bias and fulfilling earlier Catholic efforts at public service. It marked the culmination of a long process begun during the Revolutionary period by the participation of the Maryland Catholic, Charles Carrol, in the Continental Congress and by George Washington's proclamation suppressing traditional antipapal demonstrations on November 5 (Guy Fawkes or Pope's Day). Kennedy's election was also the culmination of more than a century and a half of intensive Catholic involvement in grass-roots politics.[30] The

circumstances of the 1960 campaign added even greater symbolic importance to Kennedy's election. His famous campaign speech before Protestant ministers in Houston seemed to convince them, and many others, that a Catholic president would not imperil national integrity. Kennedy's scrupulous record on church-state matters, particularly his opposition to government aid for parochial schools, silenced many critics who feared that Catholics did not have proper national priorities. On this issue Billy Graham spoke for others by bestowing the indelicate praise that Kennedy had "turned out to be a Baptist President."[31] Moreover, the apotheosis that occurred after Kennedy's assassination left him, a Catholic, one of the most popular American presidents among the public at large. The "religious issue" in American politics, though not yet dead, had suffered a crushing blow. Even Kennedy's misdeeds have helped defuse interreligious antagonisms, for his womanizing and power-grabbing were "ecumenical" in resembling the misdeeds of politicians who happened to be Protestant.

2.    The Kennedy phenomenon was less significant for long-term improvement in Protestant-Catholic relations than the more strictly religious events, which, after having been set in motion in Rome, led to great changes in America. The new situation between Catholics and evangelicals is a subset of a much larger reorientation of Catholic and Protestant relations. Ripple effects from Pope John XXIII's ecumenical spirit were not long in coming. Even before he convened the Second Vatican Council (1962–65), the pope had sent Catholic observers to the 1960 assembly of the World Council of Churches in New Delhi and had established a Secretariat for Promoting Christian Unity. In the wake of the council's Decree on Ecumenism, which "commends this work to the bishops everywhere in the world for their diligent and prudent guidance," the Conference of American Bishops in November 1964 set up its own Ecumenical Commission. This agency sponsored subcommissions that very soon were deep in discussion with the Orthodox Church in the United States and with several of the major Protestant traditions.[32] Of these meetings, that between Lutherans and Catholics has produced the richest fruit, with a series of agreements on the Nicene Creed, baptism, the Eucharist, and, most importantly, justification by faith.[33] Catholic entrance into ecumenical activity has continued on a broad level. Although the Church does not belong to either the National Council or World Council of Churches, it takes an active observer's role in the

deliberations of these bodies. Moreover, it has become a member of the National Council's Commission on Faith and Order, an agency whose staff now regularly includes Catholics.[34] Catholic-Protestant discussions, instructions, debates, and dialogue are now a regular feature at nearly all the major inter-faith forums on almost every imaginable issue.

3.    In light of how important the civic sphere has always been for Catholic-evangelical relations, it is not surprising that an alteration in po-litical perception contributed greatly to the changes of recent decades. Several developments since the 1960s have conspired to extinguish (or at least greatly diminish) the evangelical fear of Catholicism as a civil threat. Some of these developments have been literary and theoretical. On the home front, American Catholics were among the leaders at the Second Vatican Council in securing strong statements in behalf of civil liberty. Although American evangelicals did not read widely in John Courtney Murray and other American Catholic proponents of civil lib-erty, their work nonetheless undermined historic evangelical fears of Catholic tyranny.[3b] In the international arena, even more damage was done to Protestant notions of Catholic tyranny by the contribution of the Catholic Church to the Solidarity movement in Poland, the public leadership of Pope John Paul II in combating communism in Europe, and the pope's temperate statements on explosive political situations in Latin America, Africa, and Asia.[36] These political actions did not address doctrinal issues directly, but they did strip away much of the civil anxiety with which American Protestants had always looked upon Roman Catholics.

The practicalities of local political action have also done much to open doorways. Over the last several decades, contemporary political affairs have become so tangled that Christian beliefs and public stances on moral issues now collide in nearly every conceivable combination. The crucible effect wrought by this situation explains why many Catholic-evangelical barriers have fallen: committed toilers in the pub-lic vineyard have glanced up in surprise to find previously despised Catholics or evangelicals laboring right alongside.

The complex controversies surrounding three of America's funda-mental social concerns—sex, national self-defense, and the economy—have contributed a great deal to the withering of old interreligious antagonisms. Political debates on these issues, particularly controversy on how moral beliefs are to shape education, regularly reflect the passionate commitments of Americans from all points on the religious compass. Religiously infused arguments—especially on abortion, but also on other issues, including health care reform, the justice or injustice of specific military actions, the merits of United States foreign policy, or the character of candidates for public office—fill the air. The significant fact for contemporary interreligious relations is that allegiance to a general Protestantism or Catholicism is no longer a reliable indicator of commitments on public policy. Both theoretical questions and practical dilemmas, both theological applications and religious reflexes, are so diverse that whatever systematic differences still separate Catholics and Protestants are regularly lost in the public shuffle. In this new situation, Catholics and evangelicals often find themselves arguing the same or similar positions on public issues.

4.  On specific theological issues, the ecumenical dialogues promoted by the Second Vatican Council have gone a considerable distance toward clarifying the difference between mistaken religious stereotypes and genuine theological disagreement. All of the Catholic dialogues with different Protestant groups have highlighted areas of continuing disagreement. But those same dialogues have also cast some historic standoffs into a startlingly new light. While American evangelicals, with their twentieth-century suspicion of ecumenical activity, have usually not kept abreast of the various Catholic-Protestant dialogues, their contents make fascinating reading for anyone with even a little knowledge of the historic standoff between Catholics and evangelicals.

Of many examples that could be cited, the U.S. Lutheran-Roman Catholic dialogue on justification by faith, published in 1983, is one of the most remarkable. The promulgation of a joint statement was the product of extensive discussion over a period of several years. This complex, heavily footnoted document demanded careful reading, and yet its main points spoke directly to major sources of historic Catholic-Protestant antagonism. In particular, the document contended that much of the disagreement on this issue between Protestants (or, here, Lutherans) and Catholics was based on conditions that no longer prevailed. Specifically, both sides had been guilty of reading the Bible polemically in an effort to buttress their own positions, many "non-theological sources of division" that once separated Christians were now passé (like state-separated ecclesiastical establishments), and both Catholics and Lutherans should repent for the verbal abuse they had been hurling at each other for over four hundred years. The document spoke not of "uniformity" on the substance of the doctrine of justification, but about "a convergence" on the meaning of the doctrine. Most importantly, the elements of "material convergence" began with the assertion that "Christ and his gospel are the source, center and norm of Christian life, individual and corporate, in church and world. Christians have no other basis for eternal life and hope of final salvation than God's free gift in Jesus Christ, extended to them in the Holy Spirit." The shapers of the document concluded by saying that they could agree on "a fundamental affirmation . . . . *Our entire hope of justification and salvation rests on Christ Jesus and on the gospel whereby the good news of God's merciful action in Christ is made known; we do not place our ultimate trust in anything other than God's promise and saving work in Christ.*"[37] Further sections of the document hedged this statement around with carefully chosen words to qualify matters from both Lutheran and Catholic directions. The qualifications, however, did not undermine the manifest implication of the words that were used.

This is the sort of statement that J. I. Packer had in mind when he said he had not anticipated he would ever live to see such signs of "evangelicalism" within the Catholic Church. It is the sort of statement that, by recording a new willingness among at least many Catholics and Protestants to rethink old standoffs, heralds a new day of inter-Christian fellowship and activity.

## Catholic-Protestant Reengagement

Several signs of the recent Catholic-Protestant reengagement have special bearing for evangelical Protestants. The experience of many individuals has paralleled that of the fundamentalist leader Carl McIntyre. Where McIntyre in 1945 claimed that he would rather be ruled by communists than Catholics, by 1969 his message had changed, at least a little. By the latter date McIntyre averred, "I'm much closer to the Catholics in my belief in the Virgin Birth than I am to liberal Protestants who deny it."[38] Protestants who started out more flexible than McIntyre have moved a proportionately greater distance, but McIntyre's general observation—that on some matters, some Protestants stand fairly close to some Catholics—has proven true for many individuals.

More generally, the spread of the charismatic movement (and then of

songs, prayers, and worship styles going well beyond officially charismatic circles) has done a great deal to reduce the barriers between
Catholics and evangelicals.[39] Public taste in spiritual literature shows the
same lack of respect for the great divide of the sixteenth century, with
evangelicals buying the books of Catholics Thomas Merton and Henri
Nouwen, Catholics reading evangelicals Richard Foster and Richard
Lovelace, and Christians of all sorts devouring the books from Britain's
C. S. Lewis and G. K. Chesterton without caring a great deal that the
former grew up in an evangelical ethos before finding "mere Christianity," while the latter moved from Anglicanism to Catholicism without
ever embracing evangelicalism. American publishers have encouraged
the growing traffic between the traditions by bringing out numerous
books that treat interconfessional differences far more relatively than
authors in the 1950s could have imagined. To sample almost randomly,
it is possible to point to popular titles like Albert Boudreau's *The Born-
Again Catholic* (1980) from Living Flame Press, and more academic studies, such as George H. Tavard's *Justification* (1983) from Paulist Press,
which argues that Luther's construction of this key doctrine is compatible with the theology of Trent, or T. F. Torrance's *Theology in Reconciliation: Essays Towards Evangelical-Catholic Unity in East and West* (1976),
published in this country by Wm. B. Eerdmans.

Even on matters concerning the Bible, always a sensitive barometer
of public sentiment in America, the recent decades have witnessed a
series of marvels. From rioting over Catholic desires to read the Douay-
Rheims Bible in public school during the nineteenth century, to the
creation of mutually exclusive networks of professional Bible scholars in
the first half of the twentieth, the study and reading of Scripture has now
become a nonsectarian free-for-all.[40] Catholics currently may read the
Living Bible and the Good News Bible, both produced under Protestant
auspices, with the *imprimatur* and *nihil obstat*. Catholic scholars sit on the
revision committee of the Revised Standard Version, and Protestant
purchasers swell the sales of the Catholic Jerusalem Bible. Official delegates were exchanged between the Catholic Biblical Association and
the Society of Biblical Literature for the first time only in 1959, yet by
1966 a Catholic had been elected president of the SBL.[41] So unpredict-
able had the times become that it was a Catholic group that set records
in the distribution of Scripture, with the Sacred Heart League placing
orders from the American Bible Society for 775,000 New Testaments in
1979 and 800,000 in 1983.[42]

The recent careers of two stars in the religious media suggest how much and how rapidly things have changed. Billy Graham, of Southern fundamentalist extraction and nativist evangelical education, early in his evangelistic career enjoyed less than cordial relations with Catholics. During the 1950s Catholic officials in South America and the Philippines forbade their coreligionists to attend his meetings; in the same years local priests and bishops in the United States also often discouraged attendance at Graham crusades. During the presidential election of 1960, Graham only just succeeded in muting his enthusiasm for Richard Nixon and, again just barely, in hiding his apprehensions about a Democratic regime that would include not only a Catholic president, but also a catholic majority Leader in the Senate (Mike Mansfield) and a Catholic Speaker of the House (John McCormack). Very soon thereafter, however, Graham began to work at improved relations with Catholics. His efforts were unusually successful. Catholics now make up a considerable portion of those who attend his meetings, record decisions for Christ, and watch the crusades on television. Tangible evidence of Graham's transcendence of interconfessional antagonisms multiplied rapidly from the late 1960s. In 1977 he was granted permission to hold a crusade in one of American Catholicism's most hallowed locations, the football stadium at the University of Notre Dame. In 1978 he became the first Protestant leader to be entertained by the abbot of the shrine of the Black Madonna in Czestochowa, Poland. In 1981 he sought and was granted an audience at the Vatican by Pope John Paul II, who short years before as Cardinal Karol Wojtyla had made it possible for Graham to preach in Catholic churches during his evangelistic tour of Poland.[43]

If Billy Graham's growing friendliness with Catholics is remarkable, what may be said about the Catholic *volte-face* on Martin Luther? Although the antagonisms of centuries had cooled somewhat by the 1950s, Luther was still treated harshly or ignored entirely by most Catholics. Only two of thirty American Catholic periodicals in one survey provided reviews of Roland Bainton's life of Luther, the most compelling modern study, when it appeared in 1950.[44] Catholic reaction to the 1953 movie *Martin Luther* was also decidedly unfavorable. One commentator in *The Priest* summed up his judgment by calling Luther "a lewd satyr whose glandular demands were the ultimate cause of his break with the Christian Church."[45]

In the wake of the Second Vatican Council, however, an altogether different attitude filtered down rapidly into popular levels. By 1965 the pages of *The Priest* reflected a different picture. According to one writer, "We'd feel quite silly today declaiming against Luther in the intemperate words of yesterday."[46] Scholarly and popular reassessment of Luther went on apace until 1980 when a series of meetings to celebrate the 450th anniversary of the Lutherans' Augsburg Confession heard from many Catholics about the usefulness of that confession for their own tradition.[47] The reevaluation reached a grand climax in 1983, during the celebrations marking the five hundredth anniversary of Luther's birth. Local Catholic officials, anticipating the pope's own appearance in Rome's Evangelical-Lutheran Christ Church on December 11, 1983, accepted invitations to preach in Protestant services.[48] In that year, conciliatory Protestant titles like *Martin Luther: Prophet to the Catholic Church* were echoed by Catholic books of similar spirit like *Luther: A Reformer for the Church.*[49] It encapsulates the startling changes wrought by the passage of only a few years to note that in the mid-1950s Chicago Catholics fought to keep the Luther film off local television, while in 1983 the Notre Dame alumni magazine devoted much of one issue, including an attractive cover portrait, to a discussion of "What Martin Luther Means to Us."[50] Only two years before there had been a similar chorus of Protestant and Catholic voices to mark the eight hundredth anniversary of the birth of Saint Francis. But the dramatically altered position of Martin Luther in Catholic-Protestant relations testified especially eloquently to an unprecedented improvement in interconfessional attitudes.

The last several decades, in sum, have witnessed a major reorientation in relations between Protestant evangelicals and Roman Catholics. To be sure, echoes of old antagonisms still remain. A residual anti-Catholicism lives on in some areas of American civil life, but that anti-Catholicism is not usually a direct product of Protestant evangelical concerns.[51] More specific religious hostility lingers among a few Protestant fundamentalists and evangelicals. In the early 1980s a California publisher issued two comic books, *Alberto* and *The Double Cross,* that illustrated the lingering force of that hostility. The books purported to tell the story of a former Spanish Jesuit, who was trained to subvert Protestantism through a number of ingenious schemes, and of his sister, who endured the terrors of Maria Monk in an English convent. They used a language every bit as unreserved as the harshest polemics of the sixteenth or nineteenth centuries. The fairly wide sale of the comic books suggests that latent antagonisms remain in Protestant circles that the well-publicized Catholic-Protestant reengagements of recent years have not affected. As an indication of changing times, however, evangelicals joined other kinds of Protestants in denouncing the books; the Christian Booksellers Association, which represents largely a conservative Protestant constituency, expressed its regret over the publications; and evangelical journalists contributed much of the hard information that exposed the comic books as fraudulent.[52]

The hostilities that Greeley describes and Jack Chick markets would have been well at home in the 1840s or 1890s. Then they were in the mainstream. Now they are on the margin.

## Hints of Peace During Times of War

Before pausing for brief reflection on the meaning of the recent changes, it is helpful to take one more look into the past. Strife, in fact, was never the only reality in Catholic-Protestant exchange, even though it certainly was predominant. Simply to note that even in the centuries of intense controversy an occasional Catholic could commend an occasional Protestant, and vice versa, is to catch hints as to why Catholic-evangelical communication could blossom so rapidly since the 1960s. The key seems to have been that when "the other" manifested something self-evidently Christian (though not necessarily in the shape prescribed by either of the warring parties), then polemics could give way to dialogue. Enough of these moments existed to suggest that a dedicated search for Catholic-Protestant engagement, even in the darkest years of strife, might yield more edifying instances than the image of total war indicates. Before they broke up over the issue of ecclesiastical authority, Catholics and Protestants at the Council of Regensburg in 1541, for example, could agree that God's grace was entirely free in the salvation of sinners, and that it was wrong to separate faith and love. Not all on both sides thought this was a breakthrough, but John Calvin (though expressing what had already become a standard anti-Catholic attitude) could yet point out that something significant had occurred:

> You will marvel [Calvin wrote to William Farel] when you read the copy [of the article on justification] . . . that our adversaries have conceded so much. For they have committed themselves to the essentials of

what is our true teaching. Nothing is to be found in it which does not stand in our writings. I know that you would prefer a more explicit exposition and in this you are at one with myself. But if you consider with what sort of men we have to deal, you will acknowledge that a great deal has been achieved. [53]

Moreover, even when the early Protestants were engaged in their most brutal debate with Catholic opponents, leaders of both sides continued to draw on the Christian insight of exemplary theologians from the Catholic Middle Ages, like Bernard of Clairvaux, Thomas à Kempis, and, above all, Augustine.[54]

Somewhat later, a long line of Protestants found inspiration in the bracing Christian vision of Blaise Pascal, who was treasured both for his attacks on the Jesuits and for his positive Christian exposition. Evangelicals perhaps avoided the parts of Pascal's writings where he expressed his Roman convictions, but he remained a favorite of many of them, including the seventeenth-century Puritan Theophilus Gale and the eighteenth-century awakeners George Whitefield, John Newton, Jonathan Edwards, and the Wesleys.[55] In 1739, when Charles Wesley was taken to task by his fellow Protestant, Dean Conybeare of Christ Church, Oxford, he urged the dean to read the Catholic Pascal, among other authors, as a means for understanding "justification by faith" and "vital religion."[56] For his part, John Wesley, who associated Pascal with the emphases in Henry Scougall's Scottish devotional classic, *The Life of God in the Soul of Man*, was on occasion remarkably sanguine about Catholicism. In 1790, less than a year before his death, he wrote to a nephew who had become a Catholic but was now slipping away from all religion. To Wesley, the brand name was far less important than that the nephew practice the faith: "What do you want? not clothes or books or money. If you did, I should soon supply you. But I fear you want (what you least of all suspect), the greatest thing of all—religion. I do not mean external religion, but the religion of the heart; the religion which Kempis, Pascal, Fénelon enjoyed: that life of God in the soul of man, the walking with God and having fellowship with the Father and the Son."[57]

A similar account can be given about Protestant affection for the Catholic mystical tradition of François Fénelon and Madame Guyon. When the Holiness preacher Thomas Upham published a life of Madame Guyon in the mid-nineteenth century, denomination was far

less important to him than that Fénelon and Guyon had rightly proclaimed "the doctrine of pure or unselfish love, in the experience of
which . . .the sanctification of the heart essentially consists."[58] Throughout the twentieth century, even in decades of intense interreligious
strife, evangelical Protestant publishers more than any other kept the
works of these Catholic mystics alive.

Finally, it is appropriate to note that, in more reflective moments,
even battered veterans of the Catholic-Protestant wars could view the
struggle above the battle lines. So it was with John Henry Newman,
who had been raised an evangelical Anglican but who became the most
famous English convert to Catholicism in the nineteenth century. Late
in his life, after decades of sometimes sharp polemic with Protestants, an
acquaintance from deep in his past, the evangelical Edward Bickersteth,
sent Newman a copy of a poem he had written on the Last Judgment.
Newman's reply spoke for a reality that may have been more common
than antagonists were prepared to acknowledge: "I can but bow before
the great mystery that those are divided here and look for the means of
grace and glory in such different directions, who have so much in common in faith and hope."[59]

Beyond question, disengagement and polemic were the prevailing
moods of evangelical-Catholic engagement in the four centuries before
1960. It may just be, however, that beneath the alarums of battle, even in
the days of war, there existed voices that, could they only have been
heard, heralded the reality that has now come to pass.

## Reflections, Historical and Theological

Several observations are possible after a historical review of evangelical-
Catholic encounters. The most important concern the use of the terms
*Catholic* and *evangelical* without qualification. The time is long past when
responsible analysts could speak of Catholics and evangelicals as homog-
enous units. An awareness of pluralism has been a truism in the
discussion of American Protestants since the end of the nineteenth century, but only in recent decades have historians taken seriously the near
impossibility of lumping together (as only a partial list) Protestant
mainliners, fundamentalists, liberals, Lutherans, Pentecostals, Disciples,
Plymouth Brethren, and a thousand and one other variations.

The larger Protestant reality obtains also for evangelicals. With no formal structure uniting those who share evangelical faith, with evangelicals strewn across multitudes of denominations, with no institutional voice presuming to speak for or to all evangelical Protestants, with deep theological, ecclesiastical, and social differences dividing evangelicals from each other, and with the racial divide in American history posing nearly insurmountable obstacles between white and black evangelicals, it is presumptuous to speak casually about a common evangelical attitude to Catholics or to anything else. If it is true that the four marks of evangelicalism outlined most satisfactorily by British historian David Bebbington—conversionism, activism, biblicism, and crucicentrism (i.e., a focus on Christ's cross as the means of salvation)—in some general sense describe most of those who call themselves evangelicals, or who are lumped together by observers as evangelicals, still there is a daunting diversity at work within evangelicalism.[60] A recent survey of over four thousand Americans found adherents to the evangelical positions that Bebbington described distributed into a multitude of varying categories—including thirteen different kinds of Baptists, at least six distinct Pentecostal denominations, eight varieties of Holiness churches, five groups of Lutherans, several kinds of Methodists and Congregationalists, and many different independent and nondenominational churches.[61] To further complicate conceptual categories, an equally careful survey of Canadians recently discovered that of the 15 percent of Canadians who could be identified as evangelicals (through even more detailed criteria than Bebbington's four characteristics), a full one-third were Roman Catholic.[62] From the Protestant side, therefore, it is necessary to use extreme care in speaking about the often diverse elements that fit under the category "evangelical."

It has become almost equally true from the other side as well. Despite persisting tendencies to speak of a unified Catholic movement, such efforts are now nearly as indefensible as similar generalities applied to Protestants. Catholics do retain a structural unity symbolized by the pope and the Church's hierarchy, but it would be wise for Protestants to let Catholics say what that structure means. Speaking as a Catholic theologian, Richard McBrien can say of the current scene, "There are sometimes sharper divisions *within* the Roman Catholic Church than there are between certain Catholics and certain Protestants."[63] As a sociologist, Andrew Greeley (who is also a Catholic priest) has made the same point: "Every generalization about values that begins with the word 'Catholic' is likely to be misleading, if not erroneous, precisely because the generalization will mask substantial differences in values that exist among the Catholic subpopulations."[64] Given the situation of religious pluralism *within* the Christian families, there is much more opportunity now than even fifty years ago to find meaningful fellowship across, as well as significant strife within, traditional evangelical and Catholic communities.

At least two results flow from this new situation. First, after windows have been opened even a little between evangelicals and Catholics, there are not only more opportunities for mutual encouragement, but also more opportunities for underscoring tensions among Protestants or Roman Catholics. To look at matters from just the one side, different groups within the evangelical mosaic find significant differences in those aspects of Catholicism to which they are attracted. Pentecostal evangelicals, for example, may appreciate Catholic openness to the subjective working of the Spirit but continue to dislike formal Catholic hierarchy; Confessional Reformed evangelicals may appreciate Catholic objectivity about the sacraments but dislike Catholic ways of expressing the way that faith should be active in love; the new wave of academic evangelical philosophers may appreciate the tough-minded tradition of Catholic philosophical reflection (especially the Thomistic tradition) but shy away from the way that this sort of philosophy has been used to define expressly Catholic dogma; Anabaptist evangelicals may appreciate the dedication of the Catholic monastic tradition but worry about the application of Catholic just-war teaching to modern international conflict; Armenian evangelicals may appreciate the space that Catholics preserve for the exercise of free will but continue to express reservations about the primacy of the papacy; evangelicals of all stripes (I can testify from personal experience) may well appreciate the University of Notre Dame for constructing the best example of advanced Christian learning in North America but worry (as, again, a testimony from personal experience) about the ease with which the Notre Dame football team defeats athletic representatives of Protestant civil religion from all around the country. The opening of Catholic-evangelical dialogue means, in short, that many discussions among Protestants are also under way.

The pluralism within Catholic and evangelical communities also poses genuine problems for the practice of evangelism. Most responsible

Catholics and evangelicals recognize that it is at best dubious, and at worst simply wrong, for Catholics and evangelicals to proselytize across the Catholic-Protestant border in situations where believers are coming close to the finest standards of either faith. Most also agree that nominal religious adherence—whether Catholic or evangelical—poses a different problem. Where Catholics and evangelicals will continue to differ among themselves (as well as, to some extent, with each other) is on the question of what counts as genuine faithfulness, as opposed to nominal practice. The difficulties in such discussions are greatest where manifestations of either faith (as evangelicalism in some areas of the American South or Catholicism in many areas of Latin America) have enjoyed a cultural hegemony, for that is the very circumstance that historically called forth efforts to reform the Church. To recognize pluralism within evangelicalism and Catholicism does not by itself solve delicate questions of proselytization, but it is a precondition for discerning understanding of local conditions.

The current situation in the United States poses unusual opportunities as well as unusual perils for evangelical-Catholic discussion. Again, to look at matters from the angle of an evangelical Protestant, we can describe a curious situation. The formalism, the anthropocentric worship, the power-mongering, and the egotism—which Protestants saw so clearly in Roman Catholicism for so many centuries—now flourish on every hand within Protestant evangelicalism.[65] At the same time, an exaltation of divine grace, a concern for disciplined holiness, an expression of service to the poor in the name of Jesus, and an ability to apply the depths of Scripture to the complicated ethical questions of modern existence—which Protestantism came into existence in order to recover—now exist manifestly in one form or another throughout Roman Catholicism. Evangelicals who cherish the Reformation heritage face especially poignant issues in the modern climate. They are the ones who hold most tenaciously to the reformers' teachings about the radical sinfulness and irremediable finitude of human existence. But with fresh eyes to see, they can now observe these human traits as readily in the churches descended from the Reformation (and perhaps even in themselves) as in Catholicism. They are also able to see traits approved by historic Protestantism in the most luminous expressions of modern Catholicism, as for example the ethical wisdom of Pope John Paul II, the thought-provoking writings of G. K. Chesterton, J. R. R. Tolkien, Evelyn Waugh, and Malcolm Muggeridge; or the "works" of a different kind from Mother Teresa, Henri Nouwen, and the L'Arche community. However such observations might disconcert evangelical descendants of the Reformation, they can take heart from the Reformers' teachings about the incredible reach of divine grace and so perhaps turn toward Roman Catholics with as much charitable expectancy as fearful dread.

Contemporary pluralism may also enhance the ability to make discriminations. If relatively important theological differences still divide Catholics and evangelicals, it is also the case that the contemporary world needs to hear more about what Catholics and evangelicals share in common than about their legitimate disagreements. J. I. Packer has spotlighted this issue well by pointing to "the currently urgent task of upholding faith in the Trinity, the Incarnation, the inerrancy of Scripture, and the primacy of the evangelistic and pastoral imperative according to Scripture, against the secularist, relativist and antinomian onslaught to which these things are being subjected in our time both without and within the churches." As Packer and many others who have striven for perspective on the modern condition conclude, "the cobelligerence of Catholics and Protestants fighting together for the basics of the creed is nowadays more important [than discussion of individual doctrines], if only because until the cancerous spread of theological pluralism on both sides of the Reformation divide is stopped, any talk of our having achieved unity of faith will be so irrelevant to the real situation as to be both comic and pathetic."[66]

Finally, if this historic shift from all-out Catholic-evangelical antagonism to modest Catholic-evangelical engagement marks a genuine moment of grace in the long history of the Church, the way to exploit that grace will certainly not be simply to ignore the past, but will be to find a middle way of hope. In recent years, a number of significant voices have shown what that middle way of realistic, historically informed hope might look like. These voices usually come from those who know the past history very well but who think that the impasses of history are the result of human rather than divine purpose.

From the Catholic side, such a message was voiced by Pope John Paul II, when he spoke to the Lutherans in Rome at the observation of Martin Luther's five hundredth birthday.

So we see ourselves in the midst of all the evident separations that still exist in teaching and life deeply linked in the solidarity of all the Christians of Advent. . . . We believe, in the year of remembrance of the birthday of Martin Luther five centuries ago, that we see as if in a distance the dawning of the advent of a reconstruction of our unity and community. This unity is a fruit of the daily renewal, conversion and penitence of all Christians in the light of the eternal word of God. It is at the same time the best preparation for the coming of God in our world.

Let us follow the great figure of the time of Advent, let us follow the example of John the Baptist, the voice of the caller in the desert: "Make straight the way of the Lord" (John 1:23). Let us follow the invitation to reconciliation with God and among ourselves. Christ, the ruler of all, is not only above us but also in our midst as the Lord who was, who is and who will be in eternity.[67]

A similar voice of realistic hope came as the result of a significant series of modern discussions in Europe. The book in which those discussions were summarized was entitled, *The Condemnations of the Reformation Era: Do They Still Divide?* The answer was measured, but hopeful:

> Today it is possible to say the following: Far-reaching agreement in the interpretation of Holy Scripture, clearer insights about the historical contingency of traditional doctrinal formulations, and the new spirit of ecumenical dialogue, in awareness of the ties linking Christians of different denominational traditions through their faith in the one Lord, have all contributed essentially to the achievement of a large measure of mutual understanding. This understanding is not confined to the fundamental acknowledgment of the one Lord Jesus Christ. It applies also to central themes of Christian doctrine.[68]

The European Catholics and Protestants who published this book concluded that the condemnations of the Reformation were based on misconceptions, were aimed at extreme positions on the other side, and no longer apply to today's situations. While genuine differences remained, those differences did not appear as universal as once they seemed.

Of most relevance to American evangelicals are words written by George Carey when he was principal of Trinity Theological College in England. Since he wrote them, Carey has become the archbishop of Canterbury, and, in one of the unlikeliest surprises of recent history, he uses that ancient Anglican office to promote a program at once evangelical and catholic. Before going to Canterbury, Carey outlined his hope for the evangelical-Catholic future:

> How can Protestants with their faith anchored in the New Testament have unity with Catholics, whose official teachings include doctrines they cannot accept? The question is reciprocated from the Catholic side. How can the historical faith of the Church be reconciled with the somewhat reduced faith of the Protestants? . . . There is, I believe, a way through this dilemma. The Second Vatican Council, in fact, opened new possibilities through a statement in the Decree on Ecumenism. The decree suggested that closer agreement among Christians is possible if we think in terms of a hierarchy of truths. What the decree is getting at is this: unity is often barred by the attention given to our differences, but not all doctrines have the same importance for faith. Could we arrive at an understanding of the common core of the faith we share while allowing freedom with respect to other teachings less essential? This looks like a promising way forward. It is biblically true that not all the doctrines of the Christian faith have the same value for *saving faith* even if they are regarded as important in their own right.[69]

The voices of John Paul II, of the European Catholics and Protestants who are setting aside the anathemas of the sixteenth century, and of Archbishop Carey do not speak with American accents. Since they do not, for example, reflect the American way of intermingling religious and public life, they are not as alert as are Americans themselves to the historic role that political values have played in American interconfessional attitudes. In the end, the exhortations of outsiders require American confirmation. It remains for Americans, both evangelicals and Roman Catholics—and, even more, for divine grace—to determine whether they too can find together a middle way of historical realism and hope for the future.

# Notes

1    J. I. Packer, "Review of *The Born-Again Catholic*," *Eternity* (December. 1983): 92.
2    In the paragraphs below, I make use of historical material employed for different purposes in my essay, "The Eclipse of Old Hostilities *between* and

the Potential for New Strife *among* Catholics and Protestants since Vatican II," in *Uncivil Religion: Interreligious Hostility in America*, ed. Robert N. Bellah and Frederick E. Greenspahn (New York: Crossroad, 1987), 86–109.

3    In the literature on Catholic-Protestant hostility, one of the earliest books is still among the best, Ray Allen Billington, *The Protestant Crusade, 1800–1860* (New York: Macmillan, 1938). Other helpful discussions are found in John J. Kane, *Catholic-Protestant Conflicts in America* (Chicago: Regnery, 1955); David Brion Davis, "Some Themes of Countersubversion: An Analysis of Anti-Masonic, Anti-Catholic and Anti-Mormon Literature," *Mississippi Valley Historical Review* 47 (1960): 205–24; John Higham, *Strangers in the Land: Patterns of American Nativism, 1860–1925* (Westport, Conn.: Greenwood, 1980; orig. 1963); Richard Hofstadter, *The Paranoid Style in American Politics* (New York: Knopf, 1965); James H. Smylie, "Phases in Protestant Anti-Roman Catholic Relations in the United States: Monologue, Debate, and Dialogue," *Religion in Life* 34 (Spring 1965): 285–69; Jay P. Dolan, "Catholic Attitudes Toward Protestants," in *Uncivil Religion*, 72–85; and Barbara Welter, "From Maria Monk to Paul Blanshard: A Century of Protestant Anti-Catholicism," in *Uncivil Religion*, 43–71 (Welter's essay includes especially helpful bibliographical notes).

4    Quoted in James Morris, *The Preachers* (New York: St. Martins, 1973), 199.

5    Wilhelm Pauck, "The Roman Catholic Critique of Protestantism," originally published in *Theology Today* (1948), in Pauck's *The Heritage of the Reformation* (New York: Oxford, 1968), 231.

6    Quotation from "Controversies Aroused in U.S. by Taylor Mission to Vatican," *U.S. News and World Report*, 28 June 1946, 21.

7    John B. Sheerin, C.S.P., "American Catholics and Ecumenism," in *Contemporary Catholicism in the United States*, ed. Philip Gleason (Notre Dame, Ind: University of Notre Dame Press, 1969), 75.

8    Jaroslav Pelikan, *The Riddle of Roman Catholicism* (New York: Abingdon, 1959), 12, 176, 189, 219, 201.

9    Louis Bouyer, *The Spirit and Forms of Protestantism*, trans. A. V. Littledale (Westminster, Md: Newman, 1956), 223.

10   W. E. R. O'Gorman, *A Priest Speaks His Mind: Why He Returned to the Protestant Faith of His Fathers* (Glendale, Calif.: by the author, 1954); John Carrara, *Catholicism under the Searchlight of the Scriptures* (Grand Rapids: Zondervan, orig. 1943, 6th printing 1951); Charles Chiniquy, *Fifty Years in the Church of Rome* (Grand Rapids: Baker, printings in 1958, 1960, 1961 [orig. 1886]).

11   Loraine Boettner, *Roman Catholicism* (Philadelphia: Presbyterian and Reformed, 1962), 455, 459.

12   A. G. Dickens and John M. Tonkin, *The Reformation in Historical Thought* (Cambridge: Harvard University Press, 1985), 16, 84.

13   Quoted in Sister Mary Augustina (Ray), B.V.M., *American Opinion of Roman Catholicism in the Eighteenth Century* (New York: Columbia University Press, 1936), 128.

14  Billington, *The Protestant Crusade*, 445–82.

15  Charles Hodge, "The General Assembly," *Princeton Review* 17 (July 1845): 469–71. For a full statement, see Hodge, "Is the Church of Rome a Part of the Visible Church?" *Princeton Review* 18 (April 1846): 320–44.

16  James M. Gustafson, *Protestant and Roman Catholic Ethics: Prospects for Rapprochement* (Chicago: University of Chicago Press, 1978), 30.

17  George Whitefield, *Sermons on Important Subjects* (London: William Baynes, 1825), 56.

18  Aaron Burr, Sr., *A Discourse delivered at Newark, in New Jersey, January 1, 1755. Being a Day set apart for solemn Fasting and Prayer, on Account of the late Encroachments of the French, and their Designs against the British Colonies in America* (New York: Hugh Gaine, 1755), 16, 19.

19  John Lathrop, as quoted in Nathan O. Hatch, *The Sacred Cause of Liberty: Republican Thought and the Millennium in Revolutionary New England* (New Haven: Yale University Press, 1977), 75.

20  For two excellent discussions on the post-Revolutionary exaltation of liberty, see Robert H. Wiebe, *The Opening of American Society: From the Adoption of the Constitution to the Eve of Disunion* (New York: Knopf, 1984); and Gordon S. Wood, *The Radicalism of the American Revolution: How A Revolution Transformed a Monarchical Society into a Democratic One Unlike Any That Had Ever Existed* (New York: Knopf, 1992).

21  Sydney E. Ahlstrom, *A Religious History of the American People* (New Haven: Yale University Press, 1972), 561.

22  Quoted in Billington, *The Protestant Crusade*, 425.

23  See especially Richard J. Carwardine, *Evangelicals and Politics in Antebellum America* (New Haven: Yale University Press, 1993), 80–84, 199–203.

24  Josiah Strong, *Our Country: Its Possible Future and Its Present Crisis* (New York: American Home Missionary Society, 1885).

25  Quoted in John O. Geiger, "The Edgerton Bible Case: Humphrey Desmond's Political Education of Wisconsin Catholics," *Journal of Church and State* 20 (Winter 1978): 25. For Catholic efforts to promote Bible-reading in the nineteenth century that Protestants almost never noticed, see Gerald P. Fogarty, S.J., "The Quest for a Catholic Vernacular Bible in America," in *The Bible in America*, ed. Nathan O. Hatch and Mark A. Noll (New York: Oxford, 1982), 164–69.

26  A good recent study of these Catholic converts is Jenny Franchot, *Roads to Rome: The Antebellum Protestant Encounter with Catholicism* (Berkeley: University of California Press, 1994).

27  J. M. Foster, "Rome: The Antagonist of the Nation," in *The Fundamentals: A Testimony to the Truth*, 4 vols. (Grand Rapids: Baker, 1972; orig. 1910-15), 3:301, 313–14.

28  In the 1960 election, anti-Protestant voting against Kennedy was at least partially compensated for by the extra measure of support Kennedy won from Catholics. See Lyman A. Kellstedt and Mark A. Noll, "Religion, Voting for

President, and Party Identification, 1948–1984," in *Religion and American Politics*, ed. Mark A. Noll (New York: Oxford University Press, 1990), 361–62, 374–75.

29  Boettner, *Roman Catholicism*, 7, 459.

30  The historical background is well illustrated in John Tracy Ellis, ed., *Documents of American Catholic History*, 2nd ed. (Milwaukee: Bruce, 1962); and well told in James Hennesey, S. J., *American Catholics: A History of the Roman Catholic Community in the United States* (New York: Oxford, 1981); and Jay P. Dolan, *The American Catholic Experience* (Garden City, N.Y.: Doubleday, 1985).

31  Theodore C. Sorensen, *Kennedy* (New York: Harper & Row, 1965), 188–95, 357–65. Marshall Frady, *Billy Graham: A Parable of American Righteousness* (Boston: Little, Brown, 1979), 446.

32  Sheerin, "American Catholics and Ecumenism," 75–78. Some of the texts from these discussions from the 1970s and early 1980s are collected in Harding Meyer and Lukas Vischer, eds., *Growth in Agreement: Reports and Agreed Statements of Ecumenical Conversations on a World Level* (New York: Paulist, 1984).

33  Completed "Dialogues," as published by Augsburg Press in Minneapolis, include *The Status of the Nicene Creed as Dogma of the Church* (1965), *One Baptism for the Remission of Sins* (1966), *The Eucharist as Sacrifice* (1967), *Eucharist and Ministry* (1970), *Papal Primacy and the Universal Church* (1974), *Teaching Authority and Infallibility in the Church* (1980), and *The One Mediator, the Saints, and Mary* (1992). The report on justification is discussed below at note 37.

34  "Faith and Order U.S.A.," pamphlet from The National Council of the Churches of Christ in the U.S.A. (n.d.).

35  See especially John Courtney Murray, *We Hold These Truths: Catholic Reflections on the American Proposition* (New York: Sheed and Ward, 1960).

36  A good treatment of the role of Catholicism in the fall of communism in Poland and Czechoslovakia is George Weigel, *The Final Revolution: The Resistance Church and the Collapse of Communism* (New York: Oxford University Press, 1992).

37  "U.S. Lutheran-Roman Catholic Dialogue: Justification by Faith," *Origins: NC Documentary Service*, 6 October 1983: 277–304 (with quotations, 297–98).

38  McIntyre quoted in Morris, *The Preachers*, 200.

39  For a brief survey of the results that the charismatic movement has had on Catholic-evangelical connections, see Donald Bloesch, *The Future of Evangelical Christianity: A Call for Unity Amid Diversity* (New York: Doubleday, 1983), 38–42.

40  For background, see Hatch and Noll, eds., *The Bible in America*, 4, 8, 16n. 36, 17n. 43, and 165–66.

41  Ernest W. Saunders, *Searching the Scriptures: A History of the Society of Biblical Literature, 1880–1980* (Chico, Calif.: Scholars Press, 1982), 84.

42  As reported in *The Presbyterian Journal*, 6 July 1983, 3.

43  William Martin, *A Prophet with Honor: The Billy Graham Story* (New York: William Morrow, 1991), 278–80, 488–91; Frady, *Billy Graham*, 326, 441–46; John Pollock, *Billy Graham: The Authorized Biography* (New York: McGraw-Hill, 1966), 218–20; Pollock, *Billy Graham: Evangelist to the World* (San Francisco: Harper & Row, 1979), 129–30, 290–91, 307–10; and Richard V. Pierard, "From Evangelical Exclusivism to Ecumenical Openness: Billy Graham and Sociopolitical Issues," *Journal of Ecumenical Studies* 20 (1983): 428.

44  Survey conducted by Cy Hulse, "Luther's Changing Image Among Catholics," prepared for a course at Trinity Evangelical Divinity School, ca. 1978. This fine paper is also the source for the quotations from *The Priest* below.

45  "Should We Speak or Hold Our Tongue?" *The Priest* 12 (February 1956): 134.

46  Perplexus (pseud.), "The Charm of Melody," *The Priest* 21 (July 1965): 585.

47  For a review of this discussion, see Avery Dulles, S.J., "The Catholicity of the Augsburg Confession," *Journal of Religion* 63 (October 1983): 337–54.

48  *New York Times*, 12 December 1983, 1, 4.

49  James Atkinson, *Martin Luther: Prophet to the Catholic Church* (Grand Rapids: Eerdmans, 1983); Mark Edwards and George H. Tavard, *Luther: A Reformer for the Churches* (Ramsay, N.J.: Paulist, 1983).

50  Pelikan, *Riddle of Roman Catholicism*, 219. Kenneth L. Woodward, "Luther in Excelsis," *Notre Dame Magazine*, October 1983, 11–15.

51  For a discussion of this civil anti-catholicism, see Andrew M. Greeley, *An Ugly Little Secret: Anti-Catholicism in North America* (Kansas City: Sheed Andrews & McNeel, 1977).

52  Gary Metz, "Jack Chick's Anti-Catholic *Alberto* Comic Book Is Exposed as a Fraud," *Christianity Today*, 13 March 1981, 50–52. "Bookseller's Group May Expel Chick," *Christianity Today*, 23 October 1981, 62.

53  Calvin quoted in Peter Matheson, *Cardinal Contarini at Regensburg* (New York: Oxford University Press, 1972), 109.

54  John Calvin, for example, quoted (almost always favorably) from eleven different works by Bernard of Clairvaux in his *Institutes*. In the American edition of Martin Luther's works there is generally positive use of twenty works by Bernard. John T. McNeill, ed., *Calvin: Institutes of the Christian Religion*, 2 vols. (Philadelphia: Westminster, 1960), 11:1601; Joel W. Lundeen, ed., *Luther's Works, Vol. 55: Index* (Philadelphia: Fortress, 1986), 27–28.

55  John Barker, *Strange Contrarieties: Pascal in England during the Age of Reason* (Montreal: McGill-Queen's University Press, 1975), 17 (Gale), 186 (Whitefield), 191 (John Newton), 181–95 (the Wesleys). On Jonathan Edwards' reading of Pascal, see Norman Fiering, *Jonathan Edwards's Moral Thought and Its British Context* (Chapel Hill: University of North Carolina Press, 1981), 176.

56  Barker, *Strange Contrarieties*, 185.

57  Ibid., 191.

58  Thomas C. Upham, *Life and Religious Opinions and Experience of Madame de la Mothe Guyon: Together with Some Account of the Personal History and Religious*

*Opinions of Fenelon, Archbishop of Cambray* (New York: Harper & Brothers, 1846), vi. I am indebted to Patricia Ward for pointing out the consistent Protestant use of Madame Guyon.

59 Quoted in Sheridan Gilley, *Newman and His Age* (Westminster, Md.: Christian Classics, 1990), 372.

60 David W. Bebbington, *Evangelicalism in Modern Britain: A History from the 1730s to the 1980s* (London: Unwin Hyman, 1989), 2–19. For recent accounting of evangelical diversity, see Mark A. Noll, David W. Bebbington, and George A. Rawlyk, eds., *Evangelicalism: Comparative Studies of Popular Protestantism in North America, the British Isles, and Beyond, 1700–1990* (New York: Oxford University Press, 1994).

61 From "Akron Survey of Religion and Politics in America," carried out with a grant from the Pew Charitable Trusts in 1992; the scholars who conducted this survey were John Green, University of Akron; James Guth, Furman University; Lyman Kellstedt, Wheaton College; Corwin Smidt, Calvin College.

62 George Rawlyk, forthcoming publications on an Angus Reid survey; for preliminary results, see "God Is Alive: Canada Is a Nation of Believers," special report in *Maclean's,* 12 April 1993, 32–50.

63 Richard P. McBrien, "Roman Catholicism: *E Pluribus Unum*," in *Religion and America: Spirituality in a Secular Age*, ed. Mary Douglas and Steven M. Tipton (Boston: Beacon, 1983), 181.

64 Andrew M. Greeley, *The American Catholic: A Social Portrait* (New York: Basic Books, 1977), 252.

65 See David F. Wells, *No Place for Truth: or, Whatever Happened to Evangelical Theology* (Grand Rapids: Eerdmans, 1993); and Michael Scott Horton, *Made in America: The Shaping of Modern American Evangelicalism* (Grand Rapids: Baker, 1991).

66 J. I. Packer, foreword to George Carey, *A Tale of Two Churches: Can Protestants and Catholics Get Together?* (Downers Grove, Ill.: InterVarsity Press, 1985), ii.

67 "Text of John Paul's Sermon at a Lutheran Church," *New York Times,* 12 December 1983, 4.

68 Karl Lehmann and Wolfhart Pannenberg, *The Condemnations of the Reformation Era: Do They Still Divide?*, trans. Margaret Kohl (Minneapolis: Fortress, 1990), 27.

69 Carey, *A Tale of Two Churches*, 160, with Carey's own list of six "central points" that he regards as essential to Christian communion on 161–62.

# 4

# The Unity for Which We Hope

Avery Dulles, S.J.

*As people who are divided,
we can also be one.*

*Joseph Ratzinger*

T HE PRESENT search for greater cooperation between evangelicals and Catholics recalls the vigorous discussion about models of Christian union and unity that took place in ecumenical circles in the 1970s. Key turning points of this discussion were the Louvain meeting of the Faith and Order Commission in 1971, the Salamanca Consultation convened by Faith and Order in September 1973, and the Fifth Assembly of the World Council of Churches at Nairobi in 1975. Since that time many attempts have been made to categorize the various models or strategies. For example, the Lutheran / Roman Catholic Joint Commission in 1985 devoted thirteen pages of its document *Facing Unity* to a survey of "Concepts of Unity and Models of Union."[1] Drawing on these sources and the work of several recent authors,[2] I suggest the following six models as patterns for possible interchurch cooperation and unity.

## Models of Union

1. *Organic Union.* This goal, commonly understood as one form of corporate union, has been dominant in the Faith and Order movement and in the World Council of Churches almost from the beginning. At New Delhi in 1961, the Third Assembly of the World Council of Churches gave classic formulation to the vision that had by then become "the inspiration of our ecumenical endeavor":

> *We believe that the unity which is both God's will*
> *and his gift to the church*
> *is being made visible*
> *as all in each place*
> *who are baptized in Jesus Christ and confess him*
> *as Lord and Savior*
> *are brought by the Holy Spirit*
> *into one fully committed fellowship,*
> *holding the one apostolic faith,*
> *preaching the one gospel,*
> *breaking the one bread,*
> *joining in common prayer*
> *and having a corporate life reaching out*
> *in witness and service to all*
> *and who at the same time are united with the whole*
> *Christian fellowship in all places and all ages*
> *in such wise that ministry and members are accepted by all,*
> *and that all can act and speak together as occasion requires*
> *for the tasks to which God calls his people.*[3]

At its Nairobi Assembly, the World Council of Churches adopted a new constitution proclaiming as the first purpose of the council "to call the churches to the goal of visible unity in one faith and in one eucharistic fellowship expressed in worship and in common life in Christ, and to advance towards that unity in order that the world believe."[4] This formulation may be interpreted as a condensation of the New Delhi statement on unity.

Commentators on this first model frequently declare that organic union is a "costly act" involving the death and rebirth of existing confessional churches. The united Church, it would seem, will be a new entity rising from the ashes of its predecessors.[5]

2. *Conciliar Fellowship.* Fears were expressed in many quarters that the model of organic union seemed too monolithic and that the imagery of death and resurrection overlooked the promise of Christ that the Church built on the apostles would endure to the end of time (Matt. 16:18; 28:20). Partly to meet these criticisms, the Salamanca Consultation of 1973 proposed that the united Church should be understood as a differentiated conciliar fellowship of preexistent churches. "The one Church," it declared, "is to be envisioned as a conciliar fellowship of local churches which are themselves truly united." The relationships among sister churches are to be "expressed in conciliar gatherings whenever required for the fulfillment of their common calling." These conciliar gatherings are to be representative of the member churches.[6]

The Nairobi Assembly, in its report "What Unity Requires," took pains to show that "conciliar fellowship" was not an alternative to "organic unity" but only a further elaboration of it. There was no thought of reconceiving the goal of ecumenism as a glorified World Council of Churches. Assemblies such as those of the World Council, said the report, are "preconciliar." They are not councils in the full sense but imperfect anticipations of the full conciliar fellowship for which we hope.[7]

The goal of conciliar fellowship adds to that of organic union the suggestion that unity is to be achieved gradually from below, as local churches enter into regional or national unions, which in turn establish communion with other united churches. The "fully united Church," which expresses its union through councils, is not described as having any permanent governing body with authority over the member churches.

The Salamanca proposal was in part inspired by the example of the regional "united churches" that were being formed in various parts of the world, beginning with the Church of South India, which in 1947 brought together Anglican, Methodist, Reformed, and Congregational streams. This pattern was followed in other countries and continents. In the United States the most ambitious attempt was the Consultation on Church Union, launched by Eugene Carson Blake in 1962. Originally intended as a merger including Presbyterians, Episcopalians, and others, the proposal was gradually trimmed back until in 1988 it called only for "churches in covenant communion"—an instance of "unity in diversity" according to the fifth model we shall consider.

Communions that have a keen sense of confessional identity on the world level did not readily accept the idea of being absorbed into regional or national "united churches" having no particular denominational stamp. The different direction pursued by these "world confessional families" or "world communions," many of which were engaged in bilateral conversations with one another, is reflected in the following two models.

3. *Communion of Types.* This model was suggested by the coexistence within the Catholic Church of the Latin church and a variety of Eastern churches, such as the Melkite, Maronite, Ukrainian, and others. These churches, some of which have been called "uniate" because of their entry into union with Rome after a period of separation, have their own liturgical rites and discipline, stemming from the patristic heritage they have received in an Eastern form.

Some have proposed "uniatism" as an ecumenical strategy, but Emmanuel Lanne, in several important articles, pointed out that uniatism tended to introduce an unfortunate "dissociation between liturgical rite and discipline on the one hand, and theological, doctrinal, confessional typology on the other."[8] As an alternative he advocated the inclusion of several "typologies" within the same ecclesial allegiance. Building on this proposal, Cardinal Jan Willebrands, President of the Secretariat for Promoting the Unity of Christians, proposed the idea of distinct *typoi* or "types," and offered the following description: "Where there is a long coherent tradition, commanding men's love and loyalty, creating and sustaining a harmonious and organic whole of complementary elements, each of which supports and strengthens the other, you have the reality of a *typos.*"[9] Among the elements constitutive of a *typos,* Willebrands mentioned a characteristic theological approach, liturgical expression, spiritual and devotional tradition, and canonical discipline.

This model has found favorable reception in some churches with a high ecclesiology, including the Anglican and Lutheran, although the Orthodox have been wary, perhaps because of old controversies about uniatism. John Macquarrie, writing as an Anglican, holds that the "uniate model" (by which he seems to mean a communion of *typoi*) might serve as the next stage of ecumenism. On the ground that "the main traditions of the Christian church—Roman, Orthodox, Anglican, Lutheran, Reformed, Methodist, and others—have an integrity and distinctiveness that ought not to be sacrificed," Macquarrie regards this model as preferable to "organic union," as usually presented.[10] He also repudiates an ecumenism based on the creation of national union churches that would break up the existing international Christian communions.[11]

4. *Solidarity in Action.* This model has a long pedigree, going back at least to the kind of interchurch cooperation promoted by the Swedish Archbishop Nathan Söderblom, the guiding genius behind the Universal Christian Conference on Life and Work held at Stockholm in 1925. After falling out of favor during the dominance of neoorthodoxy, this tendency resurfaced with added vigor in the 1960s under the rubric of "secular ecumenism." Theologians such as Robert McAfee Brown and Lewis S. Mudge were among its prominent champions.[12] In the 1970s and 1980s it was taken up by liberation theologians such as Jon Sobrino, who maintains that the churches cannot find true unity except by practicing solidarity with the poor.[13]

Proponents of this model maintain that the principal obstacles to union among Christians are not doctrinal but socioeconomic, not theoretical but practical. The fundamental division, some of them assert, is between the rich and the poor, between the oppressors and the oppressed. By working for a just and peaceful world order Christians can find one another in unity. According to Mudge the presence of Christ is found at the point where Christians become creatively involved in the world's struggles. It is here, most of all, that they experience solidarity with one another.[14] Through "practical ecumenism," it is hoped, Christians may find the key that enables them to resolve previously intractable doctrinal differences.

5. *Reconciled Diversity.* This model was proposed in 1974 by the World Confessional Families as their response to the model of conciliar fellowship elaborated at Salamanca the previous year. The Lutheran World Federation, meeting at Dar es Salaam in 1977, gave a very positive endorsement to this model. It differs from the models of organic union and conciliar fellowship insofar as, like the *typos* model, it favors the retention of the distinct heritage of the different confessional bodies as a valuable enhancement of the life of the universal Church. While this model can lead to friendly association and in some cases to "pulpit and altar fellowship," it does not seem to provide any mechanism whereby the churches can decide and act together. To that extent it stops short of the goal of full Christian unity.[15]

Oscar Cullmann in his important little book, *Unity through Diversity,* develops his own version of this model, pleading for a "harmonious separation" of churches.[16] He holds that in a union of churches each should preserve its own structure and heritage, but he insists that the uniting churches must agree on what he calls "the primary truth of the gospel."[17] On the ground that structured ministries are divinely given charisms, necessary for the functioning of an ecclesial body, he maintains that "the planned community of churches, though it is itself not a church, should have some sort of superstructure, even if fairly loose, a superstructure which respects the churches which it unites: here too, *unity in diversity*."[18] Further on in his book he suggests that a conciliar form of government would be the most practical. While Catholics would continue to regard the papacy as a divinely instituted "Petrine" ministry, other member churches would not so regard it.[19]

6. *Spiritual Ecumenism.* Many Protestants think of the Church, the body of Christ, less as an organized society than as an invisible communion of the faithful in Christ, their common Lord. Every institutional realization of the Church is more or less deficient. For that reason incorporation in a preferred church or denomination does not itself guarantee that one is a true believer, nor does membership in a less acceptable denomination debar one from faith and salvation. The Spirit can raise up true Christians wherever the Scriptures are read and wherever prayer in the name of Jesus is practiced. The Church, thus conceived, is not totally invisible. It emerges into visibility when believers confess and practice their faith in Christ and the gospel in whatever church they happen to belong to. This less institutional conception of the Church is sometimes supported by reference to the saying of Jesus, "Where two or three are gathered in my name, there am I in the midst of them" (Matt. 18:20 RSV).

Christian unity on this theory is achieved to the extent that believers, as individuals or in groups, hear and obey the Word of God. Church union, therefore, is not achieved primarily through interchurch negotiations but through the continual conversion of individuals and congregations to Christ, who is the source of the only kind of unity worth having. Karl Barth, who may be taken as a proponent of this model, writes:

In the realization of faith in the one Church in the face of its dividedness, the decisive step must be that the separated churches should honestly and earnestly try to hear, and perhaps hear, the voice of the Lord as it is disclosed through them and for them, and then try to hear, and perhaps actually hear, the voice of the others. Where a church does this, in its own place, and without leaving that place, it is on the way to the one Church.[20]

This model holds little promise of institutional or organic union, but it does provide for significant rapprochement between groups as widely separated as Catholics and evangelicals.

## Catholic and Evangelical Options

Catholics and evangelicals have alike been reserved or even adverse to the first two models, organic union and conciliar fellowship, as these models are commonly understood in ecumenical circles. Partly for that reason, they tend to avoid membership in organizations such as the World Council of Churches and involvement in schemes such as the Consultation on Church Union, especially in its original, more ambitious form. They are convinced that the word of God, as they have heard it, must be forthrightly proclaimed and is too precious to be compromised by interchurch negotiations and mergers. However much they may mutually disagree about certain other points of doctrine, evangelicals and Catholics agree in placing supreme value on the gospel truth and in their resolve to bear witness to the gospel as they apprehend it in faith.

In view of the wide discrepancies among Christian churches, the prospect of a broadly inclusive corporate union is, under present circumstances, unrealistic and uninviting. A single united Church, though it might boast of millions of members, Protestant, Catholic, and Orthodox, would be bland and unexciting. Constrained to satisfy an enormous and widely diverse constituency, this mass-church would be incapable of speaking out prophetically on contentious issues. Although the advocates of church union surely intend no such thing, their efforts, if successful, could hardly fail to produce such colorless amalgams.

The third model, communion of types, appeals to Catholics because of the highly traditional and sacramental character of their ecclesiastical polity. This model seems to be most promising for the relationships among high church communions, such as the Orthodox, the Anglican, and some varieties of Lutheranism, that preserve their roots in the patristic age. It is more difficult to conceive of evangelical or liberal Protestant communities as sister churches within a single ecclesial allegiance. Nonsacramental churches have been predictably cool toward this model.

The fourth model, solidarity in action, has real though limited appeal to Catholics and evangelicals. Vatican II exhorted all Christians to work together to relieve human afflictions and pointed to the value of such cooperation for expressing the bond that already unites Christians and for setting the features of Christ the Servant in clearer relief (*Unitatis Redintegratio*: Decree on Ecumenism, 12). Evangelicals and Catholics in the United States have experienced the need for certain common programs of social action, such as those aimed against pornography, abortion, and euthanasia. Work for peace and justice may be effectively pursued in solidarity with Christians and non-Christians alike, but the coalitions often tend to reflect political orientations more than religious principles. In any case, sociopolitical engagement cannot dispense the parties from faithful adherence to the revealed word of God, which is "the power of God for salvation to every one who has faith" (Rom. 1:17 RSV). Social action cannot by itself effect ecclesial reconciliation. Doctrinal divergences, in fact, often impose limitations on the possibilities of practical cooperation.

The fifth model, reconciled diversity, is vague enough to accommodate a diversity of reactions. If it is to mean real ecclesial unity, rather than mere amicability, it needs to be clearly distinguished from a simple legitimation of the existing separations or a mutual endorsement of the confessions of faith of the different denominations.

Yves Congar, commenting on this model from a Catholic perspective, points out that the confessional formulas inherited from the sixteenth century give very imperfect expression to the reality of the Church, which contains within itself a fullness that cannot be constructed by patching together the disparate confessions.[21] Reconciliation, he insists, must involve change and renewal within the partner churches. Furthermore, the resulting union must include a commonly recognized ministry of unity.[22] It is hard to see how Catholics could consider themselves to be fully reconciled with churches that did not acknowledge the papacy as the bearer of a divinely instituted "Petrine ministry" within the universal Church. In view of the continuing disputes about ministerial orders and sacraments, many doctrinal obstacles still stand in the way of "pulpit and altar fellowship" between Catholics and Protestants. Some of these obstacles, but not all, could be removed if the parties were to agree that the condemnations of the sixteenth century no longer apply to the churches as they exist today.[23]

It will be for evangelicals themselves to say whether, and under what conditions, they regard the model of reconciled diversity as helpful for Catholic-evangelical relations. Many of them, I suspect, would be opposed to any kind of structural union with Roman Catholics, even the loose "federal" type of union advocated by Cullmann.

Evangelicals, if I am not mistaken, will be inclined to hold, with the sixth model, that the most promising ecumenical strategy is to build up living faith in Christ as Savior among Christians of whatever denomination. Such faith, they might say, can become tangible and unitive when expressed in basic Christian confessions with a strong biblical grounding. As this occurs, true believers can joyfully recognize one another across denominational lines.

If such is indeed the proposal coming from evangelicals, it will be for Catholics to respond to it. Some evangelical literature gives the impression that Catholics, regarding membership in their own Catholic Church and participation in its sacraments as necessary and sufficient for salvation, would deny the possibility of any genuine fellowship between believing Catholics and evangelicals. But such an impression would not take adequate account of the teaching of Vatican II.

The recent council taught that all the essential features of the Church of Christ "subsist" in the Catholic Church (*Lumen Gentium*: Dogmatic Constitution on the Church, 8; *Unitatis Redintegratio*, 4) and that full communion requires acceptance of the "whole structure" of the Church, including "all the means of grace that have been established within it" (*Lumen Gentium*, 14). In this connection the council reasserted the traditional fourfold bond of profession of faith, sacraments, ecclesiastical government, and communion. But Vatican II declared also that external membership is not sufficient for salvation. To be saved it is necessary to have living faith in Christ, which is a gift of the Holy Spirit (*Lumen Gentium*, 14). The "Constitution on the Church" can therefore quote Augustine as saying: "It is certainly clear that when we speak of 'within' and 'without' with regard to the Church, our consideration should be directed to what is in the heart, not to what is in the body."[24]

Vatican II, moreover, recognized that the Catholic Church, although it will never lose the essential marks of the Church of Christ, is in perpetual need of purification and renewal (*Lumen Gentium*, 8; *Unitatis Redintegratio*, 4), and even, in some respects, of "reformation" (*Unitatis Redintegratio*, 6). The increase of fidelity to the Church's own calling is of supreme ecumenical importance. The soul of the ecumenical movement consists not in theological theories or diplomatic negotiations but in a change of heart and holiness of life. "All the faithful should remember that the more effort they make to live holier lives according to the gospel, the better will they further Christian unity and put it into practice. For the closer their union with the Father, the Word, and the Spirit, the more deeply and easily will they be able to grow in mutual love" (*Unitatis Redintegratio*, 7).

Although communion between Catholics and other Christians is still far from perfect and complete, Vatican II recognized that Catholics already enjoy a genuine spiritual community with baptized believers of other confessional allegiances. "Those who have been justified by faith through baptism are incorporated in Christ, and have a right to be called Christians, and so are deservedly recognized as brothers and sisters in the Lord by the children of the Catholic Church" (*Unitatis Redintegratio*, 3). To enter into a saving relationship with God in Christ is the principal and all-embracing goal of the Christian life. In relation to that interior and spiritual union, the doctrinal, ministerial, and sacramental structures of the Church are important but subsidiary. These institutional elements promote, safeguard, and express the inner spiritual union.

Catholics, therefore, do not at all object to the view that true solidarity exists among all who sincerely believe in the Lord Jesus, place their hope in him, and lovingly commit their lives to his service. Indeed, this is exactly what the Catholic Church teaches. But Catholics have the further conviction that the divine Founder has equipped the Church with certain visible structures that are ordinarily necessary to preserve the faithful in the truth and unity that God intends for them. Evangelicals and Catholics have different views about whether, and to what extent, the Church and its structures are divinely ordained. They must therefore engage in dialogue about the matter.

# Biblical Perspectives

As already seen, evangelicals and Catholics have a common ground insofar as both groups accept the reality of a spiritual unity based on faith, hope, and charity. They also recognize the canonical Scriptures as a peremptory norm, one that may under no circumstances be contradicted. Holy Scripture therefore provides a common resource for giving specific content to the prayer of Christ for unity. It helps us to know what kind of unity prevailed among the early Christians and to identify the signs by which that unity was expressed and the means by which it was maintained.

As any reader of the New Testament can easily verify, Christianity in the lifetime of the apostles was in some sort a universal religion, embracing in a single fellowship adherents of every race, nation, and linguistic group. The risen Jesus is depicted in the Gospels as instructing his disciples to go forth and preach the good news to all nations, baptizing them in the name of the three divine persons (Matt. 28:19; compare Mark 16:15; Luke 24:47). The Book of Acts describes the Holy Spirit as descending on a diverse multitude consisting of Parthians, Medes, Elamites, Egyptians, Libyans, Romans, Cretans, and Arabians, among others, all of whom hear Peter speaking in their own native tongues—a powerful symbol of the worldwide mission and unitive power of the Christian religion (Acts 2:52–13). The Pauline epistles repeatedly assert that there is in Christ neither Jew nor Greek, for all alike are spiritual heirs of Abraham according to the promise (Gal. 3:28–29). The Letter to the Ephesians eloquently describes how Christ has broken down the wall of enmity between Jew and Gentile, so that he might reconcile both parties to God in one body (Eph. 2:14–16). In the Book of Revelation those saved in Christ are depicted as an immense multitude from every nation, race, people, and tongue (Rev. 7:9).

Christians from the beginning were keenly conscious that they belonged to a community that was not bounded by any political or geographical frontiers. In New Testament times apostles, prophets, and missionaries, such as Peter and Paul, Barnabas and Mark, Titus and Timothy, moved freely from one community to another and were everywhere received as brothers in the faith. Paul writes to the church in Rome, a community he has never visited, in full confidence that its members accept the same gospel as his own. Christians all over the world constitute a single people, a single society, a single communion, in which they are made, in some mysterious way, members of one and the same body.

A difficulty against the universality of the Church can be raised on the basis of the Greek word *ekklēsia* (church) as used in the New Testament. Paul, especially in his early letters, probably the first parts of the New Testament to have been written, often uses the term to mean a local congregation. He sometimes speaks of "churches" in the plural (for example, Gal. 1:2). In his salutations he often addresses a particular church such as that of Thessalonica and Corinth (1 Thess.1:1; 2 Thess. 1:1; 1 Cor. 1:2; 2 Cor. 1:1). Not infrequently, he uses the term *ekklēsia* to mean a "house church" (for example, Rom. 16:5, 14, 15; 1 Cor. 16:19; Col. 4:15; and Philem. 2). Although Paul is conscious that all Christians are "one body," he never uses the term "one church." Thus an argument can be made that the Church is primarily the local congregation and only secondarily the totality of such congregations.

In my opinion this objection is unconvincing. Study of the term *ekklēsia* in the New Testament can yield various conclusions. The term is frequently used, even by Paul, in the singular to designate what we call the universal Church. This is true not only in the Captivity Letters and the Pastorals, which are not incontestably written by Paul himself, but also in some of the earlier letters that are universally admitted to be authentic (for example, 1 Cor. 15:9, Gal. 1:13, and Phil.3:6). In many instances one may understand *ekklēsia* to mean the universal community as concretely realized in a given locality—for instance, the Church of God that is at Corinth (1 Cor.1:2; 2 Cor.1:1). In the letters to the Colossians and the Ephesians *ekklēsia* is predominantly used in a strictly theological sense to signify the whole body of Christ, where the mystery of grace and salvation is at work in the world. This is at the opposite extreme from the empirical sense in which the term means a house gathering or a town congregation.

Outside the Pauline letters the term *ekklēsia* is comparatively rare. The word appears twice in the Gospels, both times in Matthew. In Matthew 16:18 it clearly refers to the universal Church, but in Matthew 18:17 it means, to all appearances, a local community. In the letters of John and James and in the Book of Revelation the term appears several times, in each case with the meaning, apparently, of local church.

Although it can be plausibly contended that *ekklēsia* as used in the

New Testament signifies primarily the local community and only secondarily the universal, the opposite conclusion is also defensible. The examination of this one word can hardly be decisive. In the Bible the term *ekklēsia* is not a distinctively theological term, and it cannot always be translated "church." The term, in a secular context, means simply a gathering or assembly, and it is used three times in Acts (19:32, 39, 41), with no religious overtones, to designate a town meeting. The New Testament authors had no one term that clearly referred to what we mean by Church. In its religious sense *ekklēsia* may sometimes be translated "church," but it is often equally well or better translated by terms such as "assembly" or "congregation." One must therefore be cautious in drawing theological conclusions from the fact that Paul speaks of "house churches." The Greek term might just as well be rendered into English as "house meetings" or "gatherings."

The ecclesiology of the New Testament has to be teased out of a great variety of terms, each of which is sometimes used to designate what we call the Church. One such term is *laos theou* (people of God; 1 Pet. 2:10); another is *synagōgē* (assembly; James 2:2); a third is *koinōnia* (fellowship; Acts 2:42). In addition, we have a whole panoply of metaphors such as the new Israel, the body of Christ, Bride, and Temple. Although the term *ekklēsia* can surely be used of the local church or congregation, these other terms, in their ecclesiological application, are used only in the singular, designating the universal Church. To the New Testament authors it was evident that there could be only one body or bride of Christ, one temple of the Holy Spirit, one new Israel. Christians were conscious of belonging to a single, all-embracing fellowship or society.

Notwithstanding the nature of the Church as a universal (or "catholic") entity, the fact remains that it existed sociologically in the form of a multiplicity of congregations. These local congregations were inevitably stamped with a certain particularity corresponding to the language, culture, customs, and native characteristics of the members. Christians were therefore faced with the problem of how to realize the unity of the universal Church in spite of the diversity of the congregations, with their divisive tendencies.

It is fair to say, I suppose, that the principal bonds of unity were the spiritual ties of a single faith, a common hope, and a universal charity. But it could not be taken for granted that all who professed the Christian name did in fact share the same faith and the same life of grace, or that their beliefs and way of life would continue to be cohesive. For this reason Christians, assisted by the Holy Spirit, sought to establish structures that would promote, express, and assure their interior, or spiritual, solidarity. Jesus himself had provided the fundamental structures.

One safeguard of unity was the body of teaching common to all local congregations. From the New Testament it is evident that there were certain creedal and confessional formulas, such as "Jesus is the Christ," "Jesus is Lord," and "Christ is risen," that were badges of Christian identity. They were considered as binding on all Church members. One New Testament text declares that anyone who does not confess the coming of Jesus Christ in the flesh is to be shunned (2 John 7–10).

Besides these basic declarations of faith, there were more extended oral traditions, such as those concerning the Last Supper and the Resurrection that we find in Paul's First Letter to the Corinthians, chapters 11 and 15. Paul insists that he is faithfully transmitting the common doctrine of all the apostles (11:23; 15:3, 11). The words and deeds of Jesus seem to have been handed down as an oral gospel transmitted by "ministers of the word," such as those whom Luke claims to have consulted in composing his Gospel (Luke 1:2).

In addition to this body of oral materials, there was a large and growing body of written literature. All Christians accepted the Jewish Scriptures, often read in the Greek Septuagint version. These were supplemented by apostolic letters such as those we have in our New Testament and, by the second half of the first century, by written Gospels.

Yet another structure of unity was the hierarchical vigilance exercised by the apostles and their associates. At the beginning, presumably, the teaching and practices of Christians were determined by the Twelve. Others such as Paul, Barnabas, and James the "brother of the Lord" gradually came to share in the authority of the original apostles. This top leadership was assisted by a body of lieutenants or delegates, including figures such as Timothy, Titus, Mark, and Epaphroditus. The principal leaders, with the help of these assistants, exercised control over large regions. On a lower level were the bishops and presbyters whom the apostles and missionaries placed in charge of local communities. Through frequent visitations and correspondence, the highest leadership maintained close supervision of the young churches. In writing to the churches Paul does not hesitate to invoke his apostolic authority (see 1 Cor. 9:1–3; 15:8–9; Gal. 1:11–16).

When problems arose, the leaders could and did confer. Paul, for example, occasionally consulted with the leaders reputed to be the "pillars" at Jerusalem, including Peter, James, and John, receiving from them the "right hand of fellowship" (Gal. 2:9). On one occasion, reported in the fifteenth chapter of Acts, there was a council or conference to decide to what extent the Jewish dietary laws and the practice of circumcision should be binding on converts from paganism.[25]

Among the visible bonds uniting Christians to one another, common practices of worship should not be overlooked. Paul speaks of "one baptism" (Eph. 4:5), by which Christians are united to Christ in a death like his and are assured of their coming resurrection (Rom. 6:5). Baptism was regarded as admission to the Church and more broadly as insertion into the total Christian mystery. "By one Spirit we were all baptized into one body—Jews and Greeks, slaves or free—and all were made to drink of one Spirit" (1 Cor. 12:13 RSV).

Of equal unitive significance with baptism is the one eucharistic bread, the means whereby the baptized partake of the body of Christ and become one body in him (1 Cor. 10:16–22). The one cup of blessing is the blood of Christ, by the partaking of which the faithful enter into his saving death (1 Cor. 10:16; compare 11:25). Through the one loaf and the one chalice, all were brought into intimate union with the one Christ.

In the New Testament we begin to find hints that Christians regularly assembled for the Eucharist on the first day of the week (Acts 20:7–8), observing it as the Lord's day (Rev. 1:10). They had prayers in common such as the Lord's Prayer and the *maranatha* (1 Cor. 16:22; compare Rev. 22:20). Pliny the Younger, in his letter to the Emperor Trajan, remarked on the way in which the Christians at their Sunday worship sang hymns to Christ as to a god (similar, no doubt, to the Christological hymns that have found their way into the New Testament).[26] As believers have experienced in every generation, such congregational singing has remarkable power to bring people together in active participation.

The solidarity of Christians in a single body was expressed and strengthened by their mutual charity. They welcomed visitors from other local churches and took up collections to relieve poverty in distant churches, as instanced in the offerings for the needy of Jerusalem, the first of the local churches (Rom. 15:26; 1 Cor. 16:1–4; 2 Cor. 8–9).

These indications, which I have surveyed all too hastily, make it evident that the unity of the Church was not merely spiritual and interior. To be a Christian was to confess the apostolic faith, to be baptized, to partake of the Eucharist, to join in the traditional hymns and prayers, to practice mutual charity and solidarity, and to accept the leadership of the duly designated leaders, whose function it was to maintain orthodox belief and good order in the community. It may be hoped that on the basis of the New Testament, Catholics and evangelicals might be able to agree today on something resembling this vision of unity.

## The Catholic System

The system of unity in the Roman Catholic Church, as it has developed since early patristic times, is grounded in the order of the apostolic Church as attested by the New Testament. It is not a rigid perpetuation of that order but an adaptation to the needs of a later age, retaining the same essential structures in a variety of forms that have unfolded under the aegis of the Holy Spirit.

According to the Catholic view, the universal Church, without ceasing to be a mystery of grace, has the unity of a single, organized society. The members are linked together in a communion of spirit that has palpable social effects. The Second Vatican Council, a generation ago, propounded the idea of the Church as a communion of local churches, in each of which the one Catholic Church is truly present and operative (*Christus Dominus*: Decree on the Bishops' Pastoral Office in the Church, 11). Each local church is realized most palpably by the gathering of a representative body of the faithful at the Eucharist under the presidency of the bishop, surrounded by members of his clergy (*Lumen Gentium*: Dogmatic Constitution on the Church, 26; *Christus Dominus*, 11).

Far from imposing uniformity, the Catholic unity of the whole church requires the protection of legitimate differences. The Catholic vision of multiform unity is eloquently synthesized in Vatican II's "Constitution on the Church." After pointing out how Christ came in order that God's scattered children might be gathered together into one (see John 11:52), the council explains that by its quality of universality, which is a gift from the Lord himself, "the Church efficaciously and unremittingly seeks to recapitulate the whole of humanity, with all its riches, under Christ the head in the unity of his Spirit" (*Lumen Gentium*, 13). The universal Church is made up of a variety of components, each of which, rather than obstructing unity, applies its own gifts for the benefit of the other parts and of the whole.

Later on, the "Constitution on the Church" explains that certain churches have, by the dispositions of divine providence, become organically united into groups that enjoy their own discipline, their own liturgical usage, and their own theological and spiritual patrimony. "This variety of local churches, in harmony among themselves, demonstrates with greater clarity the universality of the undivided Church" (*Lumen Gentium,* 23). In this paragraph the council anticipates what Cardinal Willebrands would later describe as the union of *typoi.*

The "Decree on Ecumenism," taking up the theme of variety in unity, points out that the heritage handed down from the apostles has been received in different ways, thanks to the variety of natural gifts and conditions of life. The council praises the spiritual traditions of both East and West, and affirms that the theological formulations of the two regions, though differing from each other, alike derive from Scripture and apostolic tradition, so that the two ways of speaking are often complementary rather than conflicting (*Unitatis Redintegratio,* 14–17). The "Pastoral Constitution on the Church in the Modern World" teaches that each nation should develop the ability to express Christ's message in its own way (*Gaudium et Spes,* 44). The "Decree on the Church's Missionary Activity" makes ample room for what has subsequently come to be called inculturation (*Ad Gentes,* 22).

The unity of the whole body is expressed and maintained by manifold signs and instruments that are attested in the New Testament and in patristic tradition. Among these bonds are liturgical worship, canonical Scriptures, creeds, and a hierarchical system of government.

Liturgical worship includes most prominently baptism and the Lord's Supper. Baptism, the basic sacrament of incorporation, is necessarily "one" according to the Nicene-Constantinopolitan Creed, which in this assertion follows the teaching of Ephesians 4:5. By incorporating Christians into Christ, baptism makes them members of one another. According to the "Decree on Ecumenism" any valid baptism, even when administered outside the Catholic Church, causes the baptized to be "truly incorporated into the crucified and glorified Christ, and reborn to a sharing of the divine life. . . . Thus baptism establishes a sacramental bond of unity existing among all who have been reborn by it" (*Unitatis Redintegratio,* 22).

Of all the sacraments, the Lord's Supper or Eucharist is seen especially as the bond of unity. The Eucharistic prayer, in the original form given to it in the first-century *Didache*, was a petition for the unity of the church: "As this broken bread was scattered upon the mountains but was brought together and became one, so may your Church be gathered together from the ends of the earth into your kingdom, for yours is the glory" (*Didache*, 9). For the fathers and medieval doctors, the Eucharist was the supreme sign and instrument of the Church's unity. The "Decree on Ecumenism" describes it as "the wonderful Sacrament . . . by which the unity of the Church is both signified and brought about" (*Unitatis Redintegratio*, 2).

As a result of long discussions from the second to the end of the fourth century, the Church acquired its own canonical Scriptures, consisting of its own version of the Jewish Scriptures together with a collection of apostolic writings known as the "New Testament." Consensus regarding this canonical collection was achieved in the second half of the fourth century by local councils in both the East and the West. The canon drawn up in these councils still governs the Catholic Church today and is retained in substance by most Christian churches. Vatican II was therefore able to speak of the inspired Scriptures as "precious instruments in the mighty hand of God for attaining that unity which the Savior holds out to all" (*Unitatis Redintegratio*, 21).

The brief confessional formulas of the New Testament were gradually expanded into a "rule of faith," from which in turn the early baptismal creeds took their rise. The Apostles' Creed, still prevalent in the West, is a form of the Roman baptismal creed. Seen essentially as summaries of biblical teaching, the creeds were used for the instruction of catechumens. Later, as the problem of heresy arose, additions were made to the baptismal creed. Conciliar creeds such as that of Nicaea-Constantinople deliberately went beyond the letter of Scripture so as to exclude prevalent errors; they were imposed on bishops as tests of orthodoxy. The Apostles' Creed and the Nicene-Constantinopolitan Creed are still acknowledged as normative for Christian faith by most Christian churches.

On the organizational level, the unity of the early Church was maintained by the hierarchical system of government. In the course of the second century all the local churches came to be governed by bishops, who were assisted by presbyters and deacons. Individually and collectively the bishops were considered to be successors of the apostles, in the sense of inheriting the transmissible functions of the apostolic office. As a qualified bearer of the apostolic tradition, the bishop was a judge of orthodoxy. The bishop was also the principal celebrant of the Eucharist, so that no valid Eucharist could be held unless celebrated, or at least approved, by him. In addition, the bishop controlled access to the sacraments, and he could excommunicate Christians who did not exhibit the necessary faith or probity of life.

The bishops, constituting as they did a single order, were the vital links between different local churches. When a new bishop was ordained, usually by a group of bishops from neighboring churches, letters were sent out notifying other bishops so that they could be certain about the leader with whom they should be in communion.

Quarrels and disagreements between local bishops occasionally broke out, especially when they differed about what doctrines should be proscribed or about who was to be excommunicated. Councils of bishops modeled on the apostolic Council of Jerusalem were frequently convened to reach collective decisions about such matters. Provincial councils were a regular feature of Church life.

Ecumenical councils, which were first able to meet after the legal recognition of Christianity by Constantine in the fourth century, had special importance for the unity of the Church—an importance they continue to enjoy in contemporary Catholicism. When the bishops in an ecumenical council achieved virtual unanimity in formulating the faith of the Church, their collective decisions were considered binding and irreversible, inasmuch as the bishops were the qualified bearers of the apostolic tradition. Since these councils (up to and including Vatican I) have been assembled under the invocation of the Holy Spirit, their decisions are attributed to the Holy Spirit acting through the bishops, as was the case when the apostolic leaders conferred at Jerusalem (Acts 15:28).

From the beginning, certain bishops were recognized as having higher authority within the college. The apostolic sees—those that traced their foundation to apostles—enjoyed special prestige, and among them Rome was recognized as having preeminence. This preeminence was apparently due to convergence of several factors, but the reason most strongly emphasized in the patristic literature is that Rome was the site of the martyrdom of the two leading apostles, Peter and Paul. As time went on, the bishop of Rome was increasingly recognized as the successor of Peter, who had been entrusted with the "keys of the kingdom" (Matt. 16:19) and with pastoral care for the whole flock of Christ (John 21:15–17). It was considered that the structure of government of the primitive Church was given by its divine Founder and was intended to endure. Just as the collegial structure of apostolic leadership was to be continued in the episcopate, so its primacy, having been given to Peter, was to be perpetuated in a Petrine succession. The only serious contender for the position of successor to Peter among the bishops was, and is, the bishop of Rome.

In Catholic teaching the papacy is understood preeminently as a unitive agency. In the words of the First Vatican Council, repeated almost verbatim by the Second Vatican Council: "In order that the episcopate itself might be one and undivided, and that the whole multitude of believers might be preserved in unity of faith and communion by means of a closely united priesthood, [Christ] placed blessed Peter at the head of the other apostles, and established in him a perpetual principle and visible foundation of this twofold unity"[27] (compare *Lumen Gentium*, 23).

According to the Catholic understanding, then, the visible unity of the church, as intended by Christ, includes three constitutive elements: the sacramental, the doctrinal, and the governmental. The members of the Church are in communion with one another to the extent that they enjoy the same sacramental life, profess the same faith, and acknowledge the same authoritative leadership. This vision of unity is concisely summarized in the "Decree on Ecumenism":

> Through the faithful preaching of the gospel by the apostles and their successors—the bishops with Peter's successor at their head—through their administration of the sacraments, and through their loving governance of the Church, Jesus Christ wills the growth of his people and perfects their fellowship in unity: in the confession of one faith, in their common celebration of divine worship, and in the fraternal harmony of God's family (*Unitatis Redintegratio*, 2).

Within this unity of faith, worship, and polity, considerable scope is allowed for diversity of styles and practices. This variety, far from impairing the unity, enriches it.

# Between Evangelicals and Catholics

For reasons that should be obvious, it does not seem practical today or for the foreseeable future to envisage a union between evangelicals and Catholics that would fully correspond to the Catholic view just described. Evangelical Christianity exhibits some but not all of the traits of a distinct *typos* according to the conception propounded by Cardinal Willebrands. The *typos* notion has thus far been applied only to churches of a distinctly hierarchical and sacramental character with a highly articulated system of dogma. Thus it must be asked whether it is possible to find some other model of unity, acceptable to both Catholics and evangelicals.

As noted above, some theologians propose models of union that do not require the acceptance of the same doctrines, sacraments, and ministerial structures. Cullmann, in his *Unity through Diversity*, rejects the goal of merger as impractical and undesirable. Writing in continental Europe, he makes no specific reference to evangelical Christianity, as that term is understood in the English-speaking world, but much of what he says may be applicable to evangelicals. He maintains that the presently separated churches are bearers of distinct charisms, comparable to those discussed by Paul in the twelfth chapter of First Corinthians. Protestants, Catholics, and Orthodox, he contends, have characteristic traits that should be cherished, not suppressed, for the benefit of the whole body of churches. He acknowledges, however, that any particular charism, cultivated in isolation, is liable to one-sidedness and distortion.

In Protestantism Cullmann finds the charisms of "concentration on the Bible" and freedom, "which fosters openness to the world."[28] These charisms, pursued unilaterally, could lead to narrow biblicism, anarchic liberalism, or false accommodation. The Catholic charisms, according to Cullmann, are universalism and institutional organization. Universalism runs the risk of falling into syncretism; institutional strength incurs the peril of totalitarian institutionalism. In the Orthodox churches Cullmann finds a laudable appreciation of the living presence of the Holy Spirit and a reverent adherence to traditional liturgical forms. As possible weaknesses in Orthodoxy, Cullmann mentions rigidity and formalism.

For Cullmann the goal of ecumenism is to achieve a visible manifestation of unity without the suppression of the diversity of the distinct charisms. This can be achieved, he believes, in a community of independent churches that cross-fertilize one another, both enriching the others with their own gifts and submitting to criticism by the others. While he opposes merger, he does not exclude the erection of certain common structures to sustain the relationship between the churches. He speaks tentatively of a "federal" union, while cautioning that the political use of this term can lead to misunderstandings. He also makes it clear that such a union would be open only to churches that adhere to the basic Christian faith, as expressed in the early creedal and confessional statements found in the New Testament.

An American Southern Baptist, C. Brownlow Hastings, has come up with an ecumenical proposal somewhat similar to Cullmann's.[29] The present-day ecumenical movement, he protests, is not ecumenical enough, since it virtually excludes nonsacramental churches like his own. The Southern Baptist Convention, he notes, was originally committed to the quest for Christian unity, but it has tended to withdraw into its own denominational shell out of fear that ecumenical ties might impose excessive uniformity and put restrictions on its own missionary endeavor. After a survey of models of unity, he notes that Southern Baptists tend to prefer a kind of "spiritual unity" that recognizes the presence of the true Church in many denominational churches. But it would be a mistake, he holds, to base one's ecumenical strategy on a particular vision of the final outcome, which is in God's hands.

As a strategy he repudiates organized structural union and recommends harmony as "the *only* model that they [ecumenical leaders] may offer to the largest Protestant denomination in America."[30] Such harmony, he believes, can and should be pursued among bodies that accept the "one gospel" and eschew latitudinarianism. This strategy enables the churches to celebrate the unity they already have, to cooperate in matters of common concern, and to undertake a critical examination of their own beliefs and practices in the light of the heritage of other Christian communities.

Through open dialogue the churches must positively engage one another and seek to overcome misleading stereotypes. Without indicating very precisely how the demands of the kingdom differ from those of the Church as the body of Christ, Hastings admonishes Christians to subordinate the interests of the Church to the higher interests of God's kingdom. He alludes to the imperative of Jesus, "Seek first his kingdom

and his righteousness, and all these things shall be yours as well"
(Matt. 6:33 RSV).

Cardinal Joseph Ratzinger, writing from a Roman Catholic perspective, proposes an ecumenical strategy surprisingly similar to those of
Cullmann and Hastings.[31] As a Catholic he accepts the goal of full visible unity set forth in the "Decree on Ecumenism" and other official
Catholic documents, but he recognizes that the attainment of that goal
depends upon a special initiative of the Holy Spirit, and lies beyond our
power of disposal. It would be too much to expect that church authorities could achieve institutional union by diplomatic negotiations or that
theologians could settle all the doctrinal conflicts by superior scholarship. This does not mean, however, that we must simply resign ourselves
to the existing divisions. Leaving to God what God alone can do, we
must seriously take up our own tasks.

Paul in 1 Corinthians 11:19 says that there must be factions. The early
fathers of the Church, meditating on this text, held that although
schisms come about through human faults, they fall within the providential plan of God. They have a certain necessity, since only God can
decide when the time has come to restore unity. During the present
phase of history, they may be seen as a kind of *felix culpa*— a "happy
fault" insofar as we may profit from them. They exercise our patience
and our charity; they provide opportunities for humility, self-criticism,
and spiritual growth.

Ratzinger therefore proposes a two-pronged strategy. The first task
consists in working for eventual complete unity, by which he presumably means the kind of visible corporate union envisaged in the standard
Catholic ecumenism. The second task, to which Ratzinger here gives
greater prominence, is to pursue intermediate goals similar to those we
have studied in the writings of Cullmann and Hastings. He does in fact
refer favorably to Cullmann's *Unity through Diversity*. This second field of
activity, he says,

> would presuppose that we know neither the day nor the hour, nor are
> we able to determine, when and how unity will come into existence.
> For that what applies, really and in its full rigor, is Melanchthon's *ubi et
> quando visum est Deo* ["where and when it pleases God"]. In any case it
> should be clear that we do not create unity, no more than we bring
> about righteousness by means of our works, but that on the other hand

we should not sit around twiddling our thumbs. Here it would therefore be a question of continually learning afresh from the other as other
while respecting his or her otherness. As people who are divided we can
also be one.[32]

## Interim Strategy

In the light of the studies just surveyed, it seems clear that, although
Catholics and evangelicals will articulate the final goal in different ways,
there are intermediate goals and strategies to which they can jointly
commit themselves. They can surely strive for the kind of "peaceful
coexistence" or "harmony" advocated by Cullmann and Hastings. With
some dependence on Ratzinger and on chapter 2 of the "Decree on
Ecumenism," I should like to propose a ten-point program, the various
elements in which can be implemented simultaneously. Some items in
this program are admittedly challenging and might not be acceptable to
everyone, but I regard them all as valid and important.

    1.   In the interests of truth and justice, not to mention charity, we
must seek to correct the misleading stereotypes of the past. Catholics
must overcome the impression that Protestants usually put their private
judgment above the Word of God. Protestants, for their part, should put
to rest any suspicions that Catholics consider it possible to be justified by
good works without grace and faith, or that Catholics deny the unique
mediatorship of Christ as universal Savior. Other examples of common
misimpressions could readily be supplied.

    2.   Both evangelicals and Catholics should allow themselves to be sur-
prised at the graciousness of God, who continues to bestow his favors
even upon those whose faith comes to expression in ways that we may
consider faulty. For instance, Catholics may be edified to see how
evangelicals, who deny the Real Presence of Christ in the consecrated
elements, celebrate the Lord's Supper with reverence, devotion, and
spiritual profit. Conversely, evangelicals may be surprised to see how
Catholics are confirmed in their faith when they engage in the invocation
of saints or in other practices that evangelicals regard as superstitious.

    3.   Recognizing that probity and holiness are present outside their
respective churches, Catholics and evangelicals should be stimulated
to enter into a holy rivalry, making better use of the means of grace

available in their own communions. They should strive to excel each other not in wealth, power, and prestige but in virtues such as honesty, self-sacrifice, care for the poor, faith in God's Word, and hope of eternal life.

4.   We must find ways of overcoming the mutual suspicion, fear, and resentment that have plagued our relations in the past. As Ratzinger says, we must remove the poison of hatred from our divisions and seek rather to help and serve one another.[33] Cullmann has several times suggested the practice of taking up a collection in each group for the charities of the other.[34] Going beyond this proposal, the divided churches may appropriately assist one another spiritually, by prayer, advice, and mutual support, in the hope that the ministries of the others may be blessed with greater fruitfulness.

5.   In the course of their dialogue, evangelicals and Catholics must respect each other's freedom and integrity. They must be careful not to force anything on the other that would threaten the other's Christian identity. For example, Catholics should not pressure evangelicals to accept the papal-episcopal structure of apostolic succession or to insert the Word of God into a sacramental context that would seem to evangelicals to inhibit the freedom of that Word. In return, evangelicals should refrain from putting pressure on Catholics to allow Eucharistic sharing with members of churches not in communion with Rome. According to Catholic conviction, the bodiliness of the sacrament cannot rightly be dissociated from the bodiliness of the Church.

Cardinal Ratzinger, who gives these examples, insightfully remarks that this kind of self-restraint arises from recognition that, since schisms "must be," there is an element of necessity in our divinely permitted separations. Far from impeding rapprochement, such restraint can give rise to greater closeness and love than would "forceful pressure, which creates resistance and finally refusal."[35]

6.   Instead of following the path of reduction to some common denominator, the parties should pursue an ecumenism of mutual enrichment, asking how much they can give to, and receive from, one another. Neither evangelicals nor Catholics should prematurely surrender their distinctive characteristics and heritage for the sake of easy unity. What each group affirms in faith may be seen as held in trust by them for the whole *oikoumenē*. In God's good time the moment may come when each will welcome what the other has to offer, accepting it at least in a

modified form, purged of any unilateralism and polemical distortions. Meanwhile, the two groups can learn from one another to overcome their own narrowness and imbalances.

7.   We may likewise rejoice at the very significant bonds of faith and practice that already unite us, notwithstanding our differences. It is no small thing that we can jointly read the same Scriptures as God's inspired Word, that we can share in the confession of the Triune God and of Jesus Christ as true God and true man. It is a blessing to be bound together by the same essential forms of Christian prayer, based on Holy Scripture, and by common commitment to the way of life held forth in the Ten Commandments as interpreted in the light of the New Testament. We are privileged to share in the same hope of eternal life in the kingdom of God.

8.   On the basis of their shared patrimony, evangelicals and Catholics can engage in a measure of joint witness and social action. Without minimizing the real disagreements between them, they may jointly profess their common faith in the one Lord and Redeemer. The statement "Evangelicals and Catholics Together" calls attention to the many issues in the social and public life of our nation on which our two communities have taken a common stand. We agree, for instance, that the inalienable dignity of the individual person cannot be secure without recognition that human beings are made by God and in the image of God. In resisting moral evils and in working to preserve the Christian heritage of our nation against militant secularism, evangelicals and Catholics can find common ground.

9.   The interim period of mutual separation provides an occasion for growth in peace and patience. The realization that our divisions are, humanly speaking, insuperable and that they can be transcended only through a miracle of grace, should not be discouraging but liberating. It relieves us from feeling under an obligation to accomplish what exceeds our powers.

10.   We may and must pray, separately and together, for full realization of Christ's petition that we may all be one in a manifest way that induces the world to believe. In union with our great High Priest, we may beseech the Lord of all things to bestow full unity and concord "when and as it may please the Holy Spirit."

## Mutual Learning

The sixth proposal in the strategy just outlined calls for an ecumenism of mutual enrichment, in which the two groups learn from one another in order to supplement their respective deficiencies and remedy their respective weaknesses. This point may call for some elaboration. If Catholics and evangelicals trust and respect one another, they can learn a great deal that would not be accessible if their own expression of Christianity were all that existed. Perhaps God, in permitting the existing differences, intends that one style of Christianity may provide a home for ideas and practices that the other community is not yet prepared to accept. In dialogue we can learn things that we could not teach ourselves.

As I see it, Catholics have a great deal to learn from evangelicals, who often experience a strong personal relationship to Jesus as Savior and who display a contagious enthusiasm for the gospel. They can help Catholics to find God's living word in the Bible, and to make the Bible a basis for their daily life. They can show Catholics how to preach with greater energy and power and to witness courageously to their faith before the whole world. Evangelicals have succeeded better than Catholics, at least in this part of the world, in forming warm and welcoming communities in which the members feel themselves to be actively involved. Catholics may be able to learn from evangelicals better ways of engaging the laity at all levels of Christian life and witness. Some evangelicals have succeeded in giving a healthy autonomy to local churches without loss of confessional identity. Evangelical Christianity in the United States has stood valiantly for the principle of freedom of conscience, which was accepted rather tardily in official Catholic teaching.

Conversely, evangelicals may come to see in dialogue that they have more to learn from Catholics than they would previously have suspected. In their intense devotion to the Word of God, evangelicals have tended to neglect the sacraments, which have enormous power to mediate a living communion with God, and they have generally given insufficient attention to tradition, to which they often adhere without being fully conscious of so doing. Although the autonomy of each local church is considered an ideal by evangelicals, they are in fact ruled to a great extent by elected delegates and office-holders in their assemblies or conventions. Sometimes these officials are more authoritarian than

Catholic bishops, who must operate collegially under Roman supervision and who are bound by the prescriptions of canon law. The Catholic balance between local authority and universal authority, between a rule of persons and a rule of law, may contain important lessons for evangelicals.

In addition, the catholicity of the Church in space and time could hold an appeal for many evangelicals, who belong to churches that, by comparison, have rather shallow historical roots and a relatively narrow cultural matrix. It would also appear that the Catholic theological tradition could help evangelicals to offset the anti-intellectualism from which many of them are seeking to escape. Catholicism, especially in Europe, has had an enriching association with culture, including philosophy, architecture, music, painting, and letters. Fundamentalism, both past and present, has sometimes provided an example of the anti-intellectualism to which evanglicalism is subject.

Undoubtedly, some Catholics and some evangelicals will resist the mutual learning that is offered by the incipient dialogue. Caution, indeed, is warranted, because each group has a legitimate interest in preserving its own distinctive character. If either indiscriminately appropriated the emphases of the other, the two styles of Christianity might be too quickly blended into a featureless conflation. But, on the other hand, by isolating itself from contact with others, any church can degenerate into sectarian narcissism.

The question of mutual learning holds an integral place in the discussion of the unity for which we hope. Unity is not an either/or matter, but something to be progressively realized, in the measure that the Holy Spirit is pleased to grant it. The new relationships that could arise through dialogue and cooperation pertain intrinsically to the idea of unity itself. In cultivating such relationships the churches can form a certain kind of community, this side of full corporate union.

## Types of Community

To clarify the relationships among churches, it is helpful to distinguish between two types of community: homogeneous and heterogeneous.[36] Too often ecumenists have taken it for granted that true community cannot exist except between groups that share the same beliefs, behavioral standards, and styles of worship, as occurs in homogeneous communities. It is important indeed to have the support of fellow believers who inhabit the same spiritual home. This is the case in small parishes and base communities within a single religious denomination. The denomination itself might be described as the religious counterpart of an extended family, or family of families. The inner solidarity of homogeneous groups brings solid spiritual benefits to the members.

No family, however, can effectively live without contact with outsiders. Friends with different backgrounds help to keep the family from becoming too set in its ways and insufficiently open to alternative ideas and practices. The friend who visits the family is expected to bring the challenge of new experiences, new ideas, and new points of view. It is not necessary that friends should always agree. On the contrary, some of our best friends are those with whom we vehemently differ. The deeper the friendship, the more capable it is of sustaining disagreements that, without love, could be divisive.

Although classical ecumenism was aimed at organic union, it did not accomplish many significant mergers. But it did, perhaps unintentionally, bring about stimulating contact with new and unfamiliar styles of Christianity. That is, and remains, one of its greatest attractions. It helps to overcome the excessive inbreeding of churches and to bring the benefits of heterogeneous community.

The goal of corporate reunion, leading to a single religious family, is quite legitimate for groups that have a large common heritage, as do, for example, Orthodox and Catholics. But that goal is neither realistic nor desirable for communities as widely separated as evangelicals and Catholics. For the present and the foreseeable future the two will continue to constitute distinct religious families. This does not mean, however, that they must resign themselves to loveless separation. They can enter into warm personal relations corresponding to friendship among individuals. Individual Catholics and evangelicals can, indeed, be close friends. While they are able to find much in common (as friends normally do), they are sufficiently different to make their relationship exciting. By challenging one another, they may even fortify their friendship. They can help one another to see how the Christian faith can appear when seen through other eyes. Perhaps one of the blessings that the Lord intends to give in permitting long-standing divisions among Christians is to offer the churches the possibility of heterogeneous community.

Within this type of ecclesial friendship there is no lack of things that Catholics and evangelicals can do together. They can join in their fundamental witness to Christ and the gospel. They can affirm together their acceptance of the apostolic faith enshrined in the creeds and dogmas of the early Church. They can labor side by side in defending the religious heritage of the nation, to the extent that this is authentically biblical and is consonant with the eternal law of God. They can jointly protest against the false and debilitating creeds of militant secularism. In all these ways they can savor and deepen the unity that is already theirs in Christ.

Although the goal of full visible unity may lie beyond their powers, evangelicals and Catholics can cultivate true friendship in the Lord. Such friendship does not demand that they conceal their differences. On the contrary, it permits them to be quite frank in expressing their disagreements and in defending their divergent points of view. Even if each is convinced that the other is wrong, they must not forgo the possibility of learning from a lively exchange of views.

All these steps admittedly fall short of the ultimate goal, the perfect ecclesial unity that continues to elude us. As far as Catholics are concerned, full unity involves agreement regarding the apostolic faith, the observance of the same essential forms of worship, and acceptance of the same system of pastoral government. Between Catholics and evangelicals this type of unity seems to be beyond present prospects. It may not even seem desirable to all evangelicals, at least in the form that Catholics would understand it.

With regard to the ultimate goal, it will be sufficient for evangelicals and Catholics to pray together for that unity that Christ wills for his Church. The final achievement, we can agree, transcends all that can be accomplished by human efforts. We place our trust in the prayer of Christ, in the love of the Father, and in the power of the Holy Spirit.

# Notes

1    Roman Catholic / Lutheran Joint Commission, *Facing Unity: Models, Forms and Phases of Catholic-Lutheran Church Fellowship* (Geneva: Lutheran World Federation, 1985), 8–20.

2 John F. Hotchkin, "Probing the Possibilities," *Interface,* no. 2 (Spring 1980): 1–11; Paul A. Crow, Jr., "Ecumenics as Reflections on Models of Christian Unity," *Ecumenical Review,* 39 (1987): 389–403.

3 Willem A. Visser't Hooft, ed., *The New Delhi Report: The Third World Assembly of the World Council of Churches* (New York: Association Press, 1962), 116.

4 David M. Paton, ed., *Breaking Barriers: Nairobi 1975: The Official Report of the Fifth Assembly of the World Council of Churches* (Geneva: World Council of Churches, 1976), 317–18.

5 See the report "What Unity Requires," *Breaking Barriers,* 59–69, esp. 63–65.

6 Report of the Salamanca Consultation convened by the Faith and Order Commission, World Council of Churches, on "Concepts of Unity and Models of Union," in *What Kind of Unity?* Faith and Order Paper 69 (Geneva: World Council of Churches, 1974), 119–26, at 121.

7 Paton, *Breaking Barriers*, 60–61.

8 Emmanuel Lanne, "Pluralism and Unity: The Possibility of a Variety of Typologies within the Same Ecclesial Allegiance," *One in Christ,* 4 (1970): 430–51, at 443–44.

9 "Cardinal Willebrands' Address in Cambridge, England [January 18, 1970]," *Documents on Anglican/Roman Catholic Relations* (Washington, D.C.: United States Catholic Conference, 1972), 32–41, at 39.

10 John Macquarrie, *Christian Unity and Christian Diversity* (Philadelphia: Westminster, 1975), 46.

11 Ibid., 25–26.

12 Robert McAfee Brown, *The Ecumenical Revolution: An Interpretation of the Catholic-Protestant Dialogue* (Garden City, N.Y.: Doubleday Image, 1969), 396–413; Lewis S. Mudge, *The Crumbling Walls* (Philadelphia: Westminster Press, 1970).

13 Jon Sobrino, "Bearing with One Another in Faith," in *Theology of Christian Solidarity,* ed. Jon Sobrino and Juan Hernández Pico, (Maryknoll, N.Y.: Orbis, 1985), 1–41, esp. 24–31.

14 Mudge, *The Crumbling Walls*, 88–89.

15 The Leuenberg Agreement of 1974, embracing a number of Lutheran, Reformed, and United churches in Europe, seems to me to examplify the "reconciled diversity" model, even though *Facing Unity* places it in a distinct category. It is a fellowship between churches "with different confessional positions" that continue to adhere to their own confessions, while according one another "table and pulpit fellowship." Harding Meyer, in a critique of the agreement, points out that it "is very cautious when it comes to ways and means indispensable for common decision making and common action." He asks whether it would not be appropriate "to strengthen the structural element in the concept of church fellowship." See Harding Meyer, "Critique of the Leuenberg Agreement as an Ecumenical Model," in *The Leuenberg Agreement and Lutheran-Reformed Relationships: Evaluations by North*

*American and European Theologians,* ed. William G. Rusch and Daniel F. Martensen (Minneapolis: Augsburg, 1989), 53–66, at 63.

16   Oscar Cullmann, *Unity through Diversity* (Philadelphia: Westminster, 1988), 31.

17   Ibid., 28.

18   Ibid., 43.

19   Ibid., 62.

20   Karl Barth, *Church Dogmatics,* IV/1 (New York: Scribners, 1956), 684; translation modified in light of the original, *Die Kirchliche Dogmatik,* IV/1, 2d ed. (Zurich: EVZ-Verlag, 1960), 764.

21   Yves Congar, *Diversity and Communion* (Mystic, Conn.: Twenty-Third Press, 1985), 150–51.

22   Ibid., 156–58.

23   For a preliminary report on this question see Karl Lehmann and Wolfhart Pannenberg, eds., *The Condemnations of the Reformation Era: Do They Still Divide?* (Minneapolis: Fortress, 1990).

24   LG 14, quoting Augustine, *De Bapt. c. Donat.* 5:28:39 [PL 43:197].

25   I have tried to describe the interplay of the various groups at the Council of Jerusalem in my article, "An Ecclesial Model for Theological Reflection: The Council of Jerusalem," in *Tracing the Spirit: Communities, Social Action, and Theological Reflection,* ed. James E. Hug (New York: Paulist, 1983), 218–41.

26   Pliny, Letters, Bk. X, letter 96, §7 in Pliny, *Letters and Panegyricus,* trans. B. Radice (Cambridge, Mass.: Loeb Classical Library, 1969), 2:289.

27   H. Denzinger, ed., *Enchiridion Symbolorum, Definitionum et Declarationum de Rebus Fidei et Morum,* rev. A. Schönmetzer, 36th ed. (Freiburg, Herder, 1976), 3051.

28   Cullmann, *Unity through Diversity,* 20.

29   C. Brownlow Hastings, *Harmony among Christians: A Model Other Than Structural Unity* (Louisville, Ky.: Glad River Publications, 1992).

30   Ibid., 22–23.

31   Cardinal Joseph Ratzinger, *Church, Ecumenism and Politics: New Essays in Ecclesiology* (New York: Crossroad, 1988), 135–42.

32   Ibid., 140.

33   Ibid., 139.

34   Cullmann, *Unity through Diversity,* 30. See Cullmann's earlier work, *Message to Catholics and Protestants* (Grand Rapids: Eerdmans, 1959).

35   Ratzinger, *Church, Politics and Ecumenism,* 141.

36   See Avery Dulles, "Ecumenical Strategies for a Pluralistic Age," in *The Resilient Church* (Garden City, N.Y.: Doubleday, 1977), 173–90, esp. 180–85.

# 5

# Crosscurrents among Evangelicals

J. I. Packer

Here I stand. I cannot do otherwise.
God help me. Amen.

*Martin Luther*

WHEN I WAS YOUNG I saw the film *Martin Luther* and was deeply impressed by its portrayal of Luther's response at the Diet of Worms in 1521 when the Holy Roman Emperor's spokesman asked him to disown the books he had written because of their allegedly heretical content. With the camera closing in on his working face and the volume of his strong voice rising, Luther declaimed his famous words in a way that made this for me the high spot of the movie:

Unless I am convinced by Scripture and plain reason . . . I do not accept the authority of popes and councils, for they have contradicted each other . . . my conscience is captive to the Word of God. I cannot and will not recant anything, for to go against conscience is neither right [i. e., because it cannot please God] nor safe [i.e., because it endangers the soul]. Here I stand. I cannot do otherwise. God help me. Amen.

I did not at that time expect ever to be in circumstances that would make me feel like Martin Luther at Worms, nor for more than forty years was I. But during the past few months I have constantly identified with his words quoted above, as I have answered a stream of letters telling me that I should withdraw my name from the published list of supporters of "Evangelicals and Catholics Together" and thus recant my endorsement of its contents. Politicians may recant to order, but those who serve God can hardly do that, and I have had to tell my correspondents that my endorsement, which was conscientiously given, remains unchanged. Some of the letters, however, reflected an inadequate grasp of what ECT aims at, and I would like, therefore, first, to review criticisms of ECT from concerned evangelicals; second, to clear ECT of misunderstandings that the criticisms reflect; and third, to reargue ECT's case for parachurch cooperation in Christian mission activities.

Some of my correspondents have wondered whether my attitude to Roman Catholics and the Roman Catholic Church has changed over the years. I wish, therefore, to state explicitly that so far as I am aware everything I have ever put in print on this subject still stands. Over the years I have had Roman Catholic friends, read Roman Catholic writings, and worked with Roman Catholics in literary and conference projects, but I myself write as the Protestant evangelical that by conviction I am; in Luther's words, I cannot do otherwise. More than one of my correspondents have asked how I view participation in a common mission with Catholics in light of these two biblical passages:

> I am astonished that you are so quickly deserting the one who called you by the grace of Christ and are turning to a different gospel—which is really no gospel at all. Evidently some people are throwing you into confusion and are trying to pervert the gospel of Christ. But even if we or an angel from heaven should preach a gospel other than the one we preached to you, let him be eternally condemned! As we have already said, so now I say again: If anybody is preaching to you a gospel other than what you accepted, let him be eternally condemned!

> Am I now trying to win the approval of men, or of God? Or am I trying to please men? If I were still trying to please men, I would not be a servant of Christ (Gal. 1:6–10 NIV).

> Do not be yoked together with unbelievers. For what do righteousness and wickedness have in common? Or what fellowship can light have with darkness? What harmony is there between Christ and

Belial? What does a believer have in common with an unbeliever? (2 Cor. 6:14–15 NIV).

In what follows, I hope to make clear my answer to the questions. This is, of course, a personal piece in which I speak for nobody but myself. If, however, it throws any light on the integrity of other Protestants who have backed ECT, I shall be very thankful.

## ECT Under Evangelical Fire

The letters, sometimes with public documents enclosed, started arriving soon after ECT hit the stands in the May 1994 issue of *First Things*. The reason why was clear. ECT applied what was once called the "Lund principle" (so named from the ecumenical gathering that formulated it), that ecclesiastically divided Christians should try not to do separately what their consciences allow them to do together. The document urged that Protestant evangelicals and believing Roman Catholics act together as far as possible in both the societal and the evangelistic tasks of the Christian mission, which is in truth the mission of the Triune God, carried out through God's people. Agreement is first announced on the Apostles' Creed, on the proposition that "we are justified by grace through faith because of Christ," and on the membership of all believers in the family of God. A commitment follows to seek more love, less misrepresentation of each other, and more clarity about continuing doctrinal differences. ECT then declares war on government-enforced secularism and specifies social values that must be fought for in North America today. Finally, it sketches out a goal of nonproselytization amongst believers and joint action for the conversion and nurture of those currently outside the faith. Grass-roots "cobelligerence," to use the late Francis Schaeffer's term, is ECT's theme. It identifies common enemies (unbelief, sin, cultural apostasy) and pleads that the Christian counterattack on these things be cooperative up to the limit of what divergent convictions allow. The assumption—indeed, the argument—throughout is that those whom, with apologies for the patronizing sound of my phrase, I shall call good quality evangelical Protestants and good quality Roman Catholics have enough in common to make this agenda both realistic and wholesome. That is what the protesters challenge.

*Who are the protesters?*

Those who protest are evangelicals who have an informed commitment to a traditional Protestant vision, heritage, and policy. That statement, however, needs a good deal of analysis before its meaning is clear.

*They are evangelicals.* What does that imply? Since the middle of this century the word has gained virtually universal currency as a label for a particular type of Christian faith and life that appears in most Protestant denominations and generates a sense of worldwide spiritual unity across denominational lines that is strikingly similar to the sense of global identity exhibited by Roman Catholics. There are perhaps a billion people in the world who claim to be Catholic and something approaching half that number who identify themselves as evangelical. Etymologically, the word appeals by pointing to the evangel, that is, the God-given gospel, on which Christianity is founded. Historically, evangelical identity has been shaped and fertilized by a complex of movements: the Protestantism of the sixteenth century, the Puritanism of the seventeenth, the Pietism of the eighteenth, the religious populism of the nineteenth, and the Pentecostalism, including the charismatic renewal, of the twentieth. Theologically, evangelicalism defines itself against naturalistic Pelagianism by affirming the need for radical renewing of our sinful hearts by the Holy Spirit and against mechanical sacramentalism by affirming the directness of the Spirit's regenerating work in our hearts with and through the gospel Word. In the Christian world, evangelicalism is recognized by its proclaimed and practiced adherence to the seven principles that follow:

1. The supreme authority of the sixty-six-book canon of Holy Scripture as the self-authenticating, self-interpreting Word of God. This is sometimes expressed as the sufficiency of Scripture to mediate all of God's guidance for faith, life, knowledge of Christ, and securing salvation, and it is sometimes abbreviated into the Reformation slogan *sola scriptura* ("by Scripture alone"). Views claiming biblical warrant are respected while their credentials are examined, but any that appear to go beyond or fall short of scriptural teaching are rejected as mistaken and dishonoring to God.

2.    The majesty of Jesus Christ as God incarnate, mediator of the new covenant of grace, substitutionary sin-bearer, perfect Savior, risen, reigning and returning Lord, head of his Church, and director of his disciples. Christ is the immediate focus of the faith, hope, love, and loyalty that in a more inclusive way acknowledge and rest on the grace and saving work of the Father, the Son, and the Spirit together. Typically, this redemptive Christ-centeredness leads to a strong insistence that our present justification through faith in Christ—that is, our acquittal from the guilt of sin and acceptance as heirs of glory—is grounded entirely on his righteousness—that is, his law-keeping, sin-bearing obedience—now imputed to us. This is referred to as *sola fide* ("by faith alone").

3.    The lordship of the Holy Spirit as source and sustainer of all spiritual life and communion with God. The Spirit works in us understanding of the gospel, conviction of sin, regeneration of heart, faith in Scripture and its Christ, assurance of salvation, love and obedience, worship and prayer, giftings and ministry, the bondings of fellowship, and the fruit of holy and Christlike character.

4.    The necessity of personal conversion, in which recognition of one's helplessness in sin leads to total trust in Jesus Christ as Savior, Lord, God, lover, brother, and friend, with consequent joyful assurance from the Holy Spirit of the reality of one's new life. Conversion (the subjective side of being "born again") brings eternal life and adoption into God's family, and it sets the pattern for the daily discipline of repenting of sin and finding the forgiveness of one's heavenly Father.

5.    The priority of evangelism in the Christian life as a way of obeying and glorifying God and practicing love of our neighbor. Christians should share the gospel.

6.    The need for community in the Christian life. The Church is essentially a fellowship of believers in Christ with Christ; it manifests its reality in local churches (gatherings committed to do all the things the Church does) and also in parachurch bodies (associations committed to do some of the things the

Church does). Such bodies may be small, large, national, institutional, denominational, or transdenominational—indeed, ecumenical. Since no Christian is spiritually self-sufficient and coming together is the revealed will of God, every Christian should join a local church and will ordinarily benefit from parachurch involvements as well.

7. The practice of administering the ordinances or two sacraments that Jesus instituted, i.e., baptism and the Lord's Supper. Many, if not all, see these rites as means of grace, conveying and confirming the benefits they signify, through the active exercise of faith that they evoke. The Lord's Supper, in particular, becomes an event of spiritual refreshment through thankful, intentional remembering of Christ's cross and self-offering to him in gratitude for it.

In North America, as throughout the Christian world, different sorts of evangelicals are found: pietists and institutionalists; dogmatists and devotionalists; covenantal and dispensational interpreters of Scripture; committed adherents to the Lutheran, Calvinists, Wesleyan, and Pentecostal heritages; organized churchpeople and disorganized freewheelers; denominationalists and transdenominationalists; fideists and rationalists; combative fundamentalists, and academic postfundamentalists, plus revisionists of many kinds with a wide range of preoccupations and proposals. But all evangelicals find their identity in the seven principles stated, and it is against the background of this consensus that the objections to ECT are made.

*The critics have an informed commitment to a traditional Protestant vision, heritage, and policy.* What does that mean? The Protestant *vision* has historically been that the Roman Catholic Church should break up and dissolve (or reform itself in classic Protestant terms, which would amount to the same thing); and that as a means to this end Protestants should constantly speak against Roman Catholic teaching about the Church, the papacy, the gospel, the Mass, the priesthood, Mary, and the Christian life, not only to keep the unwary from embracing these ideas, but also to hasten their demise.

The figure in Bunyan's *Pilgrim's Progress* of the almost paralyzed Giant Pope reminds us that until early in the last century most Protestants believed that the Roman Catholic Church had received a mortal blow and really was on the way out, and its more recent resurgence has left many feeling threatened. To any who see the vision of Rome vanishing as expressing God's goal, the current call is for redoubled efforts in rebuttal of Rome's teaching, and anything less appears as crass and perhaps treasonable folly.

The Protestant *heritage* is a body of learned polemic against specific Roman Catholic tenets as expressed in the deliverances of the Council of Trent, the catechism of Pius V, the two Vatican Councils, the papal promulgations of Mary's Immaculate Conception (1854) and her Assumption (1950), and most recently in the *Catechism of the Catholic Church* (1994). Since Rome sees conciliar statements and papal definitions *ex cathedra* as infallible and irreformable, nothing changes here, and most of the polemical arguments go back in substance to the sixteenth century. Over and above objections to Church infallibility as such, their burden was and is that Roman teaching obscures the gospel and indeed distorts it in a tragically antispiritual and unpastoral manner, in at least three ways.

First, the doctrines of transubstantiation and the Mass-sacrifice in which, according to the Council of Trent, "the same Christ" is sacrificed "in an unbloody manner, who once offered himself in a bloody manner on the altar of the cross," obscure the finished character of Christ's atonement and encourage people to look to ongoing masses rather than to Christ's once-for-all historic death for the forgiveness of their sins.

Second, Rome's Mariology, Mariolatry, and regular invocation of other saints too, asking them to present and support requests to Jesus, obscure the loving availability of Jesus in his glory and discourage people from directly approaching "the throne of grace with confidence, so that we may receive mercy and find grace to help us in our time of need" (Heb. 4:16 NIV).

Third, the Tridentine exposition of justification as a salvation process functioning through the efficacy of the ongoing sacramental system to produce what would once have been called meritorious righteousness obscures the biblical meaning of justification as the here-and-now acceptance of the believing sinner on the basis not of our own righteousness (we have none), but Christ's. As Michael Horton puts it, the Tridentine equation of justification with sanctification "rejects Paul's whole point in Romans 4:1-5, that justification comes only to those who (a) are wicked and (b) stop working for it."[1] Thus is the New Testament gospel overlaid in the Roman Catholic system. Those who think that the Protestant task is to keep pointing this out, as emphatically as possible, naturally view anything less as a sign of failure to care sufficiently about God's life-giving truth.

Finally, the Protestant *policy* has always been isolation from Rome, as the best way not only of avoiding doctrinal entanglement for oneself and others but also of hastening the death of the unacceptable Catholic system. Catholics have practiced isolation from Protestants for similar reasons, and so there has been a good deal of duplication and rivalry and inflammatory long-range criticism fed by mutual suspicion and dislike. Inevitably, therefore, some now feel that by commending a pattern of cooperation with Roman Catholics, however limited, Protestants like myself are implicitly sanctioning and so strengthening the Roman church system, and thus betraying, or at least frustrating, the essential Protestant purpose. (Whether there are comparable feelings on the Catholic side I do not know, but I should certainly be surprised if there were not.)

### Specific Criticisms

The specific criticisms that to my knowledge have been leveled, publicly or privately, against ECT from a Protestant evangelical point of view are as follows:

1. Since the official Roman Catholic faith is not the gospel of grace, but a legalistic perversion of it, Roman Catholics are not ordinarily Christians, and so it is entirely wrong to say, as ECT does, "Evangelicals and Catholics are brothers and sisters in Christ." The situation (it is said) is not saved by the previous sentence, "All who accept Christ as Lord and Savior are brothers and sisters in Christ," because such acceptance of Christ, in the evangelical sense of the phrase, is not something that Roman Catholics are taught to do. So the assertion of brotherhood is an unreality, as well as a weakening of the traditional Protestant hard line, which the critics see as correct and obligatory.

2. It is inept, or disingenuous, to say, "We affirm together that Christians are to teach and live in obedience to the divinely inspired Scriptures, which are the infallible Word of God," when Roman Catholics are required by their system to take their understanding of the Scriptures from the magisterium (teaching office), rather than from within the Bible itself. The situation is not saved by the next sentence, "We further affirm together that Christ has promised to his Church the

gift of the Holy Spirit who will lead us into all truth in discerning and declaring the teaching of Scripture," because Rome equates this leading of the Holy Spirit with the dictates of the magisterium.

3. It is inept, or disingenuous, to follow a paragraph declaring that Jesus Christ is the Lord of the universe and humankind's only Savior with the words, "We affirm together that we are justified by grace through faith because of Christ." For although this is an echo of the Reformers' *per fidem propter Christum* ("through faith because of Christ"), it is a statement that, as it stands, is no less compatible with the Tridentine doctrine of justification than it is with the Reformational view. What is the use of a professed agreement that certainly means different things to the parties who agreed on it? Does the failure of the evangelicals to insist on the formula "through faith *alone*" mean that they no longer regard Paul's teaching on justification as spelled out by Luther as central to the gospel and essential to the Church's health? No other explanation (it is said) seems to fit the facts, and this is very ominous.

4. It is inept, or disingenuous, to say that "Christian witness is of necessity aimed at conversion" when conversion is not defined as the decisive initial turning to Christ in faith that brings present justification but is instead spoken of as a lifelong process, thus covertly opening the door once more to the Roman concept of justification as meritorious sanctification progressing from baptismal regeneration to final post-purgatorial glory. Certainly, the difference is noted between the Catholic belief in baptismal regeneration, with its corollary that "baptismal grace is to be continuingly reawakened and revivified through conversion," and the Protestant belief that in conversion we receive "the new birth for the first time." But then the difference is left unresolved and treated as if there is no need to resolve it, and it is too important a matter to be dismissed in this way.

5. It is inept, or disingenuous, to affirm that "as much as we might believe one community is more fully in accord with the gospel than another, we as evangelicals and Catholics affirm that opportunity and means for growth are available in our several communities," and therefore, "Those converted [i.e., those who have come alive spiritually] . . . must be given full freedom and respect as they discern and decide the community in which they will live their new life in Christ." This (it is said) is pastorally irresponsible, since whatever may be true of

the Catholic community as a whole, individual congregations lack the biblical teaching that makes for Christian maturity.

6. Some of the critics, perhaps following some writers in the public press, view the document as reaching after some actual rapprochement with the Church of Rome as such. They describe its agendas as cooperation with *the Roman Catholic Church* and read into it (for it is not possible to read out of it) a proposed moratorium on planting Protestant churches in Roman Catholic countries, as part of the rapprochement diplomacy. The words thought to imply this are, "In view of the large number of non-Christians in the world and the enormous challenge of our common evangelistic task, it is neither theologically legitimate nor a prudent use of resources for one Christian community to proselytize among active adherents of another Christian community"—an affirmation preceded by this definition of proselytizing: "'sheep stealing' . . . the practice of recruiting people from another community for purposes of denominational or institutional aggrandizement." But the offending words only announce priorities (it is "neither theologically legitimate nor a prudent use of resources" to get your priorities wrong), and an attentive reading of ECT as a whole will show that the rapprochement idea is misleading—as I hope to make clear at some length in the next section of this essay.

The most poignant expressions of these criticisms come from middle-aged and elderly individuals who found Christ and spiritual life in evangelicalism after failing to find either in the Roman Catholicism of their birth and who cannot believe that Protestants who back ECT know what they are doing. I hope the following discussion will address and allay some of their concerns.

## The Parachurch Perspective

ECT announces itself as a statement on a particular theme—"The Christian Mission in the Third Millennium"—and refers specifically to those parts of the world where evangelicals and Roman Catholics are found side by side. When I put my name to it I did not expect it to be read as implying that its evangelical supporters thought fit to end the historic war with Rome about gospel doctrine and to start treating Rome as we treat evangelical congregations and denominations other than our own—not, of course, as perfect, but not as convictionally or ecclesiastically off-limits for church communion purposes. When I found that the statement was being read this way, I received most gracious cooperation from Michael Horton in bringing to birth another statement that was printed in the July-August 1994 number of *Modern Reformation*, the house magazine of Christians United for Reformation (CURE), the agency that Horton serves. This statement picks up on the following comments from ECT on a list of sample "points of difference in doctrine, worship, practice, and piety that are frequently thought to divide us":

> On these questions, and other questions implied by them, Evangelicals hold that the Catholic Church has gone beyond Scripture, adding teachings and practices that detract from or compromise the Gospel of God's saving grace in Christ. Catholics, in turn, hold that such teachings and practices are grounded in Scripture and belong to the fullness of God's revelation. Their rejection, Catholics say, results in a truncated and reduced understanding of the Christian reality. . . .
>
> We can and do pledge that we will continue to search together—through study, discussion, and prayer—for a better understanding of one another's convictions and a more adequate comprehension of the truth of God in Christ.

### Clarifications: The CURE Statement of August 1994

Titled "Resolutions for Roman Catholic and Evangelical Dialogue," the new statement offered seven representative confessional theses from the evangelical side as agenda items for study, discussion, and prayer. Its preamble declared that as ECT was "crafted to encourage cooperation on the basis of a consensus deemed sufficient for the purpose, though confessionally incomplete, so the following statements seek to identify issues of concern to evangelical Protestants that the thrust of the document raises. What follows is intended to encourage further discussion of the possibilities and problems of acting together." The text was printed over the signatures of 35 evangelical leaders[2] and reads as follows:

> 1. While both Evangelicals and Roman Catholics affirm the ecumenical Creeds, we do not see this catholic consensus as a sufficient basis for declaring that agreement exists on all the essential elements of the Gospel.

2. The doctrine of justification by grace alone through faith alone because of Christ alone has since the Reformation been acknowledged by mainstream Protestants as "the article by which the Church stands or falls," and the tenet that distinguishes a true from a false Church. While affirming an indissoluble bond between justification and sanctification, this doctrine insists that justification itself is God's present forensic declaration of pardon and acceptance, and that the righteousness required for this declaration is neither attained by human effort nor infused or worked internally by God in the human soul, but is the righteousness of Jesus Christ imputed to those who believe. The Council of Trent anathematized those who embrace this doctrine, and all subsequent magisterial declarations, including those of the Second Vatican Council, continue to bind Roman Catholics to the conviction that this Gospel of free justification by faith alone, apart from works, and the assurance of salvation that springs from it, is not consonant with Roman Catholic teaching. While gladly noting in modern Roman Catholic exposition a growing emphasis on Christ and the biblical promises as objects of faith and trust, we see justification by faith alone as an essential of the Gospel on which radical disagreement continues, and we deny the adequacy of any version of the Gospel that falls short at this point.

3. Furthermore, while rejoicing in our agreement that God in the Gospel offers salvation in Christ to all who will receive it, we radically disagree with the teaching of the Second Vatican Council that unbelievers may be saved by their good works, apart from faith in Christ.

4. The extent of the creedal consensus that binds orthodox Evangelicals and Roman Catholics together warrants the making of common cause on moral and cultural issues in society. Roman Catholics and Evangelicals have every reason to join minds, hearts and hands when Christian values and behavioral patterns are at stake. Yet it is incorrect to regard such cooperation among Christians as common ecclesial action in fulfilling a common ecclesial mission. The mission of the Church as such is primarily the fulfilling of the Great Commission of Christ through the ministry of Word and sacraments, and cultural, moral, political and social concerns in which Christians rightly engage must not be thought to determine the relationship of ecclesial communions, or allowed to become decisive in the setting of their respective agendas.

5. We affirm that Christ's prayer for unity requires vigilant patience and diligence as we seek a greater visible unity. We deny that this prayer refers merely to the spiritual or invisible Church. We further affirm that

the unity we seek is shaped, bounded, and controlled by the teaching of the canonical Scriptures, the written Word of God, comprising the Law and the Gospel in its message of reconciliation with God and new life in Christ. To this Word the Church must submit and by it must correct its understandings, so that its unity will be unity in truth. The Roman Catholic Church claims to be graced with an infallibility that attaches to conciliar declarations and Papal pronouncements ex cathedra, such that these are in principle irreformable, and must be treated as decisive guides to the theological interpretation of the Bible. We deny that the defined doctrines of the Church's infallibility, Papal primacy, justification according to Trent, transubstantiation and eucharistic sacrifice, and the immaculate conception and assumption of Mary, can be proved from Scripture, and we cannot accept any form of joint action that appears to imply agreement with them. Also, we deny that visible unity has been or can be achieved where a common confession of the Gospel in all its essential elements is lacking.

6. We affirm that individual Roman Catholics who for whatever reason do not self-consciously assent to the precise definitions of the Roman Catholic magisterium regarding justification, the sole mediation of Christ, the relation between faith and the sacraments, the divine monergism of the new birth, and similar matters of evangelical conviction, but who think and speak evangelically about these things, are indeed our brothers and sisters in Christ, despite Rome's official position. We perceive that the Roman Catholic Church contains many such believers. We deny, however, that in its present confession it is an acceptable Christian communion, let alone being the mother of all the faithful to whom every believer needs to be related.

7. We affirm that the Great Commission of our Lord requires every Christian and every congregation to be engaged in witness to Christ, and that this is concerned not merely with conversion, but with the catechesis, nurture, and discipline of converts. Therefore, we deny that is it advisable to imply that whether one is in a church where the Word is rightly preached and the sacraments are rightly (that is, biblically) administered is no longer important; and we insist that every Christian, Roman Catholic no less than Protestant, needs regular exposure to accurate, Christ-centered preaching and exposition of the Bible.

I hoped that this statement, bearing as it did the names of three who had signed ECT (Richard Land, John White, and myself) would remove all doubt as to whether support for ECT implied any minimizing of the theological difficulties with self-defined Catholicism that classic Protestantism has felt for over four centuries. At leadership level, however, this proved not to be the case, and there were some sharp exchanges. On January 25, 1995, however, the following press release was issued:

## EVANGELICAL LEADERS RESOLVE DIFFERENCES ON EVANGELICAL-CATHOLIC PAPER

At the request of Prison Fellowship chairman Chuck Colson, a group of evangelical leaders and theologians met on January 19, 1995 to discuss a number of issues relating to the "Evangelicals and Catholics Together" (ECT) statement that was released last spring. It was the second such meeting called by Colson. The intent of both Colson and those in attendance was to achieve a measure of understanding, clarification and harmony around the truth as recognized by historic orthodoxy.

This meeting included two signers of the ECT document in addition to Chuck Colson; J. I.Packer, and Bill Bright. Also participating were John Ankerberg, Michael Horton, John MacArthur, R. C. Sproul, Joe Stowell, John Woodbridge, and D. James Kennedy, who hosted the meeting at Coral Ridge Presbyterian Church in Ft. Lauderdale, Florida.

Discussion focused on evangelical distinctives, particularly the definition and nature of the gospel. The group, without reservation, affirmed its commitment to justification by faith alone in Jesus Christ as central to the gospel.

Out of this meeting has come the attached statement, initially drafted by J. I. Packer, that will carry the signatures of Packer, Bright, Colson, and Kent Hill, one of the original ECT drafters. It is being circulated among the other Protestant signers of ECT for their signature as well.

## STATEMENT BY PROTESTANT SIGNERS TO ECT

January 19, 1995

We Protestants who signed ECT took this action to advance Christian fellowship, cooperation, and mutual trust among true Christians in the North American cultural crisis and in the worldwide task of evangelism. The same concern leads us now to elucidate our ECT commitment by stating:

1. Our parachurch cooperation with evangelically committed Roman Catholics for the pursuit of agreed objectives does not imply acceptance of Roman Catholic doctrinal distinctives or endorsement of the Roman Catholic church system.

2. We understand the statement that "we are justified by grace through faith because of Christ," in terms of the substitutionary atonement and imputed righteousness of Christ, leading to full assurance of eternal salvation; we seek to testify in all circumstances and contexts to this, the historic Protestant understanding of salvation by faith alone (*sola fide*).

3. While we view all who profess to be Christian—Protestant and Catholic and Orthodox—with charity and hope, our confidence that anyone is truly a brother or sister in Christ depends not only on the content of his or her confession but on our perceiving signs of regeneration in his or her life.

4. Though we reject proselytizing as ECT defines it (that is "sheep-stealing" for denominational aggrandizement), we hold that evangelism and church planting are always legitimate, whatever forms of church life are present already.

5. We think that the further theological discussions that ECT promised should begin as soon as possible.

We make these applicatory clarifications of our commitment as supporters of ECT in order to prevent divisive misunderstandings of our beliefs and purposes.

## Personal Persuasions

At this point I must state explicitly that I am not and could not become a Roman Catholic because of certain basic tenets to which the Roman system, as such, is committed. First, Rome's claim to be the only institution that can without qualification be called the Church of Christ seems to me theologically flawed, for it misconceives the nature of the Church as the New Testament writers explain it. In the New Testament the Church is not a sacramental and juridical organization sustained by priests channeling divine life through set rituals, but it is a worldwide fellowship of believers who share in the resurrection life of the Lord Jesus Christ and enjoy unity with each other by virtue of the spiritual union with Christ himself that their baptism proclaims. Wherever groups of believers join together to do the things that the apostolic writers tell us the Church does, there the New Testament sees the one

Church becoming visible. Bowing to Peter among the apostles as having definitive personal and pastoral authority over all the congregations, in the way that Roman Catholicism today makes acceptance of the papacy a defining mark of Catholic identity, is not however part of the New Testament picture. Nor does the fact that John Paul II is a wonderful man who has done a wonderful job as a world Christian ambassador make the papacy a credible institution or the Catholic claim to conciliar and *ex cathedra* infallibility at all plausible.

Moreover, the papacy, which is supposed to be of the Church's essence, was a relatively late development; if pipeline continuity of priestly orders and a sacramentalist soteriology, all under hierarchical leadership, are of the essence of the Church on earth, then Eastern Orthodoxy's claim to be Christ's one Church is stronger.

Again, the developed Roman Catholic teaching on the Mass and on merit, whereby the Church through its offering is given a significant share in putting away its sins and the Christian's good works are given a significant share in the securing of eventual acceptance, cuts across Paul's doctrine of present justification (pardon and acceptance for eternity) in and through Jesus Christ, a blessing that is instrumentally secured by faith alone without reference to any form of works of law. And all modes of the Marian cult, of the invoking of other saints, and of the belief in purgatory, and all reliance on the disbursing of indulgences (which still goes on, as in Luther's day, and is explained and justified in the new *Catechism*[3]), have the effect of cutting across, choking up, and damping down the full joyful assurance of present and future salvation to which, according to Scripture (see Rom. 5:1–11, 8:1–39), justification ordinarily leads through the ministry of the Holy Spirit.

Finally, the infallibility claimed for all defined church teaching and the insistence that the faithful take their beliefs from the Church as such rather than the Bible as such make self-correction as ordinarily understood virtually impossible within Roman Catholicism. The assumption that on basics the Church is never wrong is very cramping.

So, as the Horton-Packer document states, I am not able to affirm of the Roman Catholic Church that "in its present confession it is an acceptance Christian communion." What I mean by that is that Rome's official doctrinal disorders, particularly on justification, merit, and the Mass-sacrifice, so obscure the gospel that were I, as a gesture of unity, invited to mass—which of course as a Protestant I am not, nor shall be—I would not feel free to accept the invitation.

Why then should I, or any Protestant like me, want to develop mission activity in partnership with Roman Catholics? What reason is there to abandon the historic pattern of isolationism? Traditionally, as I have noted already, Protestants and Catholics have kept their distance, treating each other as inferiors; each community has seen the other as out to deny precious elements in its own faith and practice and so has given the other a wide berth. Why should anyone, and how could anyone, adjust this?

## Why Attempt Adjustment?

Despite the shortcomings of Rome's official teaching, there are many Roman Catholic Christians: believers in the Trinity, the Incarnation, the Atonement, and the historic Resurrection, present heavenly reign, and future personal return of Jesus Christ; disciples, worshipers, and lovers of Jesus; humble, self-despairing, joyful, Holy Spirit-oriented people with a story of how God made himself known to them and a spirit that resonates totally with the recent words of Roman Catholic evangelist and renewal preacher Ralph Martin:

> If you have never opened your heart to him [Jesus] before, do it now. . . . If you have never really surrendered your life to him, do so now. . . . If you have never given him your hurt, pain, and disappointment, your anger, bitterness, and resentments, do so now. . . . If you have never given him your biggest worries and greatest fears and most profound anxieties, do so now. . . . Perhaps this prayer will express something of what is in your heart:
>
> Lord Jesus, I come to you weary and burdened, guilty and fearful, hopeless even. I surrender. I give my life back to you. I put my trust in you, the true and only Savior of the world and my Savior. Forgive me my sins. Make me clean again so that the hope of eternal life may arise in my heart. Send me your Spirit, pour out your love into my heart, so I may begin again, believing, hoping, and loving, each day, until we are united forever in heaven. . . .
>
> As Catholics we are sometimes characterized by our lack of boldness and confidence when it comes to our own relationship with God

or sharing the good news with others. . . . I believe the main factor is a fundamental lack of clarity and understanding about the basis of our standing with God, about the basics of salvation. . . .

Catholics quite simply need to know Christ more. We need to know how great his love is, how great his sacrifice for us is, how steadfast his love for us is, so we can repent and believe and let the hope that brings freedom and boldness be born and grow in our hearts.[4]

I, for one, thank God for the wisdom, maturity of mind and conscience, backbone and sheer guts, reverence before God, and above all love for my Lord Jesus Christ, that I have seen many times in Catholics. I hope Catholics see fruits of grace in Protestants comparable to what this Protestant sometimes sees in them. Legalism, immorality, formalism, pharisaism (living by rule without heart), and pride are blights from which evangelicalism is observably not free, but Roman Catholics misstatings of the gospel, backed by the assurance that you can trust the Church to look after your eternal welfare, would seem to give them a head start; nonetheless, the joyful fact is that many Catholics seem unscathed by them. Such is grace!

It is Roman Catholics of this kind, with evangelical Protestants who match them, that ECT's drafters prove themselves to be when they declare that they accept Jesus Christ as Lord and Savior, affirm the Apostles' Creed, "are justified by grace through faith because of Christ," see the Christian life throughout as sustained personal conversion to Christ, and on this basis are "brothers and sisters in Christ." To want to see such Catholics and evangelicals standing and working together to uphold Christian values and spread the news about Jesus Christ is surely a natural and, if the Lund principle has any validity, a necessary desire. This, then, without going further, is sufficient reason for asking if there is a way to uncompromising and uncompromised togetherness in the mission on which Christ sends us all.

## Working Jointly through Parachurch Associations

But *how* can the desired shift—that is, from separateness to togetherness, and from rivalry to cooperation, in specific mission tasks—actually take place? Formal linkage between the mission arms of the Roman

Catholic Church and Protestant groups or churches is not possible without compromising convictions of truth on both sides, and ECT does not propose such linkage—so all the criticisms of ECT that have seen it as a call to evangelicals to fit into patterns of action set by some Roman body are mistaken. Cooperation with the Roman Catholic *Church* is not what ECT is about. The path of joint action that ECT envisages is not churchly but parachurchly.

What does that mean? The idea is no novelty, for parachurch associations have spread like wildfire during the past century. A parachurch body is a company of Christians who together pursue churchly goals—that is, goals that the Christian community as such is called to aim at—and who see themselves as an auxiliary agency, stockpiling and deploying resources to do what otherwise would not be done and thus filling a gap in the ministry of existing churches. Parachurch bodies, in the nature of the case, are independent of the churches and accountable only to their own supporters; but, since they aim to serve the churches and to serve others on behalf of the churches, it is proper, also in the nature of the case, that they keep close to the churches, report to them, plan with them, maintain with them a mutuality of interest, care, and prayer, and look to them to embrace the vision out of which the organization was born and which it now seeks to fulfill. Protestant examples include transdenominational educational units; missionary societies and student ministry structures; evangelistic agencies; and agencies for pastoral care and support.

How, in terms of theology, should we view parachurch bodies, in their association with, yet independence of, the churches? They are not themselves churches, nor are they trying to be, for they do not attempt to do everything that according to the New Testament the church does (administer communion or baptism, for instance); yet they see themselves as an arm of the church, serving the church by extending its bounds and influence and giving strength to its structures.

## The Biblical Rationale for Parachurch Associations

What biblical rationale is there for such bodies? The simplest rationale, and to my mind the soundest and truest, is in terms of the kingdom of God. Foretold by Old Testament prophets, announced by Jesus as a reality that his own ministry was effecting, and functioning as a frame of reference throughout the New Testament (where sometimes it is spoken of as the kingdom of Christ, the enthroned Lord), the kingdom is not a geographical but a relational entity, sovereign, messianic, and eschatological. It is sovereign, because it is God who in the exercise of his royal dominion over his world sets it up and creates and sustains the relationships that constitute it. It is messianic because it is by faith in Jesus the Messiah, God's appointed Savior-King, that people enter the kingdom, and it is the prophesied life of messianic *shalom*—pardon, peace, and joyful fellowship with God—that they find within it. It is eschatological because this is the start of the life of heaven, which will endure for eternity. The kingdom of God exists wherever Christ reigns as king and God's revealed will is actually done. The life of the faithful disciple is the kingdom—that is, the rule of Christ—in individual manifestation; the life of the faithful congregation is the kingdom in corporate manifestation; and the life of a faithful parachurch body is the kingdom in a form of executive manifestation, inasmuch as all the doings of such a body aim to be kingdom activities, gestures of obedience to Christ that express and extend his rule over human lives. This is evidently the kind of joint action, a parachurch togetherness in the pursuit of specific Christ-honoring goals, that ECT has in view.

In the world of English-speaking evangelicalism, with its typical activist mindset and missionary outlook, parachurch bodies that reached out to tackle churchly tasks for which the organized churches lacked expertise, resources, and sometimes focused motivation, have been establishing themselves, usually under the name of societies, fellowships, or alliances, for the best part of two hundred years. These bodies found acceptance and were blessed and used by God before any question of their theological status and legitimacy was raised. When raised, that question has regularly been resolved in kingdom terms, as stated above, and on this basis patterns of appreciative partnership between churches and parachurch agencies have emerged in the spheres of both social and evangelistic action.

ECT is tentatively feeling its way towards a pattern of this kind that would involve Roman Catholics and would seek to do so on a principled basis, without compromise on either side. The difficulties are obvious; but should the desired cooperative action prove to be practical politics, it would be an event of watershed significance. What form the pattern might take is not yet clear to anyone; what is being explored is whether the quest for such a pattern is not an idea whose time has come.

# Responding to the Critics

My own support for ECT is to be taken as support for this exploration, because I think it very possible that its time has indeed come. For half a lifetime I have publicly proclaimed and defended as biblical and true the Reformed theology that was given shape (by Calvin) in direct opposition to Roman Catholic teaching on revelation, salvation, and the Church, and I maintain this theology and this opposition still. But for the same half lifetime I have thought that informal grass-roots collaboration with Roman Catholics in ministry is the most fruitful sort of ecumenism that one can practice.

My own experience here has been happy (I know that not everyone can say that, but I can): task-force cooperation with Roman Catholics on the basis of shared loyalty to undisputed biblical teaching and to the Christ of Scripture has brought me pleasure and profit, and I have found working in Catholic-Protestant, charismatic-ecumenical networks for the faith of the creeds and the vitality of Christians consistently enriching. I notice that at ground level many Protestants in the Western world give similar testimony. Is God then starting something through ECT? I do not know, but I think it is worth giving time and labor to find out.

To avoid both being compromised and compromising others in joint evangelistic action will certainly not be easy. As section four of the Horton-Packer statement declared, when it is a matter of standing together for Christian moral and cultural values in society no problem of evangelical-Roman Catholic divergence is involved, but when the aim is to proclaim Christ the Savior together the case is different. Neither evangelicals nor Roman Catholics can stipulate that things they believe, which the other side does not believe, be made foundational to partnership at this point; so ECT lets go Protestant precision on the doctrine of justification and the correlation between conversion and new birth, just as it lets go the Roman Catholic dogmas of baptismal regeneration and the sacramental structure of the doctrine of grace. Nor may the basis for partnership be so drawn up as to invite doubt on whether either party still holds to those of its tenets that are not mentioned, or to cramp its style when the time for reasserting those tenets comes. ECT shows skill here, and those who read it as an irresponsible sellout of Protestantism have simply not appreciated what it was up to. In this connection I now respond to the six criticisms of it listed earlier:

1. The first criticism was that it is wrong to call Roman Catholics our brothers and sisters in Christ. As my quote from Ralph Martin showed, however, some Catholics do accept Jesus as Lord and Savior in a fully personal way; and it was Paul who said, "You are all sons of God through faith in Christ Jesus" (Gal. 3:26 NIV; cf. Mark 3:35). But in this connection the third point of the Fort Lauderdale statement should also be borne in mind: "While we view all who profess to be Christian . . . with charity and hope, our confidence that anyone is truly a brother or sister in Christ depends not only on the content of his or her confession but on our perceiving signs of regeneration in his or her life."

2. The second criticism was that it is unrealistic to suppose that living by the infallible Scriptures means the same for Catholics as it does for evangelicals, since the magisterium imposes its own sense on the text. In fact, though, the number of texts magisterially expounded in a sense that evangelicals must dispute hardly reaches to double figures, and for the rest Catholics are as free as Protestants to let the Bible interpret itself to them in its own terms.

3. The third criticism was that the formula "we are justified by grace through faith because of Christ" masks such radical disagreement as to express two different gospels, one of which is not a true gospel. Certainly, the Tridentine assertion of merit and the Reformational assertion of imputed righteousness can hardly be harmonized, and no doubt there are many Catholics today, as there are certainly many Protestants, who do not focus on the living Christ as Lord, Savior, and coming King, or make him the direct object of their faith and hope. (I imagine some traditional Catholics, for whom the Church rather than Christ is the primary focus of faith, will have problems with ECT at this point, though today's Catholic theologians observably do not.) But surely ECT's insistence that the Christ of Scripture and the creeds is faith's proper object, and that "Christian witness is of necessity aimed at conversion," both as an initial step and also as a personal life-process, constitutes a sufficient account of the gospel for shared evangelistic ministry. Evangelism seeks to lead people into salvation, and what brings them salvation is not any theory about faith and justification, but trusting Jesus himself as Lord, Master, and divine Savior, in line with Ralph Martin's verbalization quoted earlier. Inasmuch as this knowledge of the nature of faith is not unknown among Catholics, it would seem

simply untrue to say that the result of their holding to Augustine's theory of justification (for that is what the teaching of Trent and the *Catechism* really is) is that they have no gospel, just as it would be untrue to say that Augustine himself by the same token had no gospel.

4. The fourth criticism was that baptismal regeneration, which evangelicals see as an error that can ruin souls, is tolerated by ECT as acceptable doctrine. But ECT's real logic here, as the careful reader will see, is that agreement on the necessity of personal conversion to the Christ of the Bible and the creeds makes evangelistic cooperation fully viable despite Catholic belief about baptism, inasmuch as any thought that baptism without personal faith will save anyone is hereby ruled out. Belief in baptismal regeneration only brings ruin where baptism is thought to make conversion unnecessary. John Wesley's belief in baptismal regeneration, for instance, was harmless in practice because he stressed the universal need for conversion. And ECT's allowance of the Roman Catholic view of baptism would be harmless in practice too, for the same reason.

5. The fifth criticism was that it is irresponsible to let Roman Catholics who have been converted choose to go back to their churches, since they will not be nurtured there. But nothing in the document forbids explaining to new converts the pros and cons of choosing a church, and the importance, for growth, of being under faithful ministry of the Word, preferably in the company of people with whom one can pray about the truths being taught. In the same way, nothing in the document forbids sharing Christ with inactive, nominal, lifeless-looking adherents of any communion. All that is ruled out is associating salvation or spiritual health with churchly identity, as if a Roman Catholic cannot be saved without becoming a Protestant or vice versa, and on this basis putting people under pressure to change churches.

6. The sixth objection was that church-planting evangelism in Roman Catholic parts of the world would have to stop if ECT went ahead. This was neither said nor meant. As the Fort Lauderdale statement puts it, "Evangelism and church planting are always legitimate, whatever forms of church life are present already." Free association for religious purposes is a recognized human right, and church-planting as the next step after evangelism is a constant Christian task.

## The Case for Collaboration

Some maintain that any form of parachurch collaboration between Protestant evangelicals and Roman Catholics in evangelism will inevitably be so muted or mutilated an affair as not to be worth the effort. The reason given is that the specifics of the evangelical doctrine of justification and of regeneration, however strongly held, cannot be made standard in the enterprise, since Roman theology with supposed infallibility rejects them. Some condemn the making of the effort as undiscerning folly, on two grounds: first, no real trust in Christ for salvation is possible until the Reformational account of justification by grace alone through faith alone on the ground of Christ's imputed righteousness (merit) alone is embraced (a position implying that Athanasius, Augustine, Anselm, and Aquinas were not real believers); second, the Roman Catholic Church is fallen and has become anti-Christian by embracing false soteriology, and loyal Christians should keep away from it and oppose it at all times in matters relating to the gospel. Others, remembering Jesus' tale of the justified tax collector (Luke 18:14), his words of forgiveness to some who trusted him without knowing the doctrine of justification (Luke 5:20, 7:48), and his reminder to his disciples that "whoever is not against you is for you" (Luke 9:50 NIV), do not go so far, but still doubt whether developing evangelistic cooperation is the best option, given the restrictions that will inevitably apply. Others, however, with mission and church-planting concerns in communities where Roman Catholics are strong, will wish to explore further the vision of evangelistic partnership that ECT broaches.

History, theology, triumphalism, and old habits of vilifying the other party make this exploration a tricky business at best, over and above the unsettling fact that many of the explorers' coreligionists on both sides doubt the value of such a venture and fear its consequences. Mutual tolerance and trust, whereby all are given room to say and do what each thinks right and none try to dominate or stifle others' consciences, would seem to be very important here.

## The Value of Exploring the Vision

There are basically two reasons why some want to explore ECT's vision further:

1. *The truth calls for it.* Though Protestant and Catholic church systems stand opposed and official beliefs diverge on major aspects of the doctrine of salvation, those who love and trust the Lord Jesus Christ on both sides of the Reformation divide know that they are in a real sense united in him and are joint heirs of glory not only with him but with each other. Jesus' high-priestly prayer for the unity of his disciples as a visible reality in their life on earth (see John. 17:20-23) therefore weighs heavily on their minds. This prayer clearly entails the thought that God's one international family should seek to look and sound like one family by speaking and acting as such, and that means aiming at togetherness wherever togetherness can be achieved. The alternative is to grieve the Lord. So where there is fellowship in personal faith, fellowship in service should follow, and the cherishing of isolationism as the more comfortable and less demanding way would be sin. The quest for togetherness in mission, up to the limit of what conscience on both sides allows, is thus both permissible and desirable.

2. *The times call for it.* The present needs of both Church and community in the Western world (not to look further for the moment) cry out for an alliance of all who love the Bible and its Christ to stand together against the slide into secularism and paganism that is so much a mark of current culture. Vital for the Church's welfare and the well-being of society itself at this time is the building of the strongest possible transdenominational coalition of Bible-believing, Christ-honoring, Spirit-empowered Christians who will together resist the many forms of disintegrative theology—relativist, monist, pluralist, liberationist, feminist, and the rest—that plague organized Christianity, and the many forms of postmodern subjectivity that are disintegrating the educational, familial, and political heritage of the West. Such a coalition already exists among evangelicals, sustained by parachurch bodies, media, mission programs and agencies, and a wide range of literature. The stand for truth and wisdom would be stronger if this coalition were in closer step with the parallel Roman Catholic activities that have begun to emerge, aiming at similar goals.

Time was when Western Christendom's deepest division was between relatively homogeneous Protestant churches and a relatively homogeneous Church of Rome. Today, however, the deepest and most hurtful division is between theological conservatives ("conservationists," as I would rather call them), who honor the Christ of the Bible and the historic creeds and confessions, and theological liberals and radicals who for whatever reason do not; and this division splits the older Protestant bodies and the Roman Catholic communion equally, from the inside. Convictional renewal within the churches can only come, under God, through sustained exposition, affirmation, and debate, and since it is substantially the same battle that has to be fought across the board, a coalition of evangelical and Catholic resources for the purpose would surely make sense.

It is similarly vital for the health of society, specifically in North America, that adherents to the key truths of classical Christianity—a self-defining Triune God who is both Creator and Redeemer, this God's re-generating and sanctifying grace, the sanctity of life here, the certainty of personal judgment hereafter, and the future return of Jesus Christ to end history—should link up for the vast and pressing task of reeducating our secularized communities on these matters. North American culture generally has lost its former knowledge of what it means to revere God, and hence it is in process of losing its values and standards, its shared purposes, its focused hopes, and even its knowledge of what makes human life human. Materialism, hedonism, and nihilism, lumped together and miscalled *humanism*, is all it now has left. Again, it is the theological conservationists, and they alone, who have resources for the rebuilding of these ruins, and domestic differences about salvation and the Church should not hinder us from joint action in seeking to re-Christianize the North American milieu. But the apologia for Christian values in society is only going to carry credibility if the view of reality in which it is rooted takes hold once more of people's minds. So propagating the basic faith remains the crucial task; and it is natural to think it will best be done as a combined operation, with a combined call to Christian commitment as its focal center. Maximizing togetherness in witness at all levels will therefore be a timely move.

## Christ-Centered Unity

One swallow does not make a summer, nor does one trickle, or a set of trickles, make a river; but it is worth noting here that mission ventures involving evangelicals and Catholics side by side not only in social witness but also in evangelism and nurture have already begun to appear. Billy Graham's cooperative evangelism, in which all the churches of an area are invited to share, is one such. Charismatic gatherings where the distinction between Protestant and Catholic vanishes in a Christ-centered unity of worship, fellowship and joy, are a further example. Could it be that ECT is fuel for a fire that is already alight? Might it be right to see ECT not as running ahead of God, as some fear, but rather as responding to the Holy Spirit, formulating at the level of principle a commitment into which there has already been entry at the level of practice? It seems clear that the burden of proof must rest on any who wish to deny that this is so.

In any case, however, ECT is only a beginning. Those for whom anti-Romanism or anti-Protestantism is part of their identity and ministry will need more than ECT to alter their mindset, and there are many such. Protestants who deny that Roman Catholics can be Christians without leaving Rome will also need persuading and may well remain unpersuaded. ECT's initiative cannot be expected to make rapid head-way in the entrenched situation that so largely pertains. Also, there must be now a rigorous review of how the historic points of theological divi-sion look in light of the commitment to witness and contend together. Well does ECT say, "The differences and disagreements . . . must be ad-dressed more fully and candidly in order to strengthen between us a relation of trust in obedience to truth." Without this ECT will get no-where, nor will it deserve to.

But ECT is a good beginning. I stand with it (I cannot do otherwise) and for it I thank God. Now I wait to see what God will do with it.

## Notes

1. Michael Horton, "What Still Keeps Us Apart?" in *Roman Catholicism*, ed. John Armstrong (Chicago: Moody Press, 1994), 257.
2. The names, in alphabetical order, are as follows: John Armstrong (Reforma-tion and Revival Ministries); Steve Baugh (Westminster Theological Semi-nary); James M. Boice (Tenth Presbyterian Church, Philadelphia); Timothy Brewer (Central Presbyterian Church, St. Louis); Edmund Clowney (Westminster Theological Seminary); J. Ligon Duncan (Reformed Theologi-cal Seminary); Richard Gaffin (Westminster Theological Seminary); Ronald Gleason (Ligonier Ministries, Canada); Michael J. Glodo (Reformed Theological Seminary); W. Robert Godfrey (Westminster Theological Semi-nary); Darryl Hart (Westminster Theological Seminary); Michael Horton

(Christians United for Reformation); Frank James (Reformed Theological Seminary); Dennis Johnson (Westminster Theological Seminary); Kenneth R. Jones (Christians United for Reformation); Richard Land (Southern Baptist Convention); Art Lindsley (C. S. Lewis Institute); Erwin Lutzer (Moody Memorial Church, Chicago); James Martin (Pennsylvania State University); Allen Mawhinney (Reformed Theological Seminary); John Warwick Montgomery (Luton University, England); John Meuther (Reformed Theological Seminary); Tom Nettles (Trinity Evangelical Divinity School); Roger Nicole (Reformed Theological Seminary); Ron Noel (Reformed Theological Seminary); Joseph A. Pipa, Jr. (Westminster Theological Seminary); Robert Preus (Concordia Seminary); J. I.Packer (Regent College); Kim Riddlebarger (Christians United for Reformation); Rod Rosenbladt (Concordia University); R. C. Sproul (Ligonier Minsitries); Robert Strimple (Westminster Theological Seminary); Willem Van Gemeren (Trinity Evangelical Divinity School); David Wells (Gordon-Conwell Theological Seminary); John White (Geneva College).

3   "An indulgence is obtained through the Church who, by virtue of the power of binding and loosing granted her by Christ Jesus, intervenes in favor of individual Christians and opens for them the treasury of the merits of Christ and the saints to obtain from the Father of mercies the remission of the temporal punishments due for their sins. . . . Since the faithful departed now being purified [in Purgatory] are also members of the same communion of saints, one way we can help them is to obtain indulgences for them, so that the temporal punishments due for their sins may be remitted" (*Catechism of the Catholic Church* [Mahwah, N.J: Paulist Press, 1994], nos. 1478, 1479; 371 f.). The catechism draws on the "Apostolic Constitution of Pope Paul VI," *Indulgentiarum Doctrina*, 1 January 1967.

4   Ralph Martin, *The Catholic Church at the End of an Age* (San Francisco: Ignatius Press, 1994), 246, 258 f.

# 6

# The Catholic Difference

Richard John Neuhaus

Be not afraid!

*Pope John Paul II*

THE GREEK *kairos* suggests an opportune and decisive moment, a "fullness of time" when something can happen, when something must happen, that could not happen until then. The term is employed in the telling of the biblical story of salvation. Also in the continuing life of the Christian community, there may come a fullness of time when something new—we know not quite what—may be afoot. In his many comments on the coming of the third millennium, Pope John Paul II, while rejecting all forms of millennialistic enthusiasm, calls Christians to a heightened sense of expectation, to be on full alert to a new thing that God may be doing. In reflecting on the promise of the Christian mission in the next century, he has spoken variously about its possibly being a "springtime of evangelization" and a "springtime of Christian unity."

This is not to be confused with optimism. Optimism is simply a matter of optics, of the human propensity to see what we want to see and blind ourselves to the disagreeable. Rather, this heightened sense of expectation is a matter of Christian hope, and Christian hope is unblinkingly realistic. It is hope in the face of threats and dangers clearly posited against such hope. The Christian people are graced to live not in fear of what threatens but with hope in their promise-making and promise-keeping Lord. Such hope is always conjoined to the other two theological virtues, faith and love. Hope is not mere hopefulness but is grounded in the trust that is faith and in the gift and command that is love.

John Paul's 1994 book, *Crossing the Threshold of Hope*, bears the epigram "Be not afraid!" That was the theme of his sermon when he was inaugurated as bishop of Rome in October 1978. "Be not afraid!" he cried to the Christians then living under the Communist tyranny. But the cry was addressed to all Christians everywhere, and indeed to the whole of the human community. Be not afraid to believe, be not afraid to hope, be not afraid to love. Not only Catholics and not only Christians, but the entire world has watched with wonder as millions have responded and continue to respond to the witness of this pope. There is a tremor of an intimation that something like a *kairos* may be at hand.

## Something Like a Kairos

On a scale much smaller, a sense of heightened expectation has been stirred in many quarters by "Evangelicals and Catholics Together" (ECT). One of America's most prominent evangelical scholars told me that, upon receiving the declaration, he stayed up all night reading and rereading it, and fell on his knees to thank God that something so long prayed for was at last happening. Of course not all the responses have been so favorable, and some have been sharply, even vehemently, negative. In this essay I will address some of the criticisms that ECT has occasioned. But before doing so, we should reflect with sober hope on some of the reasons for thinking that ours may be a moment of something like a *kairos*.

ECT may be forgotten ten years from now, never mind a hundred years from now. None of us can know. I believe the declaration and the discussion it is generating will be a continuing point of reference for many years to come. I say this not because of the inherent merits of the document itself, but because it reflects a historic reorientation in our understanding of the Christian mission in and to the world. The century now coming to its close has in many respects been the bloodiest and most oppressive in human history. Utopian ideologies explicitly pitted against the Christian truth have piled up mountains of corpses and let loose rivers of blood. It has been the century of greatest Christian martyrdom and also the century of greatest missionary expansion in the two thousand year history of the Church.

The utopian impulse (which is rightly directed to the kingdom of God) will not disappear. Sinful humanity will undoubtedly come up with other proposed political substitutes for the kingdom of God. But the great and immeasurably destructive political eschatologies of this century, Nazism and Marxist-Leninism, now lie in the ashes. In addition, we are witnessing all around us the collapse of the hegemony of a secular Enlightenment, a scientism disguised as science, that succeeded for a long time in excluding Christian truth claims from public consideration. It is not too much to say that, as we enter the third millennium, the world-historical stage has been largely cleared to make room for the presentation of the Christian understanding of the human drama, the Divine-human drama that is the story of salvation. And it is not too much to believe that it is for this moment that God is bringing evangelicals and Catholics together to present to the world its promised future in Jesus Christ.

A humanity sated on the false freedoms by which it was so bitterly deceived is perhaps newly open to the One who said, "You will know the truth, and the truth will make you free" (John 8:32 RSV). An intellectual elite that so long and so smugly claimed that the question of Pilate—"What is truth?"—was the mark of enlightenment has now largely lost its confidence in the certitudes of the gospel of uncertainty. Freedom defined as freedom from the truth turns out to be no freedom at all. Freedom that is not ordered to truth and grounded in truth is but captivity to impulse, appetite, and license. In our intellectual culture, but also in large sectors of the popular culture, such false freedom is the debonair nihilism that struts about in the fancy dress of postmodernism, pretending not to be afraid of a world without truth.

So it turns out that Christianity is today the champion of universal truth and of universal human rights based on the dignity of man created in the image of God. It has been observed that history has many ironies in the fire. Few ironies are so rich as the fact that, three hundred years later, the genuine achievements of the Enlightenment, which were thought to have been secured against Christianity, are now most firmly secured and vigorously advanced by Christianity. With respect to universal human rights and the truth about the human person that undergirds the concept of human rights, I believe that future historians will recognize the conflict over abortion as a critical turning point. In the late 1960s in the United States, all the establishment institutions of politics, education, and communications favored the "liberalized abortion law" that was decreed by the Supreme Court in the *Roe v. Wade* decision of 1973 (which, in fact, did not liberalize abortion law but abolished abortion law). At the time, the only major institution in dissent was the Catholic Church. By the late 1970s, largely thanks to the remarkable ministry of Francis Schaeffer, evangelicals were alerted and activated to come to the defense of the gift of life. The evangelicals and Catholics who found one another in the pro-life cause knew they were not simply cobelligerents in a political movement. Behind the political agreement was the discovery of agreement about moral truth, expressed in terms of common grace or natural law. Undergirding it all was the discovery of a shared allegiance to the Author of truth and a shared faith in the One who is the way, the truth, and the life.

The most important affirmation of ECT is this: "All who accept Christ as Lord and Savior are brothers and sisters in Christ. Evangelicals and Catholics are brothers and sisters in Christ. We have not chosen one another, just as we have not chosen Christ. He has chosen us, and he has chosen us to be his together." Interestingly, critics on both the left and the right are skeptical about that affirmation. Liberal Christians have claimed that ECT is no more than a sociopolitical compact between Christian conservatives. In their view, the theological affirmations of the document are but a veneer thinly disguising an alliance in America's culture wars. Critics who describe themselves as evangelical or fundamentalist agree with the liberal opponents of ECT, except they claim it is and *should be* nothing more than a statement of cobelligerency in the public square. In their view, the theological affirmations of the document are not so much a deceptive veneer as they are a reflection of the naiveté of evangelicals who were taken in by their Catholic counterparts in the drafting of the statement. Sometimes this last claim has been expressed quite virulently, with ECT being condemned as part of a vast conspiracy by which evangelicals are being seduced into betraying the Reformation and "returning to Rome." Some of the promoters of this conspiracy theory evidence a mindset that is aptly described as paranoid.

At the same time, there are theologically serious critics who believe that ECT did not attend sufficiently to the distinctives of Reformation Christianity. This essay is in large part a response to those concerns. There has been little theological criticism of ECT from the Catholic side. The most obvious reason for this is that Catholics are accustomed to ecumenical engagement with other Christians, and such engagement holds no fears. By contrast, and for perfectly understandable reasons—some of which will be addressed in this essay—*ecumenical* is for many evangelicals a highly suspect term.

As one evangelical critic put it to me, "Our worry is about the third and hidden "c." By that he meant that ECT talks about "convergence and cooperation" between evangelicals and Catholics, but the worry is that behind such talk is another "c"—conversion. That worry, I am told, is not alleviated by the fact that one of the main participants in ECT is an evangelical Lutheran who became a Roman Catholic. I would be deeply grieved if my role in ECT became an obstacle to its reception among evangelical Protestants. As a Catholic, honesty requires that I represent the ecclesiological claims of Catholicism without trimming or dissimulation. For evangelicals, there would be little point in engaging in evangelical-Catholic conversation with Catholics who are not authentically Catholic. I know for a certainty with respect to my intentions, and I am confident with respect to the intentions of the other Catholic participants, that ECT is not about persuading evangelicals to become Roman Catholic.

There are, and there will no doubt continue to be, conversions: evangelical Protestants becoming Catholics and Catholics becoming evangelical Protestants. Individual Christians must earnestly seek to discern God's will and then act upon that discernment when it is given. But there is in ECT no hidden agenda of conversion harbored by either Catholics or evangelicals. In addition, any talk about "ecclesial reconciliation" between evangelicals and Catholics at this moment in history is, in my judgment, utterly premature and detracts from the great purpose served by ECT. Only God knows what the relationship between evangelicals and Catholics might be fifty or a hundred years from now. There would have to be very significant developments in both evangelicalism and the Catholic Church to make credible the discussion of ecclesial reconciliation. That is not the task of ECT. That is the task of another generation of evangelicals and Catholics together, if indeed our Lord does not first return in glory.

As for our historical moment, it is enough that, after four centuries of suspicion and hostility, we have found one another; it is enough that we are able to address our differences with candor and clarity; it is enough that we are learning to engage one another in mutual respect for the institutions, traditions, and patterns of discipleship that have developed over the years of our separation; it is enough that we discern together and embrace together the great challenges of moral and cultural renewal; it is enough that we witness to the world, and witness to one another, the saving gospel of Jesus Christ; it is enough that, toward that great end, we can admonish and encourage one another, always speaking the truth in love (Eph. 4:15). It is more than enough. It is something like a *kairos*.

## A Difference on Differences

The drafters of "Evangelicals and Catholics Together" thought they were saying something quite uncontroversial when they wrote the following: "As is evident in the two-thousand-year history of the Church, and in our contemporary experience, there are different ways of being Christian, and some of these ways are distinctively marked by communal patterns of worship, piety, and catechesis. That we are all to be one does not mean that we are all to be identical in our way of following the one Christ. Such distinctive patterns of discipleship, it should be noted, are amply evident within the communion of the Catholic Church as well as within the many worlds of Evangelical Protestantism."

From a number of evangelical friends, I have received the objection that there is only one right way of being a Christian and that is the way revealed in the Bible. True enough, and it is precisely with Saint Paul that ECT wants to underscore the varieties of gifts, service, and obedience that are all the gifts of the one Spirit (1 Cor. 12). The one biblical way of being Christian requires respect for the many ways Christians faithfully exercise the diverse gifts that the Spirit continues to bestow upon Christ's people.

In considering responses to ECT, I have again had occasion to reflect that maybe one important difference between Catholics and evangelicals lies precisely in a different attitude toward differences among Christians. I do not suggest by any means that it is the *decisive* difference between Catholics and evangelicals, or even that it is necessarily a permanent difference. But it is a factor to be taken into account when discussing "The Catholic Difference."

The term *catholic*, of course, has its roots in the Greek *kata* + *holos* ("according to" and "whole"), suggesting what is universal, general, and comprehensive. Roman Catholics are not the only ones who claim the term, for all Christians who confess the great creed of Nicaea affirm their faith in "one, holy, catholic, and apostolic Church." Similarly, nobody has a copyright on the term *evangelical*, derived as it is from the Greek *euangelion* and referring to the "good news" of the gospel that is embraced by all Christians, although they do not always articulate that gospel in the same way.

The ways in which the terms *catholic* and *evangelical* have been appropriated and employed in the last four centuries of Christianity in the West are not without importance. Words are never mere words. Their uses represent distinctive accents and sensibilities that give a recognizable form to different ways of being Christian. To say that one is an evangelical puts the accent on the message; to say that one is a Catholic puts the accent on the community that is gathered by that message. At the same time, Catholics insist that they are equally devoted to the good news of the gospel, that there is no Church apart from the gospel, and therefore they, too, are evangelical. Most evangelicals, in a similar way, would insist that they are part of the community that is given birth by the message and includes all who have embraced the message in faith, and therefore they, too, are catholic. From an evangelical perspective, this accent on the Church was strongly set forth in Charles Colson's best-selling 1992 book, *The Body: Being Light in Darkness*, which played an important part in preparing the way for the declaration "Evangelicals and Catholics Together."[1]

## Uppercase Evangelical

Just as words are not mere words, even how we write words can make a subtle but important difference. In the declaration, for example, *Evangelical* is capitalized, whereas most Protestants who call themselves evangelicals use the lower case. One reason for using the upper case in the declaration was simply stylistic, to provide a certain symmetry between capitalized Evangelical and capitalized Catholic. But the capitalized Evangelical was also meant to suggest that evangelicalism is not just a religious potpourri, a random assortment of individual Protestant Christians who happen to call themselves evangelical. Admittedly, that is what evangelicalism sometimes appears to be, both to those inside and those outside the many worlds that constitute evangelical Protestantism.

Almost all observers of our religious situation are struck by the way in which evangelicalism presents itself as a wondrously—sometimes maddeningly—individualistic and entrepreneurial phenomenon. The leadership of evangelicalism lies less with denominational officers or theological faculties than with spiritual entrepreneurs who have built their own constituencies and are frequently competing for one another's constituencies in a vast array of parachurch organizations. In view of the dominant market dynamics, it seems improbable that evangelicalism, as a distinct community, will ever constitute what in Catholic ecumenical theology is called a church or ecclesial communion. And yet, behind the appearance of unbridled individualism and entrepreneurship, evangelicalism is not without a measure of what might be called communal or ecclesial depth. If in the years ahead evangelicals develop a more communal and ecclesial understanding of what it means to be Christian, evangelicals and Catholics may come closer together in appreciating the different ways of being Christian. As we look to the possible reconfigurations of the entire Christian movement in the twenty-first century—reconfigurations that will also involve developments in the Catholic Church—the Spirit may lead us to discover ways of being together and acting together in a manner that comprehends differences that are now thought to be dividing. That at least is the hope held out by ECT.

Our different uses of a common Christian vocabulary can get confused, and the confusions are frequently related to our present unhappy divisions. In considering the term *evangelical*, for instance, we note the oddity that the only major denomination in the United States that claims the term in its name is the Evangelical Lutheran Church in America (ELCA), which is generally viewed not as evangelical but as a denomination of the Protestant mainline. On the other hand, there are a good many people in the ELCA, the Presbyterian Church (USA), the

United Methodist Church, the Episcopal Church, and other mainline bodies who do think of themselves as evangelicals. It is no secret that in recent decades the mainline bodies have been in precipitous decline, a decline that is evident in membership, resources, and morale. Some of us have written in detail about the doleful process whereby what used to be the mainline became the oldline and now appears to be the sideline of religion in American life.[2] It is both unseemly and, I believe, wrong for evangelicals or Catholics to draw any satisfaction from the disarray of what used to be the Protestant mainline. But it is a major factor in the religious situation of our time and for the foreseeable future. It also has a bearing on new ways in which evangelicals and Catholics are relating to one another.

## Negating Negations

To say that one is a Protestant is to say that one is not a Roman Catholic (or Eastern Orthodox). Today, to say that one is an evangelical is to say that one is not part of the Protestant mainline—or, if one actually is a member of a mainline body, it is to say that one is not in sympathy with the institutional directions of "the liberal mainline." A problem with this way of identifying oneself is that the identity can be construed as essentially negative; the terminology says what a person is *not* rather than what a person is. There is a sense in which all identities, religious or otherwise, necessarily imply a negative. To be X may necessarily mean, among other things, not to be Y. But the double negative in the identity of evangelical Protestantism (over against both Catholicism and liberal Protestantism) makes many evangelicals especially nervous about sympathetically engaging Christians who are different.

This nervousness is by no means universal. Witness the evangelical participants in ECT. Witness other noted evangelical theologians such as J. I. Packer, Alister McGrath, Thomas Oden, Donald Bloesch, William Abraham, and Geoffrey Wainwright. Recent years have also seen the intense involvement of evangelicals in projects such as the Center for Catholic and Evangelical Theology in Northfield, Minnesota, and its very impressive quarterly, *Pro Ecclesia*. Both among those who have welcomed and those who have opposed ECT, the idea was sometimes expressed that the declaration came, as it were, out of the blue. In fact,

ECT is born from a long gestation of evangelical ecumenical involvement, both practical and theological. Because of the liberal associations
of the term, such involvement often is not called ecumenical, but it is
the expected, indeed near inevitable, interaction among those who inhabit the world (*oikoumene*) created by a common confession of Christ,
especially when so many other worlds seem increasingly hostile to that
confession.

Yet for many evangelicals, possibly even most evangelicals, the prospect of embracing, or at least no longer opposing, certain aspects of
Catholicism runs the risk of what might be described as negating the negation that was thought to be integral to their identity as evangelical
Protestants. The declaration's use of upper case *Evangelical* may be seen
as the intimation of a hope that evangelicals will, as we move into the
Third Millennium, be understood and will understand themselves more
as a distinctive ecclesial community. Serious engagement with different
ways of being Christian requires a measure of what might be described
as ecclesial confidence. The alternative to ecclesial confidence is a debilitating fear that, through engagement with others, one's own identity is
at risk. Such fear, it seems to me, is sometimes evident among
evangelicals who have been highly critical of ECT. (I hasten to add that
the above is my gloss on the significance of upper case *Evangelical* in
ECT. It is not an interpretation that is necessarily shared by all who
signed the declaration.)

## Defining Evangelical, Once Again

Among students of contemporary Christianity, efforts to define *evangelical* seem to be never ending. The British evangelical theologian Alister
McGrath reflects a fairly secure consensus when he suggests that four
positive emphases characterize evangelicalism: (1) the authority and
sufficiency of Scripture; (2) the uniqueness of redemption through the
death of Christ upon the cross (often linked with a specifically substitutionary theory of atonement); (3) the need for personal conversion; and
(4) the necessity and urgency of evangelism. Evangelicalism, he indicates, is almost by definition transdenominational, being in many ways
"a trend within the mainstream denominations." He says it "represents
an ecumenical movement," but that it is a movement among those who

refuse "to allow any specific ecclesiology to be seen as normative, while honoring those that are clearly grounded in the New Testament and Christian tradition."[3]

The ecumenical dimension of evangelicalism would, in this view, be stretched somewhat to include Roman Catholics who insist that a specific ecclesiology is normative and that that ecclesiology is in manifest continuity with the New Testament and Christian tradition, which is the story of the Church through time. Put differently, the ecumenical dimension of evangelicalism can readily embrace individual Catholics who are thought to be evangelicals (as measured, for instance, by the four criteria mentioned by McGrath), but it has considerable difficulty with the Catholic Church.

Several distinguished evangelical thinkers (Mark Noll, Cornelius Plantinga, Jr., and David Wells) have been driven to the conclusion that the worlds described by the term *evangelical* have become so amorphous that perhaps the term itself has lost its usefulness. In a jointly authored article, they write:

> [I]t is nowadays usual to find "evangelical" used as a mute substantive that gains its voice only when coupled to another, and more clarifying, adjective. Accordingly, these days we have fewer and fewer plain garden-variety evangelicals. What we have instead is a lot of fancy evangelical hybrids: radical evangelicals, liberal evangelicals, liberals who are evangelical, charismatic evangelicals, Catholic evangelicals, evangelicals who are Catholic, evangelical liberationists, evangelical ecumenicalists, ecumenicalists who are evangelical, evangelical feminists, young evangelicals, and orthodox evangelicals. The concept *evangelical* has become so promiscuous, has enjoyed so many bedpersons, has been equally and unequally yoked so often, that its self-concept has broadened into that of a commune.[4]

One detects a measure of intentional hyperbole in that description, and it no doubt reflects esoteric varieties of evangelicalism that typically gravitate around the worlds of academe, publishing, and movement activism. It seems likely that most evangelicals do not feel a strong need for a "clarifying adjective," being content to define themselves along the lines of the four marks mentioned by McGrath. Yet there is something suggestive in the observation that evangelical self-understanding implies something like a commune. The word is right next door to *communio*, and communion. As evangelicalism develops in the future, it may increasingly evidence a sense of *communio* in search of an ecclesial form that would make it easier to conceptualize what Catholics mean by "full communion." For the present and as far as we can see ahead, however, the existing sense of *communio* in evangelicalism makes possible the growing cooperation and convergence affirmed by ECT.

## The Church and the Churches

Father Avery Dulles explains in his essay in the present volume how the Catholic Church in its many ecumenical endeavors makes distinctions among the groups with which it is in conversation. One important distinction, derived from the teaching of the Second Vatican Council, is that between *churches* and *ecclesial communities*. The churches of the East that comprise the Orthodox Church are, according to Catholic ecclesiology, fully churches. *The Catechism of the Catholic Church* quotes the statement of Pope Paul VI that the communion with the Orthodox Church is so profound "that it lacks little to attain the fullness that would permit a common celebration of the Lord's Eucharist."[5] In the relationship between Orthodoxy and Rome, it is perhaps not too much to say, somewhat paradoxically, that the main obstacle to full communion is the absence of full communion.

The situation is different, sometimes dramatically different, with other ecclesial communities and Christian groupings. In thinking about the relationship between different Christian communities, one might have in mind a spectrum of five stages: from hostility to coexistence to cooperation to sharing to full communion. How does "Evangelicals and Catholics Together" fit into that spectrum? Clearly, the declaration calls for an overcoming of hostility and moves beyond coexistence when it endorses cooperation in those things that Christians can and must do together in the world. With great care, it also invites us to share in some of those sacred activities that spring from the heart of being Christians together—evangelization, prayer, Scriptural study, and correction and edification in the gospel. As J. I. Packer asserts in his essay, referring to the well-known Lund principle, divided Christians should not settle for doing separately anything that their consciences allow them to do together.

Yet that leaves us a long way from what the Catholic Church declares to be the goal of the search for greater Christian unity, which is full communion. It may be that full communion will never be achieved between evangelicals and Catholics short of the final coming of the kingdom of God. The Second Vatican Council clearly teaches that "this holy objective—the reconciliation of all Christians in the unity of the one and only Church of Christ—transcends human powers and gifts." That is why, the council continues, we place all our hope "in the prayer of Christ for the Church, in the love of the Father for us, and in the power of the Holy Spirit." [6]

## A Communion True but Imperfect

We simply do not know what the future holds; we cannot know. We do know that we cannot be content with the continuation of existing divisions as the Christian mission moves into the next century and the next millennium. Surely there is no reason to think that the forms of division that came into being in the West in the sixteenth century of the Christian era are intended to be forever, or even for the next hundred years. In envisioning the movement from hostility to sharing, ECT calls us to be radically open to the surprises that the Holy Spirit may have in store for the church. ECT is an invitation to hope in sober recognition of all that defies our hope for a more God-pleasing manifestation of the unity that is already ours. The last point is critically important: Our purpose is not to create a unity among Christians that does not already exist. Indeed, we cannot create Christian unity at all. Unity is God's gift, not our creation.

In the words of Vatican Council II, "The Church knows that she is joined in many ways to the baptized who are honored by the name of Christian but do not profess the Catholic faith in its entirety or have not preserved unity or communion under the successor of Peter." Again, "Those who believe in Christ and have been properly baptized are in a certain, although imperfect, communion with the Catholic Church."[7] In the Catholic view, the problem posed by the division between Catholics and evangelicals is not that we are *not* united. *The problem, indeed the scandal, is that we are united but live as though we were not.* In Ephesians 4, Paul is not expressing an ideal or setting forth the program for an ecumenical movement; he is stating the fact of the matter: "There is one body and one Spirit, just as you were called to the one hope that belongs to your call, one Lord, one faith, one baptism, one God and Father of us all, who is above all and through all and in all." That reality is not something that we are to achieve; it is God's present gift. Paul's argument to the Ephesians, and to us, is that we should act upon the gift that is already ours.

## The Visibility of the Invisible

But there are those who say that, here and elsewhere, Paul is referring to "the invisible Church," and there is indeed, in Christ, a communion among all believers, living and dead, that is not apparent to our eyes. Some Protestant traditions, however, have gone considerably beyond that. For instance, Francis Pieper (d. 1931), reflecting a substantial stream of later Lutheran orthodoxy, declared: "The Church is *invisible (ecclesia invisibilis est)* because the constitutive factor of the Church, faith in the heart, is invisible for men and known only to God." In this view, the Church is essentially invisible because it is composed only of the *true believers*, and only God knows who the true believers are. True belief, in turn, is defined as accepting a particular view of Christ's vicarious satisfaction and justification by faith alone.

According to Pieper, most who think they are Christians—including Roman Catholics, Orthodox, and non-Lutheran Protestants—are not members of the true (invisible) Church, except that allowance is made for baptized children who have not yet embraced the errors of their false churches, "plus a few souls who, in the terrors of conscience and particularly in the agony of death," repudiate such erroneous beliefs.[8] I was reared in the Lutheran Church-Missouri Synod, of which Francis Pieper was the chief dogmatician at a time when it still styled itself "the true visible church on earth." Such a claim may strike most other Christians (including other Lutherans) as a curious conceit, but the claim is somewhat less curious if we keep in mind the assumption behind the claim, namely, that there is no necessary connection between the true visible church and the Church that *ultimately* matters, which is invisible. Theologians in other Protestant traditions have advanced similar ideas about the true Church being invisible. While there is not space to deal with the varieties of that argument here, we will be returning to the question of the true belief that presumably distinguishes those who are the true believers, especially as that true belief is defined in terms of "justification by faith alone."

While denying none of the mysteries of the invisible and supernatural, ECT underscores the fact that the Christian mission—which is to say Christ acting in and through his body, the Church—is a reality within history. In John 17, the unity of Christ's followers is something that the world can see, something that helps lead people to believe that Jesus is sent by the Father. Elsewhere ECT declares: "Unity and love among Christians is an integral part of our missionary witness to the Lord whom we serve. 'A new commandment I give to you, that you love one another; even as I have loved you, that you also love one another. By this all men will know that you are my disciples, if you have love for one another.' (John 13) If we do not love one another, we disobey his command and contradict the Gospel we declare." To which it must be added: If it is not visible that we love one another, it is very doubtful that we love one another.

## Community of Saints, Community of Sinners

The members of this visible community are far from perfect. In Catholic teaching, the Church is, at one and the same time, holy and inclusive of sinners. Citing 1 John 1:8–10, the *Catechism* asserts that "All members of the Church, including her ministers, must acknowledge that they are sinners." Popes, too, must confess their sins and, at least according to the great Dante's *Divine Comedy*, many of them up until his time ended up in hell for their lack of repentance and faith. The sinfulness of Christians is evident not only in our moral failings but also in our spiritual and intellectual failings, including our frequent failure to understand or accept true doctrine. In line with Paul in Ephesians 5:25–26, Vatican Council II teaches: "The Church is held, as a matter of faith, to be unfailingly holy. This is because Christ, the Son of God, who with the Father and the Spirit is hailed as 'alone holy,' loved the Church as his Bride, giving himself up for her so as to sanctify her; he joined her to himself as his body and endowed her with the gift of the Holy Spirit for the glory of God." The same document goes on to affirm, "Christ, 'holy, innocent, and undefiled,' knew nothing of sin, but came only to expiate the sins of the people. The Church, however, clasping sinners to her bosom, at once holy and always in need of purification, follows constantly the path of penance and renewal." (In support of this understanding of a holy church that nonetheless embraces and includes sinners, the Council cites passages such as Hebrews 2:17; 7:26, and 2 Corinthians 5:21.) [9]

The phrase *simul iustus et peccator* ("at the same time righteous and a sinner") is usually associated with Luther, but the truth that the expression intends to underscore has deep roots in the Catholic understanding of the Church. Just as in the Incarnation God surrendered himself to the ambiguity and God-forsakenness of the human condition, so the Church, the body of the Incarnate One, risks all in identification with sinful humanity. The Catholic sensibility does not hold out for a pure, invisible, historically unsullied Church. The only Church there is on earth is a Church of sinners; the true Church is not composed exclusively of those who are pure, whether purity be understood in terms of behavior, will, or belief. There is, to be sure, immaculate Mary in whose womb God takes on flesh, and she is the image of the *Immaculata Ecclesia* or holy Church of Ephesians 5:27. On the cross, the dying Lord entrusts Mary to John, but note the startling absence of Peter from this scene. In the New Testament, Peter represents the institutional Church par excellence. Peter is, in Catholic teaching, the rock on whom Jesus would build his Church, and he reflects at the same time the cowardice and denial that is, until the end of time, an inextricable aspect of Christ's body, the Church.

In our thinking about the Church, as in our experience with the people who are the Church (beginning with ourselves!), the image of virgin bride is in tension with another image. This other aspect of the Church as *Casta Meretrix* ("Chaste Whore") has been trenchantly examined by the late Catholic theologian Hans Urs von Balthasar:

> Nowhere is the immaculateness of the bride an established fact for the bride just to accept and not to worry about any further. The relevant text from St. Paul shows this clearly: "I feel a divine jealousy for you, for I betrothed you to Christ to present you as a pure bride to her one husband. But I am afraid that as the serpent deceived Eve by his cunning, your thoughts will be led astray from a sincere and pure devotion to Christ. For if someone comes and preaches another Jesus than the one

we preached, or if you receive a different spirit from the one you received, or if you accept a different gospel from the one you accepted, you submit to it readily enough" (2 Cor. 11:2–4). Where on earth does this susceptibility of the Church-bride come from, this curiosity and lustfulness? What makes her turn her head? Why does she heed every passer-by? Why does she not let herself be led by the apostle to her one and only Lover? Every epistle of the apostle shakes with this fear. Apostasy and relapse are always possible.[10]

Drawing on biblical and patristic materials that underscore the relationship between Israel and the harlot Rahab, and building on the prophet Hosea's understanding of redemption through union with the adulteress, von Balthasar relentlessly presses the argument that the Catholic understanding of the Church derives from the central insight that it is through the Word of God's awesome emptying of himself in the Incarnation that adulterous humanity is restored.

While one can, with care, speak of a "sinful Church," Vatican II carefully avoided the expression. Sin does not implicate the Church in its formal constituents (apostolic faith, sacraments, and ministry) but does implicate the material element (the members, both clerical and lay). By sin the members do separate themselves to some extent from the Church, and by repentance and absolution they are reconciled with the Church. The concern here is to acknowledge fully the sinfulness of the members of the Church, while taking with full seriousness the truth that the Church is the body of the Christ who is like us in all respects except sin. (Heb. 4:15). Mary from her conception (by virtue of anticipating in faith her Son's redeeming work) and the saints in their heavenly perfection are like him also in his sinlessness.

The Church described by Paul in Ephesians 4 and elsewhere is as visible and palpable as are the people, the offices, and the activities that he says are to help us "grow up in every way into him who is the head, into Christ." Of the many important differences between Catholics and most evangelicals, I believe the question of the Church must have high priority in our continuing discussions. It is not first of all or most importantly a question of the merits of this church versus that church or some other church. It is a question of *the* Church as such. Not an invisible church or a church of true believers that is conceptually removed from the ambiguities and tragedies of history, but the Church that is this identifiable people through time, a people as vulnerable to the real world of historical change as was, and is, their crucified Lord. Until he returns in glory, the form of the Church is cruciform. Part of bearing the cross is bearing with one another. We have no choice. We have not chosen one another but are together in having been chosen (John 15:16).

## The Church: Local and Universal

I noted above the significance of putting *evangelical* in the upper case, pointing to the hope that evangelicalism will increasingly manifest a greater measure of communal or ecclesial consciousness. There is another usage in ECT that should perhaps be noted. Throughout the text, *church* is lower case. This was at the urging of some evangelicals involved who argued that their constituencies might be offended by the upper case *Church* that was in the preliminary drafts, since they believe that the word *church* in the New Testament typically refers to local churches rather than to the one, universal Church that is the body of Christ. This, quite frankly, was a stylistic compromise in the document. Yet I believe the compromise does not substantively compromise the declaration, centered as it is on Christ. ECT affirms, "However imperfect our communion with one another, however deep our disagreements with one another, we recognize that there is but one church of Christ. There is one church because there is one Christ and the church is his body."

To speak about the Church is to speak about Christ, and to speak about Christ is to speak about the Church. In the New Testament, *church* also refers to local or particular churches that are fully participant in the entirety of the body of Christ. Our understanding of the Church is organic before it is organizational. An ecclesiology that is faithful to the New Testament cannot portray the Church as a multinational corporation with regional and local branches. Nor is it simply a multiplicity of local voluntary organizations brought into being by Christians to advance purposes they hold in common. The Church is conceived and constituted Christologically. "Where there is Christ Jesus, there is the Catholic Church," declared Saint Ignatius of Antioch already in the first century.[11]

Twenty centuries later, Vatican Council II elaborates that insight by affirming that in local churches "the faithful are gathered together through the preaching of the Gospel of Christ, and the mystery of the

Lord's Supper is celebrated. . . . In these communities, though they may often be small and poor, or existing in the diaspora, Christ is present, through whose power and influence the One, Holy, Catholic, and Apostolic Church is constituted."[12] The local church is understood, first of all, as the priests and the faithful gathered around their apostolically ordained bishop in a particular place. Thus each diocese is a local or particular church that is fully and rightly ordered by virtue of its communion with another particular church, the church of Rome, which, in the words of Saint Ignatius, "presides in charity" over the entire Christian people. Of Rome, Saint Irenaeus said in the second century, "For with this church, by reason of its preeminence, the whole Church, that is the faithful everywhere, must necessarily be in accord."[13]

The visible and invisible, the inward and outward, the local and the universal—these and similar distinctions accent different aspects of the one Church. They are not to be pitted against one another, as scholars of the Reformation also remind us. David Yeago, for instance, writes:

> Thus for Luther the Church, the little flock which has received the salvation of God, is at the same time the mediator of salvation to the world: we can come to Christ and be saved only by adhering bodily to the Church, sharing in the visible common life of the Church, and believing the public doctrine of the Church. It is in and through this outward and bodily involvement with the holy Christian people that we are joined to Christ as members of his ecclesial body and come to share his righteousness and, indeed all that is his. . . . Luther's theologically basic understanding of the right order of the inward and the outward seems irresistibly to invite us to speak of the Church in terms which some Lutherans, oddly, find problematic: the outward, visible church, the bodily people in the world, is like a *sacrament* of salvation, in, with, and under which we become one body together with the Lord.[14]

The Reformers recognized the schism that had occurred within the universal Church and, at least at times, expressed deep sorrow over that division. In their view, however, the fault clearly lay with Rome, and in Luther's judgment (although not in the judgment of Melanchthon and other colaborers) there was not much to be done about the broken state of the Church since he was convinced that they were living in the end time and Christ's return was a matter of months or, at most, a few years.[15]

Four centuries later, for both Catholics and Protestants, our under-standing of what God may be doing in history, of what he intends for his Church, is significantly different. Catholics have had to engage in careful self-examination. Although from the Christian beginnings the necessity of communion with the church of Rome has been maintained, the Catholic Church recognizes that Rome has not always presided "in char-ity." Most strikingly in this pontificate, and most specifically with respect to Christian unity, the Catholic Church has again and again confessed sins against what it is called and constituted to be. In his 1994 apostolic letter, "As the Third Millennium Nears," John Paul II declares, "Although she is holy because of her incorporation into Christ, the Church does not tire of doing penance: Before God and man she always acknowl-edges as her own her sinful sons and daughters." Christian unity, he says, must be pursued "without compromise in our witness to the truth," yet we must repent of the times when, "especially in certain centuries," a perverse passion for truth led to "intolerance and even the use of vio-lence in the service of truth." The Pope asserts, "The consideration of mitigating factors does not exonerate the Church from the obligation to express profound regret for the weaknesses of so many of her sons and daughters who sullied her face, preventing her from fully mirroring the image of her crucified Lord, the supreme witness of patient love and of humble meekness."[16]

## The Church: High and Low

It is conventionally said that Protestants have a low doctrine of the Church and Catholics have a high doctrine of the Church. This is par-tially understandable in light of the Reformation protest against, amongst other things, the ecclesiastical claims of Rome to authority and jurisdiction. After the sixteenth century, and before the developments of Vatican Council II, Rome was commonly understood to be claiming that the Roman Catholic Church is simply, exhaustively, and without re-mainder the Church of Christ, period. "No salvation outside the Church" was taken to mean, also by many Catholics, that only Catholics could be saved. Allowance was made for those who were "invincibly ignorant" and therefore their refusal to become Catholics did not make them cul-pable before God. (Some Protestant theologians allowed a similar salvation loophole for Catholics who by "felicitous inconsistency" did not really believe what they said they believed.) In fact, that was not and is not the teaching of the Catholic Church, but the misperception persists among many Protestants and, let it be admitted, some Catholics.[17]

Christians in the Reformation traditions understandably protested what they perceived to be the institutional arrogance of a Catholic Church that claimed to have a monopoly on, and institutional control of, God's saving grace. Because they thought the Catholic Church was pitting the Church against the gospel, it is not surprising that Protestants countered with ways of thinking that pitted the gospel against the Church. Today, especially in the light of the teaching of Vatican Council II, there is no excuse for not knowing that the Catholic Church does not claim such a monopoly or control. The dogmatic document on the Church, *Lumen Gentium*, declares: "The sole Church of Christ is that which our Savior, after his Resurrection entrusted to Peter's pastoral care, commissioning him and the other apostles to extend and rule it. . . . This Church, constituted and organized as a society in the present world, subsists in (*subsistit in*) the Catholic Church, which is governed by the successor of Peter and by the bishops in communion with him."[18]

Scholars highlight the fact that the council very deliberately said *subsistit in* and not *est*. That is, the council did not say that the sole Church of Christ *is* the Catholic Church. If one wants to know where the Church of Christ is, the answer is that it is here, it subsists here, in the Catholic Church. But it is not here exclusively, exhaustively, and without remainder. The *Catechism* draws together the teaching of the several conciliar documents in this way:

> Furthermore, many elements of sanctification and of truth are found outside the visible confines of the Catholic Church: the written Word of God; the life of grace; faith, hope, and charity, with the other interior gifts of the Holy Spirit, as well as visible elements. Christ's Spirit uses these churches and ecclesial communities as means of salvation, whose power derives from the fullness of grace and truth that Christ has entrusted to the Catholic Church. All these blessings come from Christ and lead to him, and are in themselves calls to Catholic unity.[19]

Everything is from and to Christ. All the saving and sanctifying grace that is to be found outside the visible boundaries of the Catholic Church has built into it, as it were, a God-given gravitation toward unity with the Catholic Church. But the gravitational pull, of course, works both ways. Thus Catholics are drawn to unity with other Christians. This in no way weakens or calls into question their communion with the Catholic Church; indeed they are drawn precisely because of their communion with the Catholic Church, for it is here that they have learned to recognize as brothers and sisters those who are "truly but imperfectly" in communion with the one Christ and the one Church. Again, our unity in Christ is not something that we must create; it is the gift already given. And with the gift comes the imperative to give fuller and more believable expression to the imperfect unity that is ours. Concern for Christian unity is not optional.

The Catholic claim is that the Catholic Church is the fully and rightly ordered expression of Christ's Church through time. That claim rests upon many considerations, very important among them being what many Protestant as well as Catholic scholars recognize as Christ's intention for a continuing "Petrine ministry" in his Church.[20] That Petrine ministry is, in Catholic teaching, exercised by the bishop of Rome in union with the bishops ordained in succession to the apostles. The bishop of the city of Peter's martyrdom is successor to Peter and therefore "Peter among us." If, as most Christians have held through the ages, Christ did institute a Petrine ministry with the intention that it be a permanent feature of the Church, there would seem to be no other plausible candidate for the exercise of that ministry. Of course the line of historical development from Petrine ministry to papal primacy is not undisputed, but Catholic doctrine recognizes that development as an instance of the Holy Spirit continuing to guide the Church into the fullness of truth (John 16).

If a person is convinced of the claims of the Catholic Church, that she is what she says she is, then, according to Catholic teaching, that person is in conscience bound to enter into full communion with the Catholic Church. Such full communion is required for several reasons: in order to participate unqualifiedly in the life of the Church of Jesus Christ most fully and rightly ordered, in order to advance Christian unity and the one mission of Christ, and in order to bear witness to the truth to which one has been led. ECT repeatedly insists that the only unity we can rightly seek is unity in the truth. Engagement with one another in obedience to the truth entails the risk that we will be changed; but, for both evangelicals and Catholics, that risk is welcomed if our deepest devotion is indeed to the truth and not merely to our present views or church affiliation.

A Protestant who comes to believe that the Catholic Church is in fact the most fully and rightly ordered expression of Christ's Church through time may still remain a Protestant for a number of reasons he considers compelling. He may believe the Catholic Church is simply wrong about a number of teachings, ranging from baptismal regeneration to the Immaculate Conception of Mary. In that event he does not believe that the Catholic Church "is what she says she is" when she says that she is the authoritative teacher of Christian truth. And, of course, a Protestant who may be powerfully attracted to the Catholic Church must consider prayerfully his obligations to the part of the Christian community where he is. As with salvation itself, the question of one's ecclesial duty must be worked out with fear and trembling (Phil. 2:12). In the words of ECT, those who have been converted "must be given full freedom and respect as they discern and decide the community in which they will live their new life in Christ. In such discernment and decision, they are ultimately responsible to God, and we dare not interfere with the exercise of that responsibility. Also in our differences and disagreements, we Evangelicals and Catholics commend one another to God 'who by the power at work within us is able to do far more abundantly than all that we ask or think' (Ephesians 3)."

Some critics have charged that ECT condemns the practice of evangelicals witnessing to Catholics, and vice versa. Just the opposite is the case. ECT declares, "By preaching, teaching, and life example, Christians witness to Christians and non-Christians alike. We seek and pray for the conversion of others, even as we recognize our own continuing need to be fully converted." To take one another seriously as brothers and sisters in Christ means constantly calling one another to a deeper conversion to Christ. This includes, for Catholics, bearing witness to the relationship between Christ and his Church as they believe it to be fully and rightly ordered through time. In the Catholic view, Protestant theories of the Church, whether advanced by liberals or conservatives, seem woefully inadequate. Such theories do not take with sufficient seriousness the New Testament witness to the inextricable and intimate union between Christ and his Church, the Head and the body, the Bridegroom and the Bride. And so it seems to Catholics that Protestant understandings of the

Church are in wrenching discontinuity not only with the New Testament but also with the immediate postapostolic period and with the experience through the centuries of that community to which the risen Christ promised, "Lo, I am with you always, to the close of the age" (Matt. 28:20 RSV).

As evangelicals have hard questions to put to Catholics, so we must urge evangelicals to ask themselves whether they are not seriously slighting necessary dimensions of the Church in the Bible and in the history of Christian orthodoxy. It is not a virtue to have a low ecclesiology any more than it is a virtue to have a low Christology. Most evangelicals do in fact have a high Christology, having accepted the decisions of the great councils of the fourth and fifth centuries as to the true interpretation of Scripture. Implicit in that acceptance is a trust in the Spirit's guidance of the Church, not only in recognizing and defining orthodox Christology but also in recognizing and defining the Scriptures to which orthodox teaching appeals.[21] With respect to the Bible, Christology, and much else, decisions were made at a determinate time in a determinate place by a determinate community that then called itself and today calls itself the Catholic Church. Roman Catholic and Eastern Orthodox Christians have a developed doctrine regarding their continuity with that historically determinate community. It is not sufficient for Protestants, whether liberal or evangelical, to reject such doctrine, as though ecclesiology were not part of that truth to which we are called to be faithful. More than four hundred years after the divisions of the sixteenth century, God presents evangelicals and Catholics with a moment in which we can, in mutual respect, explore the ecclesiological implications of the history of the orthodoxy that, in largest part, we both affirm.

At least in the classical Reformation traditions of Luther and Calvin, the central concern was to contend for a certain understanding of the gospel; it was not to repudiate the orthodox ecclesiology that was historically understood to be an integral part of orthodox dogma and doctrine. Separation from Rome and from the historic understanding of Catholic unity was thought by the Reformers to be justified, and finally necessary, in order to secure freedom for the gospel. As has now been acknowledged many times over, Rome bears a heavy burden of responsibility for contributing to the circumstance that led Reformers to believe that separation was justified and necessary. A similarly grave responsibility is borne by those Reformers and their heirs who broke the necessary connection between the gospel and orthodox teaching, on the one hand, and the apostolic order of the Church. Over many years of prayerful study, reflection, and conversation with those whose wisdom I respect, I came to a clear conclusion: *If, at the end of the twentieth century, separation for the sake of the gospel is not necessary, it is not justified.* Others may agree with that proposition while drawing from it a different course of action. So very much depends on that "if."

## The Article by Which the Church Stands or Falls

At this point we must take up a question that seems to move us away from our discussion of the Church, but those Christians to whom this is critically important insist that any discussion of the Church is an empty distraction unless agreement is secured on this question. The question, of course, is "justification by faith alone." Apart from that doctrine, they say, there is no true Church, for that doctrine *is the gospel* and is thus the article by which the Church stands or falls (*articulus stantis et cadentis ecclesiae.*)[22] Those who adamantly hold to this position view themselves as the champions of sixteenth-century Lutheran and Calvinist orthodoxy. The great majority of evangelicals in America and the world do not believe that those schools of theology are normative for their understanding of the Christian faith. Wesleyan, Arminian, Holiness, Pentecostal, and other evangelical traditions are much closer to the Catholic understanding of the connections between faith and the converted life, between justification and sanctification.

The more rigorous proponents of "justification by faith alone" among evangelical Protestants also have a strong and well-earned influence among those who are not part of the Lutheran or Calvinist traditions. But it is from the Calvinist theological quarter that some of the more vigorous criticism of ECT has been launched, and that criticism must be addressed here, albeit in a brief and preliminary manner. There is also a personal factor in my addressing this question. As a Lutheran Christian, my theological understanding and spiritual life were powerfully formed by the formula of "justification by grace alone, through faith alone, because of Christ alone." The truth of the gospel that that formula was intended to protect is, I am convinced, entirely compatible with ECT and with the authentic teaching of the Catholic Church.

The signers of ECT say, "We affirm together that we are justified by grace through faith because of Christ." To the charge that this statement is deceptive because it suggests that we have reached complete agreement on the central dispute of the Reformation, one must simply point out that anyone with the slightest familiarity with the history of theological controversy would immediately note the absence of the threefold "only" (the "three *solas*" as they are conveniently, if with dubious Latin, called). The *solas* are conspicuous by their absence, and it is not by accident that they are absent.

ECT does not disguise but repeatedly highlights the fact that there are important questions of continuing difference and disagreement between evangelicals and Catholics. Certainly that includes controversy over what are the most adequate formulas for describing God's work of justification. A merit of the formula chosen by ECT—"we are justified by grace through faith because of Christ"—is that all the parts of that formula are actually found in the New Testament. The advocates of "justification by grace alone through faith alone because of Christ alone" may well believe that it most adequately reflects the teaching of the Bible, but the formula itself is in fact a sixteenth-century theological construct that is not found in the Bible. Rather than enter into the many and complex controversies surrounding the history of that theological construct, ECT chose to stay with the affirmation of undisputed biblical truth.

## Protestant Reformation and Universal Church

Even friendly critics have worried in print whether ECT and the favorable discussions of it do not tend to fudge on some critical differences. This extends to a concern about whether Catholic participants in ECT have been entirely straightforward in representing the actual teaching of the Catholic Church. Alister McGrath, for instance, asks in *Christianity Today*, "Do We Still Need the Reformation?" (December 12, 1994). His answer, as one might expect, is clearly yes—and Catholics might well agree, while questioning whether the Reformation still needs churches separated from communion with Rome. In examining Catholic teaching

today, and particularly the new *Catechism of the Catholic Church*, McGrath
joins other evangelical scholars in praising the emphasis placed upon the
grace of God as the sole source of salvation and upon the unquestion-
able centrality of Jesus Christ in God's saving work from beginning to
end. But why, he and others wonder, does not the *Catechism* address
more explicitly the sixteenth-century controversies between Rome and
the Reformation? Yet more specifically, why does it not address the *sola
fide* of justification by faith alone?

In response, one points out that it is necessary to see those controversies within the entirety of Christian history. Similarly with ECT, which
bears the very comprehensive subtitle, "The Christian Mission in the
Third Millennium." While not pressing a comparison between the two,
the *Catechism* and ECT are alike in this respect: both attempt to bring
together in a positive form what can and should be said as Christians
prepare themselves for the challenge and promise of the future. The
desire is to move on, not to get bogged down in past disputes, and yet to
do so in a way that is scrupulously faithful to the truth. But, it is said, we
cannot move on together if there is fundamental disagreement about
the most foundational of truths. Some critics of ECT (not McGrath)
have cited the *Catechism* in support of their claim that Rome persists in
condemning the Reformation understanding of the gospel and that ECT
therefore falsely represents a solidarity in faith between evangelicals and
Catholics that simply does not exist. As a result, the truth about Catholic
teaching as set forth in the *Catechism* has become a factor in the discussion of ECT.

In his measured criticism, McGrath writes:

The Roman Catholic reader of this catechism will learn little, if anything, of the Reformation debates over [justification] or of Protestant
sensitivities over Roman Catholic teaching. While emphasizing that
salvation takes place by grace, on the basis of the work of Christ rather
than human effort or achievement, the catechism seems reluctant to
engage with the questions raised above and does little to reassure the
anxieties of any readers familiar with the sixteenth-century debates.

The *Catechism* is not only "reluctant to engage" the debates of the sixteenth century; it resolutely declines to do so, at least directly. And that
for the very simple reason that it intends to be what its title suggests, the

*Catechism of the Catholic Church*. Its intention is to affirm and explain the faith, life, and worship of the Catholic Church, and the fact is that— historically and theologically—the dispute with Lutherans, Calvinists, Zwinglians, and others in the sixteenth century is far from being the most formative experience in the Church's understanding of her faith, life, and worship. That is not to say that the conflicts of the sixteenth century are not of continuing importance. They are very important. But those conflicts are not the defining moment of Christian faith for most of the people to whom the *Catechism* is addressed.

That the disputes of the sixteenth century are not addressed directly does not mean that they are ignored in the *Catechism*. While the purpose is to positively set forth the faith and avoid the polemical, those intimately involved in producing the *Catechism*, most notably Joseph Cardinal Ratzinger, have throughout their lives been intensely engaged in the questions raised by the Reformation.[23] The *Catechism* does give major attention to the Council of Trent, which was Rome's reforming response to the Protestant reformers.[24] In addition, for the last three decades Rome has invested immense energy in theological dialogues with the various Protestant communities, including dialogues dealing explicitly with the controversy over justification by faith. As Cardinal Ratzinger has emphasized on a number of occasions, the acute reader of the *Catechism* will not fail to recognize that the Catholic faith is there presented in a manner that has taken into account, albeit not addressing directly, the critique advanced by the Reformation. Whether or not that critique has been *sufficiently* taken into account is, of course, something on which both Protestant and Catholic theologians may have their own views.

## A Defining Moment among Defining Moments

For many, if not most, Protestant Christians, the sixteenth century is the defining moment in their religious identity *as Protestants*. The Reformation was a protest and intended to be a corrective; the Catholic Church was the thing protested and putatively to be corrected. However warranted the corrective may have been at one time, one must ask whether it is possible to sustain the fullness of the Church upon a corrective. To be a Catholic is *not* not to be a Protestant. For Catholics in those countries strongly influenced by the Reformation traditions, the consciousness of not being Protestant is one facet of being Catholic, but being Catholic is not defined by Protestantism in the way that being Protestant is defined by Catholicism. Given this reality, it would be inappropriate for a catechism of the Catholic Church to address directly and in detail one moment—admittedly a very important moment—in the history of theological and ecclesiastical controversy. In addition, and as mentioned above, the rigorist claim that justification by faith alone is the article by which the Church stands or falls is by no means endorsed by all, or even most, evangelicals. It seems quite unreasonable to suggest that the *Catechism of the Catholic Church* address directly the specifics of a controversy that is as much an intra-Protestant dispute as a dispute between Protestants and Catholics.

While produced by the teaching authority (magisterium) of the Catholic Church for the Catholic faithful, the *Catechism* very much keeps other Christians in mind. This is frequently made explicit in relation to Orthodoxy rather than Protestantism. The Orthodox Church has pride of place on Rome's ecumenical agenda, and all Christians should understand why that is necessarily so. Only Rome is in a position to mend the schism between East and West that long predates the schisms of the sixteenth century. While the two goals should not be pitted against one another, the healing of the breach between East and West has priority over the healing of the breach between Rome and the Reformation. Orthodoxy was spared (some Protestants might say deprived of) the Reformation of the sixteenth century. Formulations such as "justification by faith alone" do not figure in Orthodox teaching. Apart from the one billion Roman Catholics, Orthodoxy is the largest ecclesial configuration of Christians in the contemporary world. The theological disputes that raged in northern Europe in the sixteenth century, and still rage in some Protestant circles, are not pertinent to the goal of reestablishing full communion between East and West.

Moreover, the great majority of the intended audience of the *Catechism of the Catholic Church* have been only marginally touched, or not touched at all, by the controversies of the sixteenth century. It might be suggested that Catholics in Latin America, for example, should know about those controversies in order to counter the arguments of evangelicals. But it seems exceedingly doubtful that evangelicals reaching out to Catholics in Brazil or Peru are themselves familiar with the theological niceties of those controversies. The arguments surrounding the *sola fide* formula are the preserve of a relatively small number of professional theologians, mainly Lutheran and Calvinist, in North America and Western Europe. That does not mean the arguments are wrong; it does mean that they are not, and cannot be, at the center of the global proclamation of the gospel and the Christian mission in the third millennium.

The *Catechism of the Catholic Church*, then, does not reject the distinctive Reformation formula that justification is by grace alone through faith alone because of Christ alone. Neither does it affirm it. It does affirm its continuity with the Council of Trent, which condemned the formula in the sense that it understood the formula at the time. But the *Catechism* refrains from directly revisiting those controversies, although, as Cardinal Ratzinger indicates, it should be obvious to all that it has indirectly taken into account the Reformation critique of Catholic doctrine and practice. Were the *Catechism* to address directly the justification formula, it would have had to go on to make clear that grace is not alone but confirms human freedom, that living faith is not alone but issues in a life of obedience, that Christ is not alone but always to be found in the company of his Church. Entering into these disputes over all the necessary distinctions and qualifications lands us right back where Protestants and some Catholics were four hundred years ago. One is inclined to believe that that is not where the Holy Spirit intends to lead the Church at the end of the twentieth century.

The *Catechism* does address more directly some theological controversies in Christian history. It must be frankly said that the sixteenth-century controversies are not the most important in the life of the Church. Certainly, for instance, the Christological and Trinitarian controversies of the early centuries have been more universally formative for Christian teaching. In those cultures that have been significantly influenced by the Protestant Reformation, such as ours, it is important for Christian thinkers to engage the controversies of the Reformation era. Even here, however, our culture today poses numerous challenges to Christian faith and life that need to be addressed as urgently as the questions to which the Reformers gave priority then.

In any event, the *Catechism of the Catholic Church* intends to be a universal (that is, catholic) catechism and is not the place to replay the controversies with Wittenberg, Geneva, and Dort. Alister McGrath is right in saying that the *Catechism* "must be in the hands of every person concerned with the future of evangelical relations with Roman Catholicism." But such persons will be greatly and rightly disappointed if they expect the *Catechism* to run the entirety of Christian faith and life through the grid of the Lutheran or Calvinist formulas of Reformation protest. Certainly the *Catechism* cannot be used fairly as an instrument to throw into question the unity affirmed by evangelicals and Catholics in ECT. Like ECT, the *Catechism* is an invitation not to refight the wars of the past but to cross the threshold of hope into a third millennium of common witness and discipleship, including, please God, greater visible unity among all who follow Christ. As for those who insist that the theological wars of the past are the wars of the present and must forever be the wars of the future—or at least until one side unconditionally surrenders—it is to be feared that they are demanding something other than unity in the gospel.

## Reconciling Christians in the Gospel of Reconciliation

In two thousand years of Christian history, the gospel has been construed in different ways. Different ways does not mean conflicting or incompatible ways. There is no one formula or theological system that can catch all the dimensions of the momentous truth that "God was in Christ reconciling the world to himself, not counting their trespasses against them, and entrusting to us the message of reconciliation" (2 Cor. 5:19 RSV). There are many ways of saying that. Paul said it in different ways, as did John, Peter, Irenaeus, Ambrose, Augustine, Maximus the Confessor, Thomas Aquinas, Teresa of Avila, Bernard of Clairvaux, Luther, Calvin, Wesley, C. S. Lewis, and Hans Urs von Balthasar. There is, as the early fathers taught, a rule of faith in the Great Tradition to which all these worthies belong, and that rule of faith, that orthodoxy, precludes some ways of saying the gospel while including diverse ways of articulating and living the wonder of Christian truth. All finally bow, with Paul, before the inexpressible mystery: "O the depth of the riches and wisdom and knowledge of God! How unsearchable are his judgments and how inscrutable his ways!" (Rom. 11:33 RSV).

Some readers may think that we are paying too much attention to critics of ECT who suggest that the evangelical signers betrayed the Reformation by joining with Catholics in publicly declaring, "We affirm together that we are justified by grace through faith because of Christ." But this criticism must be addressed seriously; first, because it is a very serious criticism and, second, because it could for some undermine their confidence in the theological integrity of a declaration that bears such high promise for our life together and for the Christian mission in the years ahead. That mission is most essentially about *salvation*—from sin, from death, and from a world that has turned away from its own true story of God's creating and redeeming love.[25]

At different times and places in Christian history, there have been different controlling concepts in how the message of salvation is expressed. These concepts do not serve equally well when judged by "the rule of faith," but theologians in one school are always duty bound to seek the ways in which the conceptualization of another school can be understood in a manner that is compatible with their understanding of the gospel. That is a duty imposed by both truth and love, which finally are not separable.[26] Theological schools produce theological systems. When theologians refuse to test a system by its capacity to comprehend the variety of ways in which the gospel has been thought and lived, the temptation is to found a "true church" in order to maintain what is claimed to be the true system. In this way churches become the servants of theological systems, rather than theology being in the service of the Church.

## Motifs of Salvation

Those who claim that there is only one way of saying the gospel and by that one way "the Church stands or falls" must attend to other ways in which the gospel of salvation has been said, thought, and lived. Among the early church fathers deification (or divinization) is clearly one of the dominant motifs in the understanding of salvation. In Athanasius, the Cappadocian Fathers and others, the Good News is that God has assumed our human nature so that our human nature can be incorporated into the life of God. This understanding of the gospel continues to be central in the faith and life of Eastern Orthodoxy.[27] In Augustine the motif is rightly ordered love and friendship with God through Christ; for Bernard of Clairvaux, it is the marriage of the soul with Christ; for Luther, it is righteousness before God; for later Calvinists, it is union with Christ; for von Balthasar, it is the drama of human participation through Christ in the glory of God; for Enlightenment Protestantism, it is moral perfection; for nineteenth-century liberal Protestantism, it is God-consciousness; for contemporary liberation theology and some forms of Calvinist reconstructionism, it is world transformation.

All of these ways of construing the gospel of salvation can and do appeal to the Bible for support. I would suggest that all but the last three (moral perfection, God-consciousness, and liberationism) can be understood as clearly being within the bounds of orthodoxy as judged by the "rule of faith" in the early Church. Luther's motif of righteousness before God, with its attendant insistence upon justification by faith alone—a motif and insistence that is historically much more Lutheran than Calvinist, although today it is pressed upon evangelicals in the name of Calvinist orthodoxy—has been embraced by many Christians as the most powerful construal of the gospel and the most faithful to Paul's understanding of salvation. But to declare it to be the article by which the Church stands or falls in a manner that excludes other ways of saying the gospel is to turn it into a sectarian doctrine. To make it such a norm of exclusion is to exclude the very tradition of orthodoxy to which Luther appealed and which he intended to serve.[28]

## The Church: Deliberating and Judging

To oppose the formula "justification by faith alone" was, in the view of some Reformers, to oppose the gospel. Some champions of that position, however, seem to come close to saying that "justification by faith alone" *is* the gospel, and the gospel *is* "justification by faith alone"— exclusively, exhaustively, and without remainder. Because there can be no Church apart from the gospel, it then follows that, where that formula is not embraced, there is no Church. But surely that cannot be right, for it would require that the entirety of the Christian reality—the Scriptures, as well as the proclamation and living of the Good News by the Christian people through time—is to be judged by a theological formula devised sixteen centuries after that reality came into being.

That Christian reality, comprehensively understood, is the Church. Surely it is the Church that judges the adequacy of theological formulations, and not vice versa. We may well disagree about how the Church should make such judgments (a question on which Catholics have rather definite views), but it should be obvious that, whether at Chalcedon in 451 or at Dort in 1618 or at Vatican II in 1964 or, for that matter, in the discussions surrounding ECT, it is the Christian people deliberating and judging theological formulas that have been proposed. The gospel is not a theological proposition or a free-floating idea that touches down here or there, bringing into being the Church wherever it momentarily rests. The gospel is the memory, the message, and the lived experience of a determinate people through time, and that people is the Church. The gospel is God in Christ continuing to reconcile the world to himself through that part of the world that is the Church, the body of Christ. Whether that way of putting the matter is satisfactory or not is a question to be deliberated and judged by the Christian people, which is to say by the Church.

In sum, it is the Church that judges the Church. The Church of the living God is "the pillar and bulwark of the truth" (1 Tim 3:15 RSV). We can say, and it is important that we do say, that the Scriptures judge the Church, even though we know that there are no Scriptures apart from the Church. We can say, and it is important that we do say, that the gospel judges the Church, even though we know that there is no gospel apart from the Church. And whether the foregoing theological assertions are adequate or not can only be deliberated and judged by the Christian people, which is to say by the Church. We who are the Church can dispute which voices, which schools of theology, and even which ecclesial communities best express the mind of the Church, but such disputes can only take place within the Church, which we are. The Church is constituted by the truth that she bears, Jesus Christ. Between the truth and the community constituted by the truth, between Head and body, no wedge can be driven, including the wedge of a theological formula claiming to be the article by which the Church stands or falls.

I expect this argument will not satisfy some of the more rigorist critics of ECT. Their syllogism is this: Justification by faith alone is the gospel; the Council of Trent condemns justification by faith alone; therefore the Catholic Church, which has not recanted the Council of Trent, condemns the gospel. It follows as night follows day that the Catholic Church is a false church because it is the enemy of the gospel. What is one to say in response to this reasoning?

First, Trent's *Decree on Justification* does declare: "If anyone shall say that by faith alone the sinner is justified, so as to understand that nothing else is required to cooperate in the attainment of the grace of justification, and that it is in no way necessary that he be prepared and disposed by the action of his own will: let him be anathema." The fathers of the council understood themselves to be saying what was said much earlier by James: "What does it profit, my brethren, if a man says he has faith but has not works? Can his faith save him? . . . So faith by itself, if it has no works, is dead" (James 2 RSV). They also thought that the *sola fide* formula promoted in the Reformation era was, among other things, a denial of human moral agency, a rejection of the role of the God-given capacities of reason and will in coming to faith, a repudiation of sanctifying grace, and an invitation to antinomianism.

Did the council fathers at Trent misunderstand what the Reformers meant by *sola fide*? Most scholars, whether Catholic or Protestant, agree that they did not understand the Reformers, especially Luther and Calvin, adequately. And there is slight disagreement, perhaps no disagreement, that the Reformers, especially Luther, could have expressed themselves more clearly, carefully, and consistently. Then too, keep in mind that, apart from Luther and Calvin, there were many who claimed to be advancing the Reformation under the slogan of *sola fide* and who were advocating precisely what Trent thought that slogan meant. Crucial to the condemnation are the words "If anyone shall say . . ." (*Si qui dixerit*). Trent did not condemn anyone by name. The council condemned anyone who taught what it understood by the formula "justification by faith alone." There were in the sixteenth century very considerable differences, also among Protestants, as to what was meant by key terms such as *justification, faith, will*, and *grace*. That there were misunderstandings is hardly surprising.

Why does the Catholic Church not recant what was said by Trent? There are at least three reasons. First, because it is Catholic teaching that a council teaches authoritatively, and the Church is not authorized to repudiate retrospectively a conciliar decree. Second, because the Catholic Church, knowing that all theological formulations fall short of expressing the fullness of truth, trusts the continuing guidance of the Spirit in a course of doctrinal development toward the ever more adequate articulation of God's Word relative to the questions posed by the time. And third, because it is historically and theologically judged that the council fathers at Trent were right in condemning what they understood by "justification by faith alone." In the intervening years, and especially in the theological dialogues of the last thirty years, Reformation Christians have made a convincing case that what they mean by *sola fide* is not what Trent condemned.

The very detailed and scholarly Protestant-Catholic consultation on these questions in Germany (*The Condemnations of the Reformation Era*) arrives at this conclusion:

> The ending of the rejections does not mean that there are no longer any differences of interpretation about the justification of the sinner, or that these are *confined* to mere misunderstandings or different modes of expression. . . . But, if our previous reflections are correct, these are not decisive questions of such a kind that the answer to them would decide about the true and false church. In other words, they are not such that with them "the church stands or falls." At the same time, they do certainly present us with theological tasks which have to be taken seriously and pursued further, even in legitimate theological dispute—*within* the one church, which must not be allowed to founder on them.[29]

In sum, the Catholic Church does not today condemn the formula "justification by faith alone," because to do so would be understood as a condemnation of heirs of the Reformation tradition who do not mean by that formula what was condemned by Trent. A statement must be understood in its historical context. The Catholic Church strives to articulate ever more adequately the truth of God's Word, including the truth the Reformers intended to protect by the language of "justification by faith alone." Those who promote the radically ahistorical syllogism mentioned above misrepresent the teaching of the Catholic Church and, I am convinced, the teaching of the Reformers.

## The Spirit of Evangelicalism

It is necessary to recall that the claim that *sola fide* is the article by which the Church stands or falls is hardly representative of evangelicalism. Much more representative is the thought and disposition of, for instance, John Wesley. With respect to soteriology, the doctrine of salvation, Wesley proposed a compelling synthesis of the Lutheran formula of "faith alone" with the historic Catholic accent on the life of holiness. The great Methodist theologian Albert Outler put it this way: In the name of a Christianity both Biblical and patristic [Wesley] managed to transcend the stark doctrinal disjunctions which had spilled so much ink and blood since Augsburg and Trent. In their stead, he proceeded to develop a theological fusion of faith and good works, Scripture and tradition, revelation and reason, universal redemption and conditional election, Christian liberty and an ordered polity, the assurance of pardon and the risks of "falling from grace," original sin and Christian perfection. In each of these conjunctions, as he insisted almost tediously, the initiative is with God, the response with men.[30]

In a moving 1749 letter to an anonymous Roman Catholic, Wesley protests the claim that he is not really a Christian because he does not accept all that is taught by the Catholic Church. Like ECT, Wesley points to the common faith represented by the Apostles' Creed. After offering a magnificent summary of the cardinal points of Christian doctrine, he concludes:

> Let the points wherein we differ stand aside: here are enough wherein we agree, enough to be the ground of every Christian temper and of every Christian action. O brethren, let us not still fall out by the way. I hope to see *you* in heaven. And if I practice the religion above described, you dare not say I shall go to hell. You cannot think so. None can persuade you to it. Your own conscience tells you the contrary. Then if we cannot as yet *think alike* in all things, at least we may *love alike*. Herein we cannot possibly do amiss. For of one point none can doubt a moment: God is love; and he that dwelleth in love, dwelleth in God, and God in him.[31]

I think it most likely that, were John Wesley still with us, he would have signed ECT. In fact, had the climate of confessional polemics not been so intense in his day, I believe he would have been instrumental in advancing the course of reconciliation between evangelicals and Catholics that is affirmed by ECT. Far from being an initiative that is abrupt and premature, ECT is simply catching up, two centuries later, with John Wesley and other defining figures of world evangelicalism.

And yet there are those for whom such a Wesleyan appeal to love is a flashing red light warning that truth is being shortchanged. So entrenched is a spirit of defensiveness, the anxiety that people might succumb to the seductions of Catholicism, the fear of losing the vibrancy of

Reformation protest, and the apprehension that Protestant identity will collapse with the negation of the negation upon which it is premised. To those who feel threatened by the convergence and cooperation encouraged by ECT, we must say, "Be not afraid!" Much has changed since the great spilling of ink and blood in the era of Augsburg and Trent.[32] Understood within the "rule of faith" to which all orthodox Christians subscribe, Reformation doctrine and much of the vibrant history of Protestantism that it helped produce can deepen our unity in proclaiming the Good News that God is in Christ reconciling the world to himself, and us to one another.

## The Final Judgment

"Yes, but," persists my evangelical friend, "do you really believe that you are saved by faith alone?" Here is what I believe as a Catholic Christian who is conscientiously resolved to be utterly faithful to the magisterium of the Catholic Church. When I come before the judgment throne, I will plead the promise of God in the shed blood of Jesus Christ. I will not plead any work that I have done, although I will thank God that he has enabled me to do some good. I will not plead the merits of Mary or the saints, although I will thank God for their company and their prayers throughout my earthly life. I will not plead that I had faith, for sometimes I was unsure of my faith, and in any event that would be to turn faith into a meritorious work of my own. I will not plead that I held the correct understanding of "justification by faith alone," although I will thank God that he led me to know ever more fully the great truth that formula was intended to protect. Whatever little growth in holiness I have experienced, whatever strength I have received from the company of the saints, whatever understanding I have attained of God and his ways—these and all other gifts received I will bring gratefully to the throne. But in seeking entry to that heavenly kingdom, I will plead Christ and Christ alone.

> *Just as I am, without one plea*
> *But that Thy blood was shed for me*
> *And that Thou bidd'st me come to Thee,*
> *O Lamb of God, I come, I come.*

And that is what "Evangelicals and Catholics Together" affirms: "We are justified by grace through faith because of Christ. Living faith is active in love that is nothing less than the love of Christ, for we say with Paul: 'I have been crucified with Christ; it is no longer I who live, but Christ who lives in me; and the life I now live in the flesh I live by faith in the Son of God, who loved me and gave himself for me.'" Saying that together, we could only at the peril of denying the work of Christ deny that we are brothers and sisters in Christ.

## Witnessing to the Church

Returning to our reflection on ecclesiology, a word is in order about another section of ECT that has come in for criticism, namely, its statements about evangelizing and proselytizing. ECT could hardly be clearer about the right and obligation to evangelize everybody, which includes Catholics witnessing to evangelicals and evangelicals witnessing to Catholics. There is not always a *bright line* (to use the lawyer's term) between evangelizing and proselytizing. In the section titled "We Witness Together," however, indicators are given to help us tell the difference between the two in practice. Nonetheless, both Catholic and evangelical critics have had difficulties with the assertion that "the decision of the committed Christian with respect to his communal allegiance and participation must be assiduously respected." To respect a decision does not mean to approve of it. In this connection, to respect a person's decision does not mean that we agree with what he decided but that we respect the person who conscientiously makes the decision even when we think he decided wrongly.

The same section of ECT declares, "It is understandable that Christians who bear witness to the Gospel try to persuade others that their communities and traditions are more fully in accord with the Gospel." In the realm of personal relations, love may well compel someone to urge her Catholic friend that the opportunities for fuller growth in Christ are more available in her local Assemblies of God congregation. That is not necessarily the proselytizing that ECT criticizes. It is in the larger context of evangelistic strategy that ECT emphatically states that "in view of the large number of non-Christians in the world and the enormous challenge of our common evangelistic task, it is neither theologically legitimate nor a prudent use of resources for one Christian community to proselytize among active adherents of another Christian community."

Let it be said in all candor that the formulations in ECT are not entirely satisfactory. One declaration can only do so much. ECT was intended to propose principles and point directions. That is why the document calls for continuing and disciplined discussion among evangelicals and Catholics, and for all of us to reflect upon the meaning of these principles and directions in our evangelistic endeavors. The Catholic cannot agree with "the decision of the committed Christian with respect to his communal allegiance" if that decision means living in permanent separation from the community in which the Church of Jesus Christ, fully and rightly ordered, subsists. At the same time, the Catholic can understand, respect, and even sympathize with the reasons why a person might make that decision. Again, in Catholic teaching, every element of Christian faith and life gravitates toward Catholic unity in communion with the Petrine ministry instituted by Jesus and continued in the ministry of the bishop of Rome. This is the body of Christ most amply exemplified through time, and communion with this Church is not incidental to communion with Christ.

On the one hand, the Catholic spirit is broadly, even promiscuously, embracing. St. Paul writes, "Therefore I want you to understand that no one speaking by the Spirit of God ever says 'Jesus be cursed!' and no one can say 'Jesus is Lord' except by the Holy Spirit" (1 Cor. 12:3 RSV). Everyone who sincerely says "Jesus is Lord" has been moved by the Spirit of God, no matter how many disagreements or difficulties we may have with that person, no matter how qualified is our actual fellowship. The Church most comprehensively understood is coterminous with Christ, which is to say that where Christ is there also is the Church. Again, whoever claims Jesus Christ as Lord and Savior and is baptized is "truly but imperfectly" in communion with the Church. At the same time, that imperfect communion has built into it, so to speak, the desire and imperative for full communion.

In 1959 Yale University's Jaroslav Pelikan, a Lutheran, wrote a much discussed book, *The Riddle of Roman Catholicism*. Pelikan, who describes himself as an "evangelical catholic," has a profound sense of the empirical Church through time. Yet he was also candid about the problems he had with Rome's understanding of Christian unity. "Rome's eagerness for reunion," he complained, "comes in the form of an invitation—'Return to Mother Church.'" Nearly three decades later, in 1985 at the Extraordinary Synod in Rome, Jan Cardinal Willebrands, then head of the Secretariat for Christian Unity, declared, "'Return' is not a word in our ecumenical vocabulary."[33] The continuing conversion to which we are all called does entail turnings and returnings of many kinds, but the invitation that Rome issues to evangelicals and others today cannot be described simply in terms of "Return to Mother Church." Rather, Rome asks, "What can we do, and what can you do, and what can we do together to overcome the divisions that are manifestly contrary to the will of God for his Christian people?" The Catholic Church does not claim to have all the answers to those questions. Only God knows what will be the result of this encounter between evangelicals and Catholics. Certainly, both evangelicals and Catholics will be changed by it. The invitation and the questions do not come with an organizational blueprint or a schedule of ecumenical actions. To accept the invitation requires only that we be seriously asking the questions, and asking them together.

Joseph Cardinal Ratzinger, Prefect of the Doctrine of the Faith, has written witheringly about an older liberal style of ecumenism that tried to overcome division by "negotiating" differences, as though the Christian reality was a matter of diplomacy and not of divinely revealed truth. In agreement with Ratzinger, ECT insists that the only unity we can desire with integrity, the only unity that is pleasing to God, is unity in the truth. The alternative, says Ratzinger, is an "ecumenism of skepticism," based on our uncertainties, rather than an ecumenism of faith, based on God's Word. He contrasts the skepticism that has marked much liberal ecumenism in this century with the situation in the sixteenth century: "Our quarreling ancestors were in reality much closer to each other when in all their disputes they still knew that they could only be servants of one truth which must be acknowledged as being as great and as pure as it has been intended for us by God."[34]

## Christ and Church: One Act of Faith

In accord with the entirety of orthodox Christianity, from the first century to this very day, Catholics are convinced that the Church is an integral part of the truth intended for us by God. Permit me to put it more sharply, for this is at the heart of "the Catholic difference": *For the Catholic, faith in Christ and faith in the Church are one act of faith*. Faith in Christ and faith in the Church are not pitted against one another. Christ the head cannot be separated from the body, the Church. I do not love Christ if I do not love his Church. "Saul, Saul, why do you persecute me?" (Acts 9:4). In persecuting the Church Saul was persecuting Christ, and in loving the Church we love Christ. To be sure, Christ is sinless and the Church is composed of sinners; Christ is Master and the Church is the community of disciples. Christ and the Church cannot be equated; and the Church must never presume to think it has superseded Christ. That way lies the blasphemy and heresy so devastatingly depicted by Dostoyevski in "The Legend of the Grand Inquisitor" in *The Brothers Karamazov*. This is always a temptation for the Catholic Church, and sometimes its members, and no doubt some popes, have succumbed to the temptation. But the temptation and risk are inherent in the radicality of Christ's devotion to his Church; he does not want to be known or to be served apart from those for whom he died and to whom he promised his Spirit until the end of time. All of this is implicated in the declaration of Ignatius of Antioch as he made his way to be martyred in the Coliseum in Rome, "Where Christ Jesus is, there is the Church."

With Protestants and Protestantism it is different. Kevin Offner, who works with evangelical students at Harvard University, reflects on these differences in an essay titled "Different Kinds of Christians."[35] The great divide, he suggests, is between "conservative" and "cultural" Christians, the latter being of a liberal disposition and inclined to believe that Christianity should be aligned with what is culturally normative. Among "conservative" Christians, the great divide is between the "evangelical" and the "confessional," with the former being "individualistic" and the latter "churchly." This is how Offner describes the evangelical posture:

> Evangelicals by definition are individualistic. An Evangelical is one who "has a personal relationship with Jesus Christ." Most Evangelicals can point to a specific conversion experience at which they "made a decision for Christ" (which they equate with "being born again"), and can vividly recall what their lives were like before and after this decision. This most important aspect of salvation is done alone, between the individual and God, in one's own heart. Once one has been "been saved," only secondarily is he (perhaps) instructed, "Now it's important for you

to attend a local church—somewhere where the Bible is preached well and Jesus Christ is central." Often a church is looked for which will best "meet one's needs." Any relationship one has with the Church is secondary, supplemental, and intrinsically separate from one's individual relationship with Christ.

Offner suggests that there are strengths and weaknesses in each of these different ways of being Christian. The evangelical way encourages individual initiative in cultivating and sharing one's faith, a strong interest in Bible study, and activism in evangelism and Christian service. The churchly way has a greater appreciation of community, a clearer understanding of God's purposes in the secular world, and a higher estimation of theology and the importance of the intellectual life. Offner's suggestive little taxonomy of different kinds of Christians ends with the somewhat anodyne observation that "both groups need one another."

Some evangelicals would no doubt quarrel with Kevin Offner's account of the evangelical understanding of the relationship between Christ and the Church. As we have noted, on this and other questions there are notable differences between classic Calvinists, Arminians, Pentecostals, and those from sundry holiness traditions. But, whereas for Catholics faith in Christ and faith in the Church constitute one act of faith, almost all who call themselves evangelicals would say that these are two distinct, if not separate, acts. Of paramount importance is "making a decision for Christ," and the question of one's relationship to the Church is secondary, if it gets asked at all. Returning to the concern about evangelizing and proselytizing addressed by ECT, an evangelical who evangelizes a Catholic might advise him to attend a local church "where the Bible is preached well and Jesus Christ is central." That could mean a Catholic parish. A Catholic evangelizing an evangelical, however, would urge him to be part of a local church that, along with being biblical and Christocentric, is in full communion with the universal Church. That in no way prevents the Catholic from affirming wholeheartedly the assertion of ECT that "the decision of the committed Christian with respect to his communal allegiance and participation must be assiduously respected."

## Churchly Evangelicalism

A final Catholic difference is that Catholics are robustly skeptical of the claim that evangelicalism is as individualistic as many think. The person "making a decision for Christ" at an evangelistic rally, who thinks that it is an event strictly between him and God, something that is going on in the intimacy and privacy of his own heart—such a person is already deeply implicated in the one, holy, catholic, and apostolic Church. The very Bible on which such a person relies as the Word of God was not formally defined as such until the end of the fourth century, and that was done by the Church. Whether the Church *decided* which books were divinely inspired or simply *recognized* the inspired text's attestation to itself is a distinction without a difference. In either case, one trusts that the Holy Spirit guided the Church in that act of decision or recognition. Similarly, although the person making that supposedly individualistic decision for Christ may never have heard of the councils of Nicaea, Constantinople, or Chalcedon, that decision for Christ is formed by a context that assumes the rightness of the Church's Spirit-guided decision that Jesus is both God and man, and that God is Father, Son, and Holy Spirit, coeternal persons, three in one and one in three.

And so Catholics cannot easily agree with evangelicals when evangelicals say they are not "churchly" Christians. They accept a definition of Christian orthodoxy that is inexplicable apart from the controversies, reflections, and decisions of the Church through time.[36] They acknowledge as authoritative a Bible that was, under the inspiration of the Spirit, written in and by and for the Church, and thus do they implicitly acknowledge the authority of the Church. On these great questions that are constitutive of what we evangelicals and Catholics alike call orthodox Christianity, alternative interpretations were advanced in the early centuries of the Church, all appealing to the authority and texts of the Bible. The views associated with the names of Arius, Nestorius, Pelagius, and others were condemned as heretical, and today evangelicals and Catholics together agree that the Church, guided by the Spirit that had been promised, made those decisions rightly.

## Tradition Protesting Tradition

Far from rejecting the authority of tradition, evangelicals firmly embrace foundational elements of the tradition that is called orthodox Christianity. In addition, in expressing their differences with the Catholic Church, evangelicals invoke the authority of persons and theological schools that clearly constitute a tradition of their own. Among conservative Calvinists and Lutherans, for instance, the thought of Calvin or Luther is invoked with a weight of authority not accorded any one theologian or school of theology in the Catholic Church. Catholics cannot help but wonder why Protestants do not also think it a little odd when the tradition of, say, Calvin and Calvinism is invoked against Catholic teaching regarding the authority of tradition.

Beyond the formation of Scripture, dogma, and doctrine, when one examines the experiential dimensions of evangelical Christianity, it seems that evangelicals are also more churchly than they allow. Seen in the light of the sociology of religion, there are not only traditions but also hierarchies of authority, orders of ministry and accountability, doctrinal censors, forms of excommunication, and, however confusedly made, the claims of a magisterium or teaching authority. To take but a mainstream reflection of evangelicalism, even a few issues of *Christianity Today* give ample evidence of the remarkable ecclesial *thickness* (to use the fashionable academic term) of American evangelicalism. Of course there are many different initiatives, entrepreneurs, and competing programs, but all within a relatively narrow understanding of what constitutes evangelical faith and life. I say without irony that by comparison the Catholic Church, often depicted as a monolithic system, is much more capacious and diverse. And that returns us to the question with which we began, namely, different attitudes toward different ways of being Christian.

The evangelical Protestant way of being Christian, I would suggest, is in fact very churchly. This is true in terms of received definitions of orthodoxy, in terms of the experience of being converted and converting others, and in terms of organizational structure. Looked at in its sociological dynamics, in the light of what people actually do and think they are doing, the head offices of the Southern Baptist Convention and the curial offices of the Vatican are not so different as one may be inclined to suppose, and the operations of an evangelical megachurch in, say, the suburbs of Chicago are strikingly like those of a small Catholic diocese. No more than Catholics do evangelicals conceive of Christian faith and life apart from the reality of the Church. Both allow for the possibility of Christians who are unrelated to the Church, but that is clearly the exception. Evangelicals might well ask themselves whether for them, too, it is not the case that faith in Christ and faith in the Church constitute one act of faith.

Although many evangelicals are accustomed to speaking in the same way, we must question Kevin Offner's description of being born again when he says that "this most important aspect of salvation is done alone, between the individual and God, in one's own heart." God works through means. "But how are men to call upon him in whom they have not believed? And how are they to believe in him of whom they have never heard? And how are they to hear without a preacher? And how can men preach unless they are sent?" (Rom. 10:14 RSV). Put differently, there is no salvation apart from the Church. It was William James, certainly no evangelical, who wrote in *The Varieties of Religious Experience* that religion means "the feelings, acts, and experiences of individual men in their solitude." Many liberal Christians traditions agree with James, but it seems to me that evangelicals should not. Friedrich Schleiermacher (d. 1834), the father of Protestant modernism, declared that "the antithesis between Protestantism and Catholicism may provisionally be conceived in this way: the former makes the individual's relation to the Church dependent on his relation to Christ, while the latter makes his relation to Christ dependent on his relation to the Church."[37] Neither Catholics nor evangelicals should accept that antithesis today. Christ is encountered in the company of his disciples, just where he promised he would be. Becoming a Christian and living as a Christian is an intensely personal matter, but it is not a private matter.

## Grace and Mediation

As some evangelical theologians have persuasively argued, this accent on the ecclesial nature of Christian faith and life should not be viewed as something alien to evangelicalism.[38] While for perfectly understandable historical reasons many evangelicals are made uneasy by the claim that the grace of God is mediated, the experienced reality of mediation is as evident among evangelicals as it is among Catholics. There is the preacher, the essential speaker of the Word, as emphasized by Paul in Romans 10. There is God's gift of the written Word of Scripture which, although some may think it was parachuted directly from the first century to this Sunday's Bible class, is given to us through the community of faith that also defines its correct (orthodox) interpretation. And again, even those Protestant traditions most adamantly opposed to the Catholic understanding of the authority of tradition are precisely that—traditions.

Within those traditions there are theological formulas that are viewed as normative, and persons who are thought to speak with particular authority. The Catholic Church has a developed understanding of magisterium, of teaching authority in the Church. And yet, I would suggest, the *function* of magisterium is no less evident among evangelicals. Any community must have guiding rules and precedents in order to survive and flourish. Leaders are somehow selected and held accountable to lead in a way that is in credible continuity with the tradition in question. In the setting of directions and settling of disputes, the authority of defining figures is invoked. These are the names that carry magisterial weight, the giants whom one cannot explicitly oppose without risking one's standing in the community. Depending on the tradition, they include figures from the past such as Luther, Calvin, Wesley, D. L. Moody, and J. Gresham Machen, and contemporaries as various as J. I. Packer, Billy Graham, Charles Colson, Bob Jones, and R. C. Sproul.

Some evangelicals will protest the suggestion that evangelicals have a functional equivalent of a magisterium or teach in accord with authoritative tradition. They are, they say, guided only by Scripture—or, in some Pentecostal traditions, by Scripture interpreted by the direct inspiration of the Holy Spirit. They insist emphatically on the principle of *sola scriptura*, not noting the irony that *sola scriptura* does not appear in the Bible but is itself a formula of a particular Protestant tradition. To pit *sola scriptura* against authoritative tradition is to oppose tradition in the name of tradition. All Christians are "traditioned," all of us are formed by interpretive communities; the language and patterns of faith that we embrace as most personally our own are received from others. The difference is not that some Christians are more churchly than others; the difference turns on whether our understanding of the church is in faithful continuity with that of the apostolic community through time.

Certainly Catholics will take second place to none in their respect for the authority of Holy Scripture. Speaking of the magisterium and the Bible, Vatican II declares:

> Yet this Magisterium is not superior to the Word of God, but is its servant. It teaches only what has been handed on to it. At the divine command and with the help of the Holy Spirit, it listens to this devotedly, guards it with dedication, and expounds it faithfully. All that it proposes for belief as being divinely revealed is drawn from this single deposit of faith.[39]

If, as G. K. Chesterton proposed, tradition is the democracy of the dead, there is something very democratic about the Catholic understanding of teaching authority. It is not democratic, of course, in the modern sense of "one man, one vote," but in the sense that it invites the full participation of all who have contributed to the Great Tradition of orthodox Christianity. To many Catholics it cannot help but seem that Protestants posit the formal principle of *sola scriptura* but then surrender effective interpretive authority to a small school of Reformation theologians, with nobody from the previous sixteen centuries being given a voice, except, sometimes, Augustine. In fact, as I have suggested, there is a continuing magisterium in evangelicalism, but it is not conscious of itself as being such, and therefore cannot hold itself in disciplined accountability to the entirety of the interpretive community that is the Church through time.

The purpose here is not to recommend that evangelicals accept the Catholic understanding of the magisterium, but that we together recognize the inescapably ecclesial character of Christian existence. In addition to the mediation of the Word and the unavoidability of authoritative traditions of teaching, evangelicals are engaged as much as Catholics in traditions of ritual. An evangelistic crusade or charismatic rally is as fully ritualized as the Mass, and in worship nothing is so burdensomely ritualistic as the effort to be spontaneous. (That used to be the burden mainly of evangelicals, but in recent years it has been assumed by some Catholic priests who feel compelled to "liven up" the Mass with the clichés of spontaneity.) The difference is not that some churches have rituals and others do not; ritual, like tradition, is inescapable. The difference is in the richness, beauty, and expressiveness of the ritual in question, and in the degree to which it reflects the fullness of the faith and life of the apostolic community through time.

## Dichotomies That Cripple

For almost five centuries now Catholics and Protestants have lived with crippling dichotomies, such as that between the Bible and tradition, and between ritual and spiritual experience. The most grievously crippling dichotomy, however, is that between the gospel and the Church. As we have discussed, it is historically understandable that those who thought the Church was being pitted against the gospel should respond by pitting the gospel against the Church. The Catholic Church, ever in need of reform, must more convincingly demonstrate the truth that the Church exists for the gospel and from the gospel. That truth is luminously clear in the Catholic Church's official teaching, but it is far from clear in much pastoral and catechetical practice. If in Latin America, for instance, the Catholic Church had more effectively proclaimed God's saving work in Jesus Christ, it is doubtful that there would today be such controversy over evangelical proselytizing. And, of course, it is not only in Latin America that Catholics must work much harder at communicating the understanding of personal conversion expressed in the Baptist-Catholic statement that is embraced by ECT and is fully supported by authentic Catholic teaching.

To overcome the crippling dichotomy between Church and gospel, it is necessary, too, that evangelicals recognize that the Church is an integral part of the gospel, that the Good News necessarily includes the new people of God journeying through time to the final consummation. Faith in Christ and faith in the Church is one act of faith. To come to Christ is to come to the Church, indeed to become the Church. "Come to him, to that living stone, rejected by men but in God's sight chosen and precious; and like living stones be yourselves built into a spiritual house, to be a holy priesthood, to offer spiritual sacrifices acceptable to God through Jesus Christ" (1 Pet. 2:4, 5 RSV). Overcoming the dichotomy requires that evangelicals bring to consciousness and submit to careful reflection the ecclesial dimensions of their faith and life. The "Church in the gospel" can then be given fuller theological articulation, and evangelicals can make their distinctive contributions in searching for ways in which their communities might better embody continuity and faithfulness with the apostolic doctrine, order, and worship of the New Testament Church through time. From such evangelical searching and experiment, Catholics, too, will learn. The Catholic Church does not fear but strongly affirms the dynamics of Spirit-guided development, and recognizes that such development is sometimes provoked and informed by dynamics coming from outside the Catholic Church.

## Crossing the Threshold

For this we need to pray together as we together cross the threshold of the third millennium: that as the second millennium has been the millennium of Christian divisions, so the third millennium will be the millennium of Christian unity; that the suspicions and hostilities that have attended the names Protestant and Roman Catholic will give way to a common mission among all who bear the name of Christ; that the different ways of being Christian will be embodied in ecclesial forms that the world will recognize as the continuing community of his disciples from Pentecost until the end of time. Of course we cannot know what the future holds. But we can now affirm together, hope together, search together, contend together, and witness together in expectant openness to the promised Spirit; we can now act in obedience to the faith that we profess in the one, holy, catholic, and apostolic Church.

## Notes

1  Charles Colson, *The Body: Being Light in Darkness* (Dallas: Word, 1992).
2  This is a central theme of my *The Naked Public Square* (Grand Rapids: Eerdmans, 1984). The phenomenon was most influentially and presciently analyzed in Dean Kelley's *Why Conservative Churches Are Growing* (New York: Harper and Row, 1972).
3  Alister McGrath, *The Blackwell Encyclopedia of Modern Christian Thought* (Cambridge, Mass.: Blackwell, 1993), 183.
4  "Evangelical Theology Today," *Theology Today* 51 (January 1995):495–507.
5  *Catechism of the Catholic Church* (New Hope, Ken.: St. Paul Books, 1994), 222.
6  *Unitatis Redintegratio,* no. 2.

7   *Lumen Gentium*, nos. 14 and 15.

8   Francis Pieper, *Christian Dogmatics* (St. Louis, Miss.:Concordia, 1953), 397ff.

9   *Lumen Gentium*, nos. 39, 8, and *Catechism*, 218f.

10  Hans Urs von Balthasar, *Explorations in Theology*, vol. 2 (San Francisco: Ignatius, 1989), 208.

11  Quoted in *Catechism*, 220.

12  *Lumen Gentium*, No. 26

13  *Catechism*, page 221.

14  David Yeago "Luther, the Church, and the Catholic Tradition," page 18, a chapter in forthcoming book, *The Catholic Luther*.

15  Mark U. Edwards, Jr., *Luther's Last Battles* (Ithaca, N.Y.: Cornell, 1983). Luther's identification of the papacy as the anti-Christ was among the eschatological signs supporting his apocalyptic view of the imminent end of the world.

16  "As the Third Millennium Draws Near," *Origins* 24 November 1994, 33–35. See also the recent encyclical, *Ut Unum Sint* (That They May Be One), *Origins*, 10 June 1995: 1ff.

17  Also before Vatican Council II, the Roman Catholic Church had occasion to correct that misperception, as, for instance, in the case of Father Leonard Feeney, S.J., of Boston, who promoted the proposition that "outside the (Roman Catholic) Church there is no salvation." Feeney's position was rejected by the Holy Office (now called the Congregation for the Doctrine of the Faith) in a 1949 letter to Richard Cardinal Cushing of Boston that set forth the authentic teaching of the Catholic Church. That teaching is reaffirmed and elaborated in the *Dogmatic Constitution on the Church* (*Lumen Gentium*) of the Council. Today a group founded by an excommunicated French bishop, The Society of Pius X, continues to hold to the position definitively repudiated by the magisterium of the Catholic Church.

18  *Lumen Gentium*, no. 8.

19  *Catechism*, 216, conciliar footnotes omitted.

20  See Raymond Brown et al., eds., *Peter in the New Testament* (Minneapolis: Augsburg, 1973).

21  On the question of the canon of Scripture, there is of course a long-standing difference between Catholic teaching and the view of most Protestants when it comes to the Apocrypha of the Old Testament. Actually, the difference goes back much earlier. The books of the Apocrypha (1 and 2 Esdras, Tobit, Ecclesiasticus, 1 and 2 Maccabees, etc.) were received by the early Church as part of the Greek version of the Old Testament, although non-Greek Jews excluded them from their version of the Hebrew Bible. The subsequent history of the Apocrypha has been ambiguous. For instance, Jerome distinguished the apocryphal books from the rest of the canon, while Augustine assumed their canonicity. Luther included the Apocrypha (except 1 and 2 Esdras) as an appendix in his translation of the Bible and recommended them as "useful and good to read." (A warmer recommendation, one notes,

than he gave to the Epistle of James.) The council of Trent declared the Apocrypha to be part of the canon. In contemporary biblical scholarship, as in the early Church, the Apocrypha is again highly valued for the light it throws on the period between the end of the Old Testament and the opening of the New, especially with respect to understandings of eternal life, the resurrection of the body, and the expectations regarding the End Time. Recognizing that the Apocrypha was read as Scripture by the pre-Nicene Church and by many post-Nicene fathers, these books have gained increasing respect from Christian scholars, even from those who do not hold them to be equally canonical with the rest of the Old Testament. There are no substantive doctrinal differences between Protestants and Catholics that turn on the acceptance or rejection of the Apocrypha, and whether or not these books are accepted as canonical is, as I have indicated, a matter that can only be deliberated and decided by the Christian community.

22   In fact, it seems the phrase *articulus stantis et cadentis ecclesiae* first appears two hundred years after the beginning of the Reformation. (See "Justification by Faith," *Origins*, 6 October 1983, 300 f51.) It was devised by a theologian of Lutheran orthodoxy, Valentius Loescher, in order to attack the Pietists of his day. According to Loescher, faith alone (*sola fide*) condemned, among other things, the claimed necessity of an identifiable conversion experience. There is considerable irony in the fact that nearly three hundred years later some evangelicals invoke "the article by which the Church stands or falls"—a formula by which an earlier Protestant orthodoxy condemned teachings that many today assume to be essential to evangelicalism.

23   These and other questions touching on the purpose of the *Catechism* are addressed by Cardinal Ratzinger and Bishop Christoph Schönborn in *Introduction to the Catechism of the Catholic Church* (San Francisco: Ignatius, 1994).

24   For a critical appreciation by an evangelical of the degree to which Trent did actually respond to the concerns of the Reformation, see J. Daryl Charles, "Evangelical-Catholic Dialogue: Basis, Boundaries, Benefits," *Pro Ecclesia* 3 (Summer 1994): 289–305.

25   For a powerful development of this metaphor, see Robert Jenson, "How the World Lost Its Story," in *First Things* 36 (October 1993): 19–24.

26   On "the rule of faith" and commensurate theological traditions, see George Lindbeck, *The Nature of Doctrine* (Philadelphia: Westminster, 1984).

27   For an excellent introduction to this motif, see Vladimir Lossky, *Orthodox Theology* (Crestwood, N.Y.: St. Vladimir Seminary Press, 1978).

28   For a persuasive treatment of Luther's understanding of his place in relation to this tradition, see David S. Yeago, "The Catholic Luther," in *First Things* (June 1995). This is part of a forthcoming book by Yeago on the theme of Luther's catholicity.

29   Karl Lehmann and Wolfhart Pannenberg, eds., *The Condemnations of the Reformation Era* (Minneapolis: Fortress, 1990), 68. The Lutheran World

Federation in 1994 issued a document, *Church and Justification*, preparatory to an expected joint Lutheran-Catholic declaration in 1997 that differences on justification are no longer church-dividing. For a recent elaboration of the Catholic understanding of the development of doctrine, see "The Ecclesial Vocation of the Theologian," an instruction issued by the Congregation for the Doctrine of the Faith in 1988 [approved May 24, 1990; revised June 26, 1990].

30   Albert Outler, *John Wesley* (Oxford: Oxford University Press, 1964), 119.

31   Ibid., 498.

32   Of the many studies documenting these changes, the following three are especially valuable. Alister McGrath, *Iustitia Dei: A History of the Christian Doctrine of Justification* (Cambridge: Cambridge University Press,1986). For an examination of the different meanings and theological uses of *faith*, see Avery Dulles, *The Assurance of Things Hoped for: A Theology of Christian Faith* (Oxford: Oxford University Press, 1994) and *The Condemnations of the Reformation Era*.

33   The Pelikan and Willebrands views are discussed in the author's *The Catholic Moment* (NewYork: Harper & Row, 1987), 13ff.

34   Joseph Ratzinger, *Church, Ecumenism and Politics* (New York: Crossroad, 1988), 98.

35   Kevin Offner, "Different Kinds of Christians," unpublished manuscript, June 1994.

36   For an excellent discussion of the ways in which orthodoxy is a Spirit-directed development of the Church's teaching, see Robert L. Wilken, *The Myth of Christian Beginnings* (Garden City, N.Y.: Doubleday, 1971).

37   Friedrich Schleiermacher, *The Christian Faith* (Edinburgh: T and T Clark, 1928), 103.

38   This question is impressively addressed from a Baptist perspective by Stanley J. Grenz in his comprehensive study *Theology for the Community of God* (Nashville: Broadman and Holman, 1994).

39   *Dei Verbum*, 10.

# Index